★★★
NAL

DAILY NEWS

NEW YORK'S PICTURE NEW

4¢

36. No. 151   Copr. 1954 News Syndicate Co. Inc.   New York 17, N.Y., Saturday, December

UTSIDE
Y LIMITS

HEPPARD JURY
IS LOCKED UP
ut 12 Hrs., Tries Anew Today

—Story on Page 3

aits Decision in Cell. Dr. Sam Sheppard is led into cell above Cleveland courtroom where jury deliberated as to whether he killed his wife, Marilyn. After nine weeks of trial, the jurors had a choice of decisions where— could free him, send him to prison from one year to life, or send him to electric chair. At 10:35 P. M. jury retired for night. *Story on page 3*

(United Press Telefoto)

Headline Justice

Headline Justice

Inside the Courtroom:
The Country's Most Controversial Trials

Theo Wilson

Thunder's Mouth Press

Copyright © 1996 Theo Wilson
All rights reserved

First Edition
First printing, 1996

Published by
Thunder's Mouth Press
632 Broadway, 7th Floor
New York, NY 10012

Library of Congress Cataloging-in-Publication Data
Wilson, Theo
Headline justice : inside the courtroom : the
country's most controversial trials / Theo Wilson.
    p.   cm.
ISBN 1-56025-108-5
    I. Wilson, Theo. 2. Women journalists—United States—
Biography. 3. Newspaper court reporting—United States. 4.
Trials—United States. I. Title.
PN4872.W55H43   1996
070'.92'273—dc20
[B]   96-18293
                                                         CIP

Printed in the United States of America

Distributed by
Publishers Group West
4065 Hollis Street
Emeryville, CA 94608
(800) 788-3123

For Delph, who grew up during all this—
and became a mensch.

Acknowledgments

Heartfelt thanks to my family, friends, and newspaper colleagues who kept me going with continuing encouragement, gentle persuasion, and outright threats, including Delph Wilson, H. D. (Doc) Quigg, Marion Rose, Isabella Fine, Ann Ratray, Linda Deutsch, Carolyn and Jack Fox, Earl Caldwell, Evelyn Fraser, Sandi Gibbons, Mary Neiswender, Claudia Luther, Fran Lewine, Ronnie Claire Edwards, Norman Parker, Kay Finegan, Beverly and Tony Montalbano, George Burns, Sid Feingold, the late Alton Slagle, and the late Bill Farr.

My gratitude to Judge Robert Takasugi, who proved that humanity and dignity can co-exist in a high-profile trial.

My deepest gratitude to my agent, Barbara Lowenstein, who created the idea for this book and stayed with it through the years; to Corlies M. Smith, among the first to show his faith in this project; to publisher Neil Ortenberg and Matt Trokenheim of Thunder's Mouth Press, who made it possible for me to hold this book in my hands; and to my editor, Robert Weisser, who polished every word and made it all come together in dawn-to-midnight sessions.

And my love to Lois Lane, my Siamese cat-companion, who watched over me throughout the writing of *Headline Justice*, giving me great joy and comfort.

Contents

Foreword by Linda Deutsch xi
Introduction 1
1   The O.J. Simpson Trial: Flash and Trash 12
2   Bowties and Beats: Moonshine and the Law 24
3   On the Road 40
4   The *Confidential* Trial 53
5   Gag Orders and Other Pains in the Tush 69
6   The Colonel's Lady 86
7   The Joy of Writing 103
8   Oh Lawdy! How They Could Love! 121
9   In Nic's City Room 142
10   Going Crazy With Charlie 165
11   The Queen of the SLA 195
12   Jean and the Diet Doc 217

Foreword

I knew Theo Wilson before I ever met her. As a college student and later as a young reporter aspiring to the heights of journalistic accomplishment, I devoured Theo's writing in the New York *Daily News*. Her skillful coverage of such grisly trials as the Carl Coppolino murder case in my home state of New Jersey made better reading than any detective novel. I remember racing to the newsstand to get the latest installment in that gripping saga before all the papers were sold. In those days, the thought that Theo would become my mentor and best friend was more than I could have ever dreamed.

At a recent party, a colleague pointed at Theo across the room and announced, "That woman is the greatest living reporter in the world." That may sound like hyperbole, but it fits Theo.

The true genius of her reporting was evident to all those who were privileged enough to work alongside her. I have wished that she would return to the courtroom one of these days and show the novices how it's done. I should note that trials were only part of her journalistic repertoire. She covered space shots, the birth of quintuplets, hurricanes, and royal weddings with great flair. When Jacqueline Kennedy visited India, Theo went along and wrote the tale in her inimitable, colorful style.

Her energy and adventurous spirit when it came to chasing a story became legendary. Yes, she did get stuck on an elephant in India. She flew to a Texas flood in a *Daily News* plane only to land in a field full of snakes. And, in her most famous exploit, she took a Los Angeles cab several hundred miles to cover a kidnapping.

A cab? Theo was the most famous nondriving reporter in Los Angeles. Cars just didn't interest her. She had grown up in Brooklyn and worked much of her career in Manhattan, where cabs were plentiful. When she moved to the West Coast to open the *News* bureau in the 1970s, she managed to get around without a car. Other reporters, anxious to share her expertise, wouldn't leave for a big story without checking to see if Theo had a ride. But in July 1976, a story broke which required quick action. A school bus full of children had disappeared in the central California town of Chowchilla. The place was barely on the maps. I had left town that day for a speaking engagement in San Francisco unaware I soon would be recruited to go to Chowchilla. The story was big. As I drove from San Francisco, I wondered how Theo was managing. I need not have worried.

When I walked into the makeshift press center at a rural firehouse, the first person I spotted with phone in hand dictating a story was Theo. She had arrived before I did and even before those who chartered planes.

"How did you get here so fast?" I asked incredulously.

"I took a cab," she said matter-of-factly.

Word spread like wildfire and pretty soon the story of Theo's wild, $200 cab ride was grabbing headlines. Little children came to point in awe at "the lady that took the cab." It was vintage Theo. Nellie Bly had nothing on her when it came to guts and determination.

But trials were her forte. In courtrooms across the country, she charted the emotional landscape of America and took readers along for a tour they would never forget. You may ask what was so different about Theo's coverage. The answer is that many journalists have covered such stories; Theo inhabited them. She climbed into the skin of such defendants as Sam Sheppard, Candace Mossler, Jack Ruby, Charles Manson, and Jean Harris and showed what made them tick.

It is interesting to note that Theo's readers felt they were attending the trials with her even though this was long before TV cameras entered courtrooms. Ask them today if they saw Charlie Manson jump at the judge and they will probably say they did. Theo was their eyes and ears and they couldn't ask for better.

No wonder that she developed a cult following at the *News* among readers who often didn't know that *Theo Wilson* was a woman's byline. It gave her particular pleasure to receive "Dear Sir" letters suggesting that her take on a story might be different if she just had a feminine perspective.

My formal introduction to Theo came at the Manson trial, which is sort of like saying we met under bombardment in the middle of a war. As a cub reporter for the Associated Press, I had seen her from afar when I made occasional visits to the Sirhan Sirhan trial. She was always surrounded by a group of admirers. In 1970, when the trial of Manson and his three woman followers was about to get underway, advance word began to spread: "Theo is coming, Theo is coming," my reporter friends said.

I soon learned the twofold message behind these words: (1) This is an important trial or she wouldn't be here. (2) We would have a good time if we just stayed close to this tiny grand dame of journalists. To Theo, covering any story had to be fun or it wasn't worth doing. Sometimes it took gallows humor to snap reporters out of depression during a particularly grisly trial, and Theo's wisecracks, her infectious laugh, and her gift for storytelling (on paper and in person) were the remedy for trial blues. She was always surrounded by a cadre of colleagues willing to carry her notebook or to bring ice to her hotel room for after-court cocktail parties. Most of the men fell in love with her; the women became her dedicated friends.

Beyond her personal magnetism, Theo was a generous teacher of other reporters. No matter how pressing the deadline, if you needed to check a quote for accuracy, she always had the time. And she always had it right. Her notes were impeccable, written in the tiniest script in a small spiral notebook that could have doubled for a trial transcript. Once, attorney F. Lee Bailey inquired if she was wearing a wire; her quotes were that accurate.

When Theo blew into Newport, Rhode Island, for the Claus von Bulow trial, *Boston Phoenix* reporter Michael Matza was dispatched to cover Theo and the traveling press corps that surrounded her in the often chaotic world of trial coverage. He captured Theo's impact this way:

> Through this world turned upside down, seemingly never off balance, strides Theo Wilson, the acknowledged dean of the trial press corps. As one of the writers who is covering a major trial for

the first time admits, "She is the standard. You can keep score by counting the number of times she has to tell you what's going on and the number of times you get to tell her." Wilson's is the voice of experience in a milieu of hedged bets. . . . And when Wilson speaks, people listen. As well they should. "Take people into the courtroom," is the first instruction she remembers from a *Daily News* editor, and she's been doing just that for the better part of three decades.

The story went on to note Theo's tangible value to her paper. On the day of the Jean Harris verdict, for instance, the newspaper sold 100,000 extra copies.

Other reporters learned from her the Theo Wilson Cardinal Rules of Trial Coverage. These included: Never leave the courtroom except to file your story; you might miss a crucial moment. Don't give undue attention to out-of-court gossip; the only important facts are those which come from the witness stand to the jury's ears. Never forget that lawyers on both sides of a case are salespeople, and those "secrets" they may want to tell you are designed to help their clients. And most importantly, never come to a trial with your mind made up; listen to the evidence as if you were a juror and report it with a fair, unbiased approach.

Theo's readers trusted her to tell the truth, and she knew it. She trusted their intelligence and was confident that if they read her copy every day, they would reach their own sensible conclusions.

They would also have a heck of a good time. As you will see in the pages of this book, her copy was colorful, lively, sensitive, and powerful. Her instinct for what was important on any given day was unerring and her understanding of the law was so keen that lawyers would often seek her out to gain a reading on how their strategy was faring. (She was usually noncomittal.) The stuffier ones would be surprised to find such accuracy from a tabloid reporter—although the *Daily News* of Theo's day was a respected paper, unlike the tawdry supermarket dreadfuls of current journalism. When her own paper began its descent to a lower journalistic road, Theo decided to accept a buy-out and step aside. The editors who treasured her talent were gone, and the new ones just didn't seem to get it. Her readers were the losers.

But with her generous spirit still thriving, Theo has continued as an inspiration to so many of us who still call on her for journalistic counsel. In the most challenging moments of trials such as the

O.J. Simpson extravaganza, I sometimes ask myself, "How would Theo write this?"

As you read this book, the answer to that question will be evident. She would write it better than anyone else would.

Linda Deutsch
July 1996

Introduction

The most wonderful thing about starting out in the newspaper business when I did and where I did was that I was thrust into a world of fiercely independent, creative, well-read, vastly under-paid and overworked people who loved the newspaper business so much, cared about writing so passionately, that they stayed in a job distinguished by low wages and long hours.

It was these drawbacks that separated the dedicated newspaper writers from the sensible, careful people who really wanted nice jobs with regular hours, decent salaries, and the security of a little pension. The sensible people might have started a newspaper career, but they generally left as soon as possible for safer jobs that didn't interfere with family life.

What remained were born writers, frustrated poets, heavy drinkers, talented oddballs, and enough sane, educated, and ambi-tious professionals to hold everything together and get out a paper every day on time.

What also remained were the legmen—colorful characters who couldn't write or spell but who had innumerable sources and were so street smart and so fast at digging up facts that we writers were in awe of them, instead of the other way around. They gave us wonderful details on the phone, telling us that a helicopter was "hoovering over the water, you know, not moving anywhere" and carefully explaining that "a torso, without a head on it or arms or legs" had been found in a car trunk.

We were paid so little that we could tell the city editor to go screw himself; we could argue with the guys on the desk about how the copy was being handled. We were free spirits who loved being with each other and being on the inside of the stories that other people could only read about. We could stop all conversation at a bar with our shop talk, which always was the most interesting shop talk in any place where we congregated.

There are journalists today who think that *The Front Page*, with its tough-talking, unpolished reporters, epitomized newspaper work in the 1940s, and maybe in some areas it did. Where I worked we may have been zany, but we were educated professionals way past the *Front Page* era. At the Richmond (Va.) *News Leader,* for instance, my editor was a Pulitzer-winning Civil War scholar, the rewrite battery and staff included two graduates from the University of Missouri School of Journalism, one who was a graduate from both Harvard and Columbia, two graduates from the College of William and Mary, a graduate of the Columbia School of Journalism, and a Medill School of Journalism graduate. The only other woman on rewrite was a Sweetbriar alum: I was a Phi Beta Kappa with a B.A. in English. Those were reporters in the 1940s.

When I started in the business in Evansville, Indiana, a few days after graduating from the Unversity of Kentucky, there were still deskmen, pros with the special skills needed to edit copy, who followed the sun, walked into a town, headed for the nearest newspaper office, and were welcomed and given a job right away. They could stay as long as they wanted to, but they never did linger. They'd work for a while, get some money together, and as soon as the weather turned bad, they'd take off for a new town, a different newspaper, a better climate.

We writers, rewritemen, beat reporters, and legmen were made to feel that we were the heart of our newspapers. We had a passion for our jobs, and so did the people who owned the newspapers.

A few years ago Katharine Hepburn was discussing the changes she has seen during a lifetime in her profession, and talking about the old-time movie-makers, the pioneers. She said: "They were tough men but they were pushovers for this business. They wanted to make money, too, but they had a romantic attitude toward the people who make movies and the movies themselves. Now, for the most part, it's a money-making business, and the money behind the business today is cold money. Theirs [the movie moguls'] was hot money."

What Hepburn said about the movie pioneers was true of the newspaper pioneers as well. The Pattersons and the Hearsts and the McCormacks and the Pulitzers all had "hot money"—they were all passionate about their papers.

The newspaper business these days seems to be just that, a business. Reporters are probably better trained, and thanks to unions they have job security and decent wages at some newspapers. But there seems to be no passion, no deep loyalty in the city rooms. As a result, the kind of readers I had at the *News*, those millions who fiercely loved/hated the newspaper and would stand on line in sleet and rain to buy it, are disappearing. And so are the newspapers, and it breaks my heart.

What I am writing about is another time—the decades of the 1950s, 1960s, 1970s—and another kind of a newspaper, both gone forever. The *New York Daily News* started dying—or was being killed, perhaps—in the 1970s. By the time I quit, in the early 1980s, it was going downhill fast. I kept complaining and predicting, but even I did not know that eventually the *News* would lose everything—its beautiful building, its millions of devoted readers, its status as the newspaper of choice in New York, its style, its spirit, and its voice.

"I think you tinker with the spirit of a newspaper at your peril," wrote journalist-author Ward Just in 1978. "A newspaper should speak for the town in which it is published. That's what it is. The *Washington Post* is not published in New York or Warren, Vermont. It's published in Washington, D.C. and it's got the spirit of that town in it. A newspaper, if it is properly done, does have a soul and style."

The *News*, before the global heads took over and began to tinker with the spirit of it, could only have been published in New York. I remember going through the paper one day, after executive editor Bob Shand died, and circling a profusion of Washington datelines scattered throughout, small fillers as well as large items. I showed them to the editor and asked, surely, in a city as big as New York, couldn't we get New York City items to fill these spaces? Why this stuff out of Washington, which was not only uninteresting but irrelevant to our New York City readers? Later, before I got so disgusted that I quit even coming into the city room, I remember complaining about how badly local stories were being played, how color and people were being edited out, how the trials I was covering were being totally mishandled. "You want to be like the *New York Times*?" I yelled at the editor. "Then you'll wind up with the *Times'* circulation!" which at that time was quite small.

The wealthy founder of the *News*, Captain Joe Patterson, rode subways and ate in Automats so he could hear what New Yorkers were talking about and he knew what the voice of New York sounded like. For nearly six decades, until the 1970s, the *Daily News* reflected the soul and spirit of the biggest city in the country. During my life at the *News* I covered every kind of story, but my specialty was high-profile trials. When people discover I have spent a lot of my adult life covering notorious criminal cases— from Sam Sheppard in the 1950s to John DeLorean in the 1980s— either they become eager to hear the "inside dirt" they think I kept out of my newspaper stories, or they become unsettled because they think I should be a great big brassy cynical broad, although I'm quite small and very tenderhearted. Or they react like one lady at a dinner party who asked me with a slight tinge of revulsion, "Watching those sensational cases, don't you feel like a voyeur?"

My answer gave her pause: "Why no, not at all," I replied. "Is that how you feel when you go to see *Macbeth* or *Hamlet*?"

It was an easy answer for me, because I always have compared big courtroom trials to great theater, filled as those trials are with revelations of human weakness and folly, with violence and sorrow and humor and pity and passion, all the more fascinating because these are real people, real life.

Real people, victims and defendants both, are dissected at trials. We see not only what they want us to see, but what is normally hidden from us, and so these trials tell us about ourselves, our own facades and the secrets behind them, our own potential for good and evil, just as do the stage plays that most intrigue us.

There is always suspense, and there is often the added fillip that, no matter what the verdict, no matter what the testimony—we never can be sure.

It is not required, you know, for the prosecution to prove guilt beyond all doubt. Jurors are instructed to presume a defendant innocent until the prosecution has proven guilt "beyond a reasonable doubt" and has convinced them "to a moral certainty" that the defendant is guilty. Verdicts from juries, sentences from judges, and opinions from appeals courts end trials and conclude cases, but they cannot resolve the beliefs, ranging from doubt and surmise to fierce conviction, that continue to surround defendants who insist, until they die, that they did not commit the crimes with which they were charged.

We will never know, absolutely, whether or not Dr. Sam Sheppard stabbed his pregnant wife to death, as the state charged, or whether her murderer was a bushy-haired intruder who also injured the doctor, as Sheppard claimed. Twenty years later, we will never know, absolutely, whether or not Dr. Jeffrey MacDonald stabbed his pregnant wife and two little daughters to death, as the federal government charged, or whether those murders were committed by a band of junkies who also injured the doctor, as MacDonald claimed.

Once convicted and imprisoned, then granted a new trial and acquitted, Sam Sheppard went to his grave swearing his innocence. Neither verdict—conviction or acquittal—changed the minds of those who believed him and those who didn't. To this day you can start a battle by bringing up the Sheppard case, because there are those who still insist that Sam was a murderer who used the appellate system to beat the rap, and others equally fierce in their conviction that his acquittal was a long overdue triumph of a justice. (Nothing unique about the O. J. Simpson case and its aftermath here.)

It took years for the system to catch up with MacDonald, once cleared by a military tribunal, then tried and convicted in federal court. Now in prison for the murders, MacDonald continues to protest his innocence. He has supporters who believe him and refuse to accept the jury verdict, just as there are disbelievers, his late father-in-law among them, who are convinced MacDonald is a murderer and is sitting right where he belongs.

Candace Mossler was acquitted, with her nephew-lover, of the murder of her millionaire husband. She herself is dead now, but while a jury's unanimous "not guilty" decision set her and Mel Powers free, it never convinced everybody that Candy and Mel were innocent. The Manson "girls" admitted those seven murders so horrendous they will never be forgotten, but to this day, nobody—probably not even the girls themselves—knows why they did it.

Patty Hearst swore she hated her captors and claimed that every tape she made reviling her parents and the establishment, and every crime she committed, including bank robbery, was done unwillingly and under threat of death. It was a version her family wanted to, had to, believe in, but as the prosecutor said, it was a version that "didn't wash," and her jurors convicted her.

The most violent reaction I ever got from an audience was when I addressed a luncheon and indicated that the jurors in the Hearst case had done the right thing by finding the heiress guilty because they believed that on the witness stand she had lied and lied and lied. The predominantly male audience angrily rose to the defense of poor kidnapped Patty, ignoring the facts that her jury had listened to for months. As they hollered at me and at each other, I realized that, for the public, these cases will never be settled.

Did Jean Harris shoot Dr. Herman Tarnower because she was distraught with jealousy, as the state contended? Or did Tarnower die while trying to prevent Harris from shooting herself, the version that Jean offered and that the jury didn't buy? Like Patty's story, Jean's just "didn't wash," and like Patty, she was convicted. But once again, the conviction did not end the debate over whether Jean Harris deliberately or accidentally shot her lover, and her 15-year prison sentence became a bone of contention between those who felt she deserved it and those who thought it unjust.

In great plays, the audience gradually becomes aware of the truth. The truth gradually comes out in courtroom dramas, too—but always there is that haunting doubt, that "maybe" which keeps alive the stories of Sheppard and Hearst and Mossler and others I've covered like Sirhan Sirhan and Angela Davis and Jack Ruby and Carl Coppolino and Claus von Bulow and John DeLorean.

At the Angela Davis trial, I watched her attorney turn an all-white jury black, and Angela was acquitted of murder. Yet today, and probably always, there will be those who insist she was involved in that tragic Marin County Courthouse shootout.

At the Candy Mossler trial, I watched defense lawyer Percy Foreman make masterful use of that old legal bromide "the best defense is a strong offense" and win an acquittal for Candy and her co-defendant Mel Powers. But to some people, that victory simply means that Candy and Mel "got away with murder."

At the first Carl Coppolino trial, in which that doctor was accused of killing his mistress's husband, I watched a young and brilliant lawyer, F. Lee Bailey, win an acquittal despite detailed, articulate eyewitness testimony from the mistress, who swore to the jury that Carl killed her husband and she saw him do it; and despite medical testimony from the country's most famous coroner, Dr. Milton Helpern, who told the jurors that an autopsy on the exhumed body proved a homicide had been committed.

At the second Coppolino trial, in which Carl was accused of murdering his first wife by injecting her with succinylcholine chloride, I watched Lee Bailey lose the case, although this time there was no eyewitness and only circumstantial evidence.

At the Pentagon Papers trial in Los Angeles, we first heard about the White House "plumbers" and—even before the revelations of Watergate and the downfall of President Nixon—watched the lawyers for Daniel Ellsberg and Tony Russo produce so much proof of governmental misconduct that the federal judge dismissed forever charges against the two defendants that could have imprisoned them for life.

And by that time, the *News* was already deteriorating. The editors in New York downplayed and cut stories I was sending from the trial, stories that should have been front page because they were, for the first time, revealing information about the terrible machinations of the men around Nixon. The information was made available to reporters because U.S. District Judge Matt Byrne ordered grand jury transcripts from Washington unsealed in Los Angeles, a dramatic and unusual development. It wasn't until years later I discovered, to my horror, that one of the boneheads in New York scoffed at the stories I was sending because, he said, "That federal judge just wants to horn in on the publicity surrounding the Pentagon Papers." This was how the *News* was being killed.

Nothing ever is predictable at a trial, and no two trials are alike. Of all the stories I have covered—national political conventions (including the 1968 horrors in Chicago), Hurricane Carla, royal weddings and visits, First Lady Jackie Kennedy's trip to India and Pakistan, President Nixon in power and then in exile at San Clemente, all of the Mercury space shots, man's first walk on the moon—none has been as challenging, as difficult, as demanding as covering a big trial.

We had to rely solely on handwritten notes; we were not allowed to bring tape recorders inside a trial courtroom. We dictated and wrote from those notes; there were no "handouts" available, no live feed from the trial room, no time to wait for transcripts, if indeed any transcripts were available. We had to write so that our readers could see every day what transpired in a courtroom invisible to them.

During my years of covering state and federal courts in Richmond, Virginia, I learned how to read a long and complicated opinion and dictate immediately from it, how to write meticulous notes for hours every day in every kind of a court case, how to write a story, always on a deadline, so it could be understood by the readers. I knew the law and I knew how to write about it. I understood the nuances of jury selection, I watched all kinds of direct and cross examinations, and I covered all kinds of verdicts. The judges in Richmond read my reports every day; believe me, I heard about it if I goofed on the tiniest detail.

(At the *News*, no one even know about my background in law and trials; no newspaper I ever worked for ever asked me for a resume. When I was sent to cover the Sam Sheppard case, it was because it was a big story and the editors thought I should handle it. The AP sent their Pulitzer Prize winner, the UPI sent their former war correspondent, and Hearst sent two of their headliners.)

One reason trial coverage is the most challenging of newspaper stories is that you can never leave a courtroom session, not for a moment. When Charlie Manson suddenly leaped at the judge with a pencil and was hauled out of the trial room, the whole incident took a few minutes—but it was the Page 1 headline, and the reporters who had strolled out of the trial room for a brief smoke missed it all.

And to cover a trial correctly, you must have capable editors who can handle the vagaries and unpredictabilities of a trial, with leads sometimes changing three or four times within one session. Trial coverage and trial editing are not for the slow or lazy.

I have sat through entire trial days of nothing but private conferences and sidebars between judges and lawyers, nothing to write about for hours. Then, shortly before deadline, all hell breaks loose. A witness or a lawyer or a defendant says something wild, and there I am battling to file a huge and totally unexpected story at the last minute.

But at all of the trials I covered, I was the only reporter who did not have to tell the editors in advance how much space I might need for that day's story. And although I filed four, five, even ten times as much copy as any other reporter there, I was always the first one finished. I used to leave the press room listening to reporters arguing with their editors about their stories, complaining about being rewritten, screaming about being second-guessed.

I didn't have to go through that with the *News*.

I was lucky for a long time. The *Daily News* was considered the best trial paper in the country, and the editors I worked with always knew how to handle a trial. Actually, they just knew how to handle fast-breaking news of any kind, even if it meant tearing the paper apart at the last minute.

They understood news, and they understood their millions of readers. They had style, they had humor, they had grace under pressure. They were professionals. The paper could have saved enormous amounts of money by using reports from the wire services such as AP, UPI, and Reuters, for trial coverage at no extra cost. But that wasn't good enough for the *News*. Wire service stories, the editors felt, were written for readers in Chicago and in Memphis, in San Francisco and in Dubuque, for newspapers that either couldn't afford to send a reporter or weren't interested enough in the trial to staff it and didn't mind giving their readers the same story that thousands of other papers were using.

The *News* wanted its own reporter on the scene and invested thousands of dollars; it sent me out of town for as long as the trial lasted, paid for first class plane seating, paid for my hotel room and daily living expenses, paid for a direct wire from the trial press room into the *News* wire room, hired the best Western Union operator in town to work full time only for the *News*, and ran my stories front page nearly every day, stories that always were more detailed, filled with more Q and A testimony, than any coming over the wire or being printed in any other paper.

During the glory days at the *News*, if you were willing to break your neck getting a story to your editors as fast as humanly possible, the editors were willing to knock themselves out at their end. What we had was a mutual appreciation society, and nothing was ever too much effort, on either side, to get the best possible story into the paper, no matter how late the story erupted.

Nobody ever said it, but I think we shared the same feeling: our readers were spending their money for this paper and they were entitled to the best. (One of the joys of returning to New York after a long trial was listening to readers and getting letters from them, and realizing how much they knew about the case from reading the *News* every day.)

That was a big reason why the *News*, publishing in an intensely competitive market against such papers as the *Times* and the *Herald* and the *World* and the *Post* and the *Mirror* and later the *Herald-Tribune* and the *World-Telegram* and the *Journal-American*, for more than a half-century remained the largest-circulation newspaper not only in New York but in the entire country. During those years, with a circulation in the millions, this was the newspaper with the most loyal readers, the most loyal staff. And it was chosen, at one time, as one of the ten best newspapers in the United States.

I was lucky to be at the *News* when it was a world-class tabloid. And I was lucky to be at the *Evansville Press* when it was getting started and was filled with youth and energy and excitement, and I was lucky to be at the *Richmond News Leader* when its editor was a famous historian, and I was lucky to be at the *Philadelpha Bulletin* when it dominated the city and made famous its masthead slogan: "In Philadelphia Nearly Everybody Reads the *Bulletin*."

The *News Leader* closed in 1991; before that, the *Bulletin* folded. The *Daily News* nearly folded, and it has lost its circulation, its dash, its spirit. Newspapers are an endangered species, and the kind I worked on are already extinct.

John Schulian, a former newspaper columnist, reviewing Jimmy Breslin's book on Damon Runyon in the *Los Angeles Times* in September 1991, started with: "When you look at the gray tapioca that American newspapers have become, it's hard to believe they ever spawned Damon Runyon." Runyon flourished, wrote Schulian, "when newspapers weren't so tame, so timid, so full of careerists who would rather become editors than write a sentence with the rhythm of the streets in it."

How lucky I was that I, who was a writer first, became a reporter by accident, worked at a time when newspapers were most definitely not gray tapioca, and got paid to do what I love to do most—watching people, listening to people, talking to people, learning about people, writing about people so that millions of other people could understand.

On an old poster in my office is an announcement of a panel discussion sponsored by the New York Newspaper Women's Club on "Free Press Vs. Fair Trial." The date was April 29, 1965. The panelists included Theo Wilson, reporter for the *Daily News*; Jerome L. Walker, Sr., executive editor of *Editor and Publisher*; Peter T. Farrell, State Supreme Court justice; Judith Vladech, attorney for the Civil Liberties Union, and James Boylan, editor of Columbia University's *Journalism Review*. The admission was free to the press, the bar, the judiciary, and their guests, and it was held at the

Overseas Press Club, then on West 40th Street.

Three decades later, the same issues of free press versus fair trial still are being thrashed out by the press and the judiciary and the lawyers. The same arguments that I and other trial reporters made in the 1960s—that a free press and a fair trial are not mutually exclusive—are being repeated by reporters like Linda Deutsch in the 1990s.

For me, listening to and reading about the same old discussions at judicial conferences and bar associations and press groups is not deja vu. It is more like, well, duh! Not only has there been no change, but with judges refusing to allow the public to see trials on camera, we have retrogressed. The camera is the most honest tool of the criminal justice system, if it is allowed to show the public a trial, unadorned from gavel to gavel, in the courtroom—without the TV celebrities, without the brain-dead interviews, without the second-guessing pundits.

As citizens, we have a right to see our system, warts and all, and judge for ourselves. Nobody should have the power to deny us, the taxpayers, the right to watch what is happening in the courts we pay for, or should be allowed to to tell us that by watching a trial on a camera, in our homes, we are jeopardizing any other cit-izen's rights.

After the excesses of the O.J. Simpson trial, when lawyers used TV outside the courtroom to make charges that should have been reserved for the courtroom, I have no quarrel anymore with certain kinds of gag orders. Getting opinions from biased lawyers is not the way to educate the public. But the camera, that honest and unbiased eye, should be used so that the public can watch a trial, without the media circus, and see our criminal justice system in action, working as it has for centuries. It may not be the best sys-tem, it may need changes, but I know of no other in the world that is better.

1

The O.J. Simpson Trial: Flash and Trash

It was a short, sad epitaph for the O.J. Simpson trial, from one of the more thoughtful defense attorneys. Even though he was on the side that was mightily victorious, the side that got for the defendant the fastest acquittal verdict in big trial history, he said at the end: "There are no winners here."

It was Barry Scheck—what was a guy like that doing with a group like this?—and he was prophetic. The losers? The trial itself, the defendant himself, the lawyers, the judge, and the biggest loser of all—the public.

Once embarrassingly trumpeted as "the trial of the century" by reporters who apparently never before had been involved in high-profile cases, the Simpson trial now is referred to as a circus, a fiasco, an aberration in the criminal justice system by law journals, newspapers, magazine articles, and in speeches. For me, the pretrial proceedings were an early warning. I was dismayed by what I called "the flash and the trash" surrounding the case—the hype, the manipulation of unseasoned media, the bias shown by commentators even before they heard evidence from the courtroom, the publication of rumors and gossip and leaks that violated every principle of trial reporting my colleagues and I practiced.

As everybody who ever worked with me knows, my No. 1 instruction was, "Stay in the courtroom. The only important news is what the jury hears from the witness chair, what the judge rules

on, and what the lawyers say *inside the courtroom*. The rest is junk."
I preached that in the 1950s, the 1960s, the 1970s, and the 1980s. It
was encouraging to read, in the 1996 calendar distributed by the
Freedom Forum, the group organized to protect the First
Amendment, this quote: "Evidence is not evidence until it comes
from [the courtroom], not the 11 o'clock news." The quote was
attributed to Judge Lance Ito. My second most important instruction: take your reader inside the courtroom with you, describe
everything, explain everything.

Even when an important event took place outside the courtroom, as
when President Nixon declared Charlie Manson guilty while his trial
was still in progress, that story was used separately in the *News*, and
was not incorporated into the trial story except for a brief reference.
Which is why for decades, *News* readers learned every detail of the big
trials, knew exactly what the jury had heard as opposed to what had
transpired outside the courtroom, and understood why jurors
returned the verdicts they did. After the Simpson trial, however, I
could tell from the questions the public asked that the viewers could-
n't figure out what testimony had or had not been heard by the jury,
and what was plain junk from outside the courtroom.

It wasn't just the supermarket tabloids and the TV shows, which
for the first time dominated and influenced a high-profile case. It
was a magazine like the *New Yorker*, which in a pretrial article
accused a cop of a heinous crime—planting evidence against the
defendant, the bloody glove—without proof of any kind.
Obviously given to the writer by a Simpson lawyer, this was a
defense "theory," an accusation which should have been revealed
only in the courtroom. The article was written about Detective
Mark Fuhrman, who proved to be not only a disgusting bigot, but
a stupid one as well when he walked right into the trap that F. Lee
Bailey set for him in cross-examination. But nobody in this country, not even a Fuhrman, should be accused publicly without
proof, without a chance to respond, of a crime that in this case carried a penalty of life imprisonment solely because the defense wanted to plant a theory in a willing magazine.

Countless times in my career, a prosecutor or defense attorney
offered me an "exclusive" tip beneficial, of course, to his own side.
And every time I said, "That's great. When it comes out in court, I
assure you it will be my lead that day." Usually the exclusive never
surfaced again. The lawyers and I had a great understanding: if

they tried to sell and I didn't buy, well, they were just doing their job, and I was doing mine. No hard feelings.

When the trial started and the pressure mounted, the flash and trash escalated. I watched it every minute of every day, and although this was a serious trial with the accused facing life in prison, I sometimes got the feeling I was watching the Doo Dah Parade—the outrageous send-up of the pomp and ceremony of the Rose Parade. With TV and the supermarket tabloids and the magazines and mainstream newspapers flying off in pursuit of the likes of Kato Kaelin, there definitely were times when the Simpson trial became the the the Doo Dah Parade of criminal justice.

As the case continued, I became increasingly worried about how the Simpson trial would affect future coverage of high-profile trials. I had fought for years to bring cameras into the courtroom. Televising how a trial unfolds, I told judges and lawyers and other trial reporters, would enlighten those millions of citizens whose taxes pay for the courtrooms, the judges, the prosecutors, and the experts. The people have a right to see justice at work, I argued.

There was more posturing by lawyers on TV cameras outside the courtroom than inside the O.J. trial room. A gag order would have prevented that and would have stopped the lawyers from using the compliant media to air unfounded charges and to make biased and often incorrect statements to the public.

With the enormous worldwide publicity of the Simpson trial, millions got their first look, but it was a worst look, and many trial-followers, even those who believed O.J. was innocent and deserved an acquittal, were left cynical and disillusioned. The Simpson case will be remembered as the trial that got out of control, the trial that tainted nearly everyone involved in it.

O.J. Simpson, with his life returned to him, should have been the biggest winner, but he has lost and lost and lost. It becomes more evident with every effort he makes that his former life, his golden life, is gone forever.

He has lost his credibility, his popularity, his role as the real-life American success story, the poor black kid who went from ghetto rags to Brentwood riches.

He has lost his image as the sunny, funny, graceful athlete beloved by sponsors who discovered he could sell anything to anybody. He was remarkable, and the advertisers knew it, because although he was big and black and beautiful, he was nonthreatening to white buyers, the men admiring him because he was a sports legend, the women because he seemed so easygoing and articulate and charming. Now the sponsors who made him a millionaire are gone.

O.J. will go to his grave swearing his innocence, vainly trying to convince an unforgiving segment of the public that the verdict was just and that he did not get away with murder. But the acquittal verdict didn't bring closure. Simpson is still out there defending himself, claiming he was victimized by the media, even though the pretrial media coverage apparently had no effect on the jurors who acquitted him so fast. The rehashing of the trial in books and on talk shows will go on for years, like the Sheppard case.

Dr. Sam was first convicted of murdering his wife at a trial in Cleveland that was the most publicized of its time, and then was acquitted at a new trial made possible by the rising young Boston lawyer F. Lee Bailey. What the Sheppard trial taught me was that verdicts do not change public opinion. Dr. Sam, like O.J., had his defenders who published books, fought to establish his innocence when he was in prison, and exulted when he was finally exonerated. But those who were convinced more than 40 years ago that Dr. Sam killed Marilyn Sheppard believe it to this day, with Dr. Sheppard himself long dead. They believed that justice triumphed when he was convicted; they believed he got away with murder when he was acquitted.

If not-guilty verdicts could change the mindset of the public, Sheppard's son would not have spent his life trying to prove his father's innocence. In *Mockery of Justice*, published in 1995, the son offers painstakingly gathered evidence that his father did not murder his mother, that he was railroaded when he was convicted, and that he was properly acquitted at his second trial. And it really doesn't matter.

Has there ever been in our time such rancor, bad-mouthing, ill-will and contempt exhibited among famous lawyers as there was during and after the Simpson trial? High-priced the lawyers were, but not high class.

Johnnie Cochran, Jr., the lead defense attorney, was savaged not only in a posttrial book written by prosecutor Christopher Darden, but also in the posttrial book written by his teammate, Robert Shapiro. Then Shapiro and Darden got their lumps. A law journal reviewer who read both books said they were both "whiners." Darden was "a crybaby" who was "simply outmatched" by Cochran in the courtroom; Shapiro was an "opportunist" who had to undertake damage control when the case unexpectedly "took an unpopular turn."

In another book published during the trial, Cochran was described by his ex-wife as a physically abusive, unscrupulous man, and an adulterous husband who abandoned his white mistress, the mother of his only son, when he took another woman as his second wife. Would such a book have been published if the Simpson case had not become mired in dirt, unlike any other high-profile trial of our time?

Shapiro and Bailey went into the trial as longtime buddies; Bailey is godfather to one of Shapiro's sons, and Shapiro won an acquittal for Bailey in 1982 on a drunk driving charge. They came out of the trial implacable enemies. These high-priced mouthpieces didn't keep their hostility private either: Shapiro called Bailey "a snake," and Bailey called Shapiro "a sick little puppy."

They then became entangled in a federal court dispute in Florida over money from a drug dealer they had once defended. It ended with Bailey going to jail and blaming Shapiro, who testified, for his imprisonment.

Prosecutor Marcia Clark's messy divorce from her second husband and details about her first marriage were exposed in tacky detail along with stories about her hairdos and clothes, as if this had anything to do with the trial.

Clark and Darden got million-dollar contracts for books and appearances, and a bonus from District Attorney Gil Garcetti. (The bonuses and Garcetti were later denounced publicly by nearly everybody in the DA's office.) What would they have gotten if they had *won* the case! This just helped prove the trial was an aberration, since the people who should have been the biggest losers became financial winners.

Judge Lance Ito came to this trial with an untarnished reputation, but he could not handle the unprecedented publicity. He became so authoritarian that, after many of his knee-jerk rulings, I found myself yelling at the TV screen, "For God sakes, judge, who died and made you emperor?"

Ito is still getting bad press. It is a sad commentary that in May 1996 a newspaper item revealed that when Ito was invited to speak at graduation ceremonies for the University of Arizona College of Law, three dozen students, about 20 percent of the class, protested, charging that Ito was "just a California Superior Court judge" and was chosen simply because he was a celebrity. Come on, UA law students, a California Superior Court judge isn't good enough for you? Not if it's Ito, I guess.

Unfortunately, the Simpson trial turned into a zoo, and the judge was too green to control it. His one experience with a trial of national interest, the Charles Keating savings and loan fraud scandal, was no preparation for the Simpson case. Keating was an important and tragic case, but reporters weren't exactly breaking down doors trying to cover it. Unfortunately, Judge Ito—smart, witty, self-confident, an excellent lawyer—thought he knew all about the intricacies and pitfalls of high-profile trials—but he didn't.

If he got good advice, he certainly didn't listen to it, not when it came to issuing seats in the trial room (what an awful decision he made, and where were the veteran reporters to tell him it was awful?), not when it came to keeping order in the court (you don't permanently bar reporters from your fiefdom without asking questions or giving second chances), not when it came to agreeing to a pretrial television interview (the people around him should have threatened suicide and homicide before allowing him to even consider such a proposal), not when it came to threatening removal of the camera every time he got upset, not when it came to yelling at the lawyers (much as some of them deserved it for their snide, unprofessional conduct).

Ito was criticized as a star-struck judge who catered to celebrities and allowed them into his sanctum when ordinary reporters and others were not so privileged. But you have to remember that this judge was working with a mass of reporters so unfamiliar with courts and judges that they didn't realize that at big trials, veteran reporters, and veteran lawyers, and the judge can share a healthy friendship and a healthy respect; they can trust each other so much they can meet and drink and eat together throughout the trial, knowing that the after-hours get-togethers will never be publicized or even discussed. At every big trial I covered, my rooms became the press center where we got together for drinks, to relax, to plan dinners and parties. I don't know if this would have been possible at the Simpson trial; in fact, I know I could never have guaranteed, as I did at other trials, that no word of get-togethers with the judge or the lawyers would leak out.

At the Simpson trial, there was such an overblown attitude toward the judge that merely being admitted into his chambers created so much excitement one newspaper visitor had to write a non-story assuring the readers and the panting media that nothing of substance was discussed.

Bombarded during the trial by some of the most overwrought coverage in criminal trial history, exposed to bias, gossip, rumors, and plain dumbness from the mass of amateurs and on-the-job trainees who outnumbered the professional and objective press, the public now faces the loss of the one honest voice in the courtroom—the camera inside.

In what the *Los Angeles Times* described as "the rancorous aftermath" of the trial, the governor of California proposed barring all cameras; and some judges, recoiling from the excesses of the Simpson trial, refused to allow cameras inside their courtrooms.

Stringent regulations were proposed, including some that would have jeopardized the public's right to see and to understand what goes on in the courtroom. One proposal, for example, was that cameras would be allowed to film only what the jury hears. They would be forbidden to film any events in the courtoom that took place with the jury absent. What a mistake that would be! Some of a trial's most important occurrences—a motion for a mistrial, for example—happen with the jury out of the room. Why shouldn't the camera record all of a trial's highlights and happenings, with or without the jury, so long as the judge is on the bench and the trial is in process? The public is not the jury, nor is the public going to influence the jury. There is no reason why the public should not be informed of judicial rulings and legal arguments as they occur inside the courtroom, with the judge in charge.

The people watching a trial can learn how the justice system works if they are given the opportunity to see a complete trial, not selected portions. Every reporter who has covered a court beat or who has been at a high-profile trial for a long time gets to know the courthouse regulars, the seniors who spend hours every day in courtrooms following trials. Because they watch trials faithfully, these groupies learn the law much as court reporters on the beat learn it. They are marvelous sources of information about trials in progress and the personality of the judges and the lawyers. Without benefit of TV legal commentators or newspaper analysis, these regulars understand the complexities that arise, and so would the millions out there who would learn the law just by following complete trials on camera, as the regulars have done in person for many years.

The public was saturated with press coverage at the Simpson trial, some of it excellent, but there were times when the public was not served well. Take the day at the outset of the case when Cochran gave his opening statement and Simpson was permitted to show the jury the scars on his knees.

Seeing O.J. half-naked in his underdrawers in color photos and then getting a peek at his knee scars must have so bedazzled the press horde that nobody—not on TV, not on radio, not in the newspapers—bothered to warn the public that a defense admission of serious error at the end of that session had just put the entire trial in disarray.

Cochran's opening had been punctuated by objection after objection from the prosecution because he was violating the rules governing discovery, which require both sides to reveal in advance such important matters as the names of witnesses who were going to be called. Wasn't anybody listening?

No reporters that night, or even the next morning, explained high up in their stories that the trial could not possibly continue with business as usual when it resumed. Nor did anyone print in full on the day it occurred the remarkable dialogue between defense attorney Carl Douglas and prosecutor William Hodgman after Douglas admitted he was "embarrassed" over the defense "oversight" and declared: "I take full responsibility . . . this is my blame and my blame alone."

Nor did they emphasize that Hodgman, protesting the violation as "a horrible breakdown" in the judicial system, was having great difficulty talking. Douglas may have fallen on his sword, Hodgman said, but the "people were seriously prejudiced" and he begged Ito, "Do not minimize this."

Maybe the press was unhinged by O.J.'s show-and-tell, but why did Judge Ito think that the problems created by the defense's admission was something you could cure overnight, even if they claimed the wrongdoing was inadvertent?

When Ito told the prosecutors to work on the problem after court and said he'd hear them at 9 A.M. the next morning and would call the jurors in at 10 A.M. I wrote in my notebook in red ink, "Is he nuts?" Did he really believe he could cure such damage in one hour?

Were Hodgman and I the only two people who were stunned by

Ito's failure to understand how serious this problem was, that by saying he'd give an hour to it he was trivializing it? True, there was a lot
going on before Douglas made his confession, with Cochran doing a
masterful defense job trying to persuade the jurors that there was no
way O.J. could have been the killer of Nicole Brown and Ron Goldman.

When he told the jurors that a defense witness would tell them she
saw four men running from the area of Nicole's condo around the
time of the murders, there was no way the jurors could know that
Cochran was talking about a witness whose identity had never been
revealed to the prosecution—a blatant violation of court rules.

This witness, incidentally, had a rare talent. Just by looking at
four guys as they sped past, she could tell that they might be
undercover cops, Cochran said. If this lady could teach crooks how
to spot undercover cops that quickly, she could make a fortune.

As it turned out, of course, the trial was interrupted for much more
than an hour, the jurors weren't seen again for nearly a week, and
when the trial resumed before them, Cochran finally finished his opening statement. Judge Ito allowed prosecutor Marcia Clark to briefly
reopen her case because, Ito ruled, the defense had broken the law not
inadvertently but "intentionally and to gain unfair advantage."

(When Douglas made his initial admission that the defense had
violated the discovery rules, I was so amazed that I immediately
called reporters, friends, and neighbors to say that in all my years
of covering trials, I had never seen such an extraordinary development. I told them that the trial was in confusion, that when
Hodgman spoke he apparently was having difficulty breathing,
that Douglas's admission was so serious that the prosecution
should demand the right to reopen. If I could figure this out, so
should some of the jillions of reporters who were there).

Because of the initial lack of information from the huge press
corps, bad things happened.

Since the news media did not dwell on the serious nature of the
defense's law-breaking, nor on Hodgman's obvious anger and dis-
tress in open court, Cochran was able to tell reporters the next day
that the defense errors were minor and that Hodgman, who had
been rushed to an emergency room the night before, apparently
had become upset not because of the "minor" defense violations
but because of the damaging revelations Cochran had made during his opening statement. Yeah, right!

I heard not one reporter ask Cochran the big question: "If the prosecutor had violated the discovery rule in front of the jury, would you consider it minor? And if the prosecutor committed those violations, after you completed your opening statement, wouldn't you be screaming nationwide for a mistrial? And wouldn't you be claiming the prosecutors had destroyed O.J.'s right to a fair trial?"

The problem with reporters not doing their jobs properly in a trial so widely publicized is that you leave the entire country with the wrong impression. If you are unaware that a serious defense violation has been admitted, and if you didn't notice when it was happening that the prosecutor is so outraged he is having trouble speaking, then you are going to be misled, misdirected. You are going to believe the faulty thinking of some people that Hodgman was faking a heart attack. A newspaper columnist and the lady who runs the shoeshine stand at the Criminal Courts Building shared this "professional" reaction.

That was at the beginning of the trial. But at the end it was really was no better. When Judge Ito delayed the reading of the verdict for nineteen hours, not one reporter, not one lawyer, not one TV expert voiced outrage. They should have.

In every case I ever covered, lawyers and reporters were notified when a verdict was reached, and they were expected to get into the courtroom to hear the verdict within a certain time period, usually no more than two hours. If they weren't back within that time, they were locked out. We learned never ever to leave the courthouse when a jury was in deliberation.

Why did Simpson have to suffer the anxiety of awaiting the verdict for nineteen hours, when the wait should have been no more than two or three hours? Why did the jurors have to be kept sequestered for nineteen more hours? Why did the families of the victims have to be tortured by the long delay? Why was this cruel and unusual punishment not criticized by somebody in the media?

If the excuse was that security measures had to be taken, that is ridiculous. As soon as the jurors began deliberating, the police were on alert. And creating a nineteen-hour delay gave every crackpot who wanted to a chance to get down to the courthouse, along with crowds that could not have been there if the verdict had been read promptly.

This trial was not as volatile as Patty Hearst's, when Hearst Castle and other buildings were bombed by the underground; or Charlie Manson's, whose unstable followers were loose on the street protesting every day. Hearst's verdict came in on a Saturday, and the federal judge didn't kvetch about weekend overtime, as

Ito did when talking about delaying a possible Saturday verdict. The Hearst judge did what he was supposed to do: he gave the press and the lawyers the two hours he had promised, the verdict was delivered, and the trial was over. The Manson judge did the same.

When Ito first announced that he would not reveal the verdict if it was brought in on a Saturday, I called the young producer of a TV show I had been on. I told him that Ito's proposal was awful and started to explain about the Hearst trial. The young producer was polite but uninterested, and I realized he had no conception of how cruel and unnecessary a delayed verdict can be.

The Simpson acquittal did not come in on a Saturday, but Ito delayed it anyway. If, as I have been told, this was done because one of the defense lawyers had to go out of town, then I fault Ito. He should have told the attorney that the defendant, the lawyers, the families, and the jurors were not be be kept waiting at a trial already too long, and if the lawyer wanted to go out of town, he would have to miss the verdict and let the many other defense attorneys stand with Simpson. But Ito didn't.

While O.J. was captivating the world, one TV commentator said to me, "Isn't this an incredible trial? The sex! The money! The drama! It really is a giant soap opera."

And I thought, what sex, what money, what drama? Cut out the glitz and the hype and the hysteria, and the O.J. case really wasn't much of a thriller. There was more sex at the Candy Mossler trial, more money at the Patty Hearst trial, and more drama at the Claus von Bulow trial. They weren't on camera worldwide and they weren't overrun by hordes of media, but millions of *Daily News* readers were as hooked by those trials as any of the Simpson viewers. Lots of readers told us that following the *News* stories was like following a big soap opera. And none of the readers I talked to ever called any of those cases "the trial of the century."

The prosecutors who lost the case and then became instant millionaires have been second-guessed and criticized ad nauseum. Their presentation of evidence was so disorganized it was difficult for even an unbiased observer to follow or be convinced by it. Marcia Clark was overwhelmed by her sudden fame; Chris Darden may be a good lawyer, but he is too slow for the high-speed exchanges that distinguish great trial attorneys. Instead of demolishing the opposition with verbal rapiers, with icy wit, Clark resorted to angry accusations and Darden became sullen.

As for the defense: compare the low key, elegant lawyering of Leo Branton in the Angela Davis murder case with the ham-handed use of the race card in the Simpson case, and you see the difference between a great trial and a Doo-Dah.

Actually, there is no comparison. Branton and his co-counsel, Howard Moore, Jr., both black, had a challenge so much greater than the Simpson team's that the acquittal they won seems miraculous.

Their client was not a beloved sports legend accused of murders where there were no eyewitnesses. She was a controversial, militant black scholar accused of murder, kidnapping, and conspiracy in a raid and gun battle at the Marin County Courthouse on August 7, 1970.

In that raid, a white judge who was taken hostage was killed, a white prosecutor was shot and paralyzed, a white woman hostage was shot. The black leader of the raid and two escaping black prisoners were killed. The picture of the judge being led from the courthouse with a sawed-off shotgun taped to his neck was sent worldwide.

Guns used in the melee were traced to Davis, who had bought them legally. She was not at the courthouse, but immediately after the murders she disappeared, was indicted as the raid's mastermind, was placed on the FBI's most-wanted list, and finally was captured two months after the bloody shootout. Her disappearance, said the prosecutors, was proof of her guilt. Besides all of these challenges for the defense, the white prosecutor, Assistant Attorney General Albert Harris, succeeded in seating an all-white jury.

It was Leo Branton's closing, with his eloquent, softly spoken plea to the jurors to "think black, be black" so they could understand the woman they were judging, that most moved the jurors, they said later. Branton was emotional, but he never ranted or shouted. (There were no outbursts between defense and prosecution throughout the trial, and at the end, Judge Richard E. Arnason was thanked for his "evenhanded justice.") Branton begged the jurors to remember that Davis, even before the murders, had been called a "Commie bitch" and threatened with "extermination" in the hate mail she received during a dispute with the Board of Regents over her job at UCLA. He told them that after she learned her guns had been used, without her knowledge, she hid because she feared for her life. "You must realize that no black person would wonder why she fled," Branton said. "They would only wonder why she would allow herself to be caught." The jury deliberated for 13 hours, spread over three days, and acquitted the 28-year-old defendant.

2

Bowties and Beats:
Moonshine and the Law

Newspapers have been disappearing from our daily lives at a depressing rate, but I was not prepared for the news in 1991 that the Richmond (Va.) *News Leader*, where I learned how to cover courts, was one of those casualties. I thought that as a solid, reputable, local paper it was an irreplaceable part of life in that state's capital.

Soon after I read that the *News Leader* would be merged with a morning paper, I joined a unique project that became a permanent tribute to my old paper. Instead of a funeral service, the *News Leader* was given a farewell by the men and women who had worked there between 1950 and 1965 and whose memoirs were collected in a book.

The idea came from James W. Baker of Williamsburg, Virginia, who got his first newspaper job at the *News Leader* in 1951 and stayed there 12 years. After learning that the old paper would exist no more, Jim wrote to as many former staffers of the 1950-1965 era that he could find. Although I had lost touch with my Virginia colleagues, I responded as soon as I heard about the project. Apparently, so did the others, for in an incredibly short time, I received a copy of *Whatever Happened to. . . .* It contained the stories of what had happened to 37 of us who had passed through the *News Leader* city room.

Among them were Gene Miller, who went to the Miami (Fl.) *Herald* and won two Pulitzer Prizes; James Jackson Kilpatrick, who became a nationally syndicated columnist; Roger Mudd, of the *McNeil-Lehrer Newshour;* George Gill, who became president and publisher of the Louisville (Ky.) *Courier-Journal;* and John M. Lee, who is an assistant managing editor at the *New York Times.*

It was fascinating reading through the memoirs and realizing how many of us had honed our journalistic skills covering beats, and how many of us had happy memories of our time at the *News Leader.* One of the old friends, David Barnett, who went on to become a bureau chief for the North American Newspaper Alliance and eventually an editor at *U.S. News & World Report,* wrote that working in Virginia was a "special time" for him and his wife, Jeanne. "The newspaper gang operated on the social level as one big family," he wrote. "While we were there, we thought life on a newspaper staff was like that all over. We know now it is rarely so."

As a reporter covering what were known as the "Main Street" and the "Federal" beats for the *News Leader,* I learned to cover the courts that were part of both beats, and it was here that my love affair with trial reporting began.

I came to Virginia because my husband was in the wartime Navy and I followed him there from Indiana, where I had met him while working on my first newspaper, the *Evansville Press.* I had come to Evansville fresh out of college with a Phi Beta Kappa key and no formal journalism training. One of my many sisters, Matty Kaplan, lived there, and she and her husband arranged for me to stay with them and work on the *Press,* a Scripps-Howard paper, for $10 a week. I had never thought about being a newspaper reporter but I had done a lot of writing for the University of Kentucky newspaper, the *Kentucky Kernel,* where I was a columnist and an associate editor. I had been writing poetry and short stories and plays and essays all though grade school and high school in New York City; in fact, my first published byline was in a national magazine when I was eight years old. (I won first prize in a contest for a story I wrote about our pet monkey, Mickey.) Two short stories I had written as a sophomore for a summer English course had won first and third prizes in a national intercollegiate contest sponsored by the national literary sorority Chi Delta Phi. The judges didn't know until the contest was over that they had awarded the same writer two prizes, because the stories were identified by number only. I had done all kinds of writing for the school newspaper and school magazine and I wanted to keep writing, so the newspaper job seemed fine to me.

At the *Press*, I covered hard news, wrote features, and like the rest of the staff, did everything else, including obituaries. I became tri-state editor, handling news from Kentucky, Illinois, and Indiana, and when I left to marry my husband, Bob, then stationed with the Navy in Indianapolis, I immediately got a job with the *Indianapolis Times*, another Scripps-Howard paper. After a short time, Bob was transferred to Richmond and I went with him, getting a job at the *News Leader*. This was my first trip to Richmond, and I stayed until my husband's discharge from the Navy. The second time around was after our son was born and we returned to Richmond when Bob, a news commentator in civilian life, got a job with Richmond's largest radio station. I went back to the *News Leader*.

Those of us in Virginia who worked a beat were "writing reporters." There was no time to sit down and get it all down on paper, especially since often there were as many as six stories breaking at the same time. In Philadelphia and New York, the police and City Hall beats were manned by legmen, those wonderful, colorful, street-smart reporters who did no writing but gave the information to us rewritemen, who turned it into stories. But in Virginia, we couldn't do this. We dictated the story with a lead first, then the middle, and then the end. It was like working for a wire service.

And since the *News Leader* was an afternoon paper, I had to learn to dictate an instant story. Back-breaking deadlines are the biggest challenge of working for a PM daily, which has to hit the streets only hours after courts and offices open for business.

But once you've worked on a PM, it is easy forever after to handle the deadlines and time pressures on any "AM" paper, you go to. On a morning paper, you have the luxury of time—sometimes you have all day and part of the night to work on a story, which most of your readers will see at breakfast the next day.

Like a cop on a beat, in Richmond I was assigned a certain area to cover by foot every day. The retiring veteran of the beat walked me through it, giving me invaluable tips that would have taken me months to learn for myself. Although I had covered all kinds of stories in Evansville and Indianapolis, traveling the beat with a pro was an eye-opener. He pointed out not only how to recognize instantly the importance—or non-importance—of a story, but also the best and fastest way to get a big one to the paper in time for early deadlines.

My first beat included the FBI, the Alcohol Tax Unit, the Federal Court, the U.S. Circuit Court of Appeals, and the U.S. marshal's office, among others. The reporter who broke me in explained such arcane ins and outs as these: The FBI office had to be visited and the agents queried each morning about any criminal doings that may have occurred. But no FBI agent outside of the special agent in charge was allowed to talk to a reporter about a case, and the special agent never gave out anything without clearing it with Washington. And when a truly important arrest was made in the Richmond area, the story had to be released simultaneously in Richmond and in Washington, quoting God himself, J. Edgar Hoover. So—"Get in and get out, don't waste time there, you'll never find out anything in a hurry from those guys," the veteran reporter told me.

If there was any hint that an important story was breaking, it wasn't a good idea to wait for the FBI to futz around with its bureaucratic folderol. With our early deadlines, waiting on the FBI could mean missing the whole story, and—God forbid—getting scooped by the competition. The trick was to figure out who else might have the information. If there was a big FBI bust, the U.S. marshal's office at the federal courthouse had to know about it, because that was where the FBI brought federal prisoners and where a U.S. commissioner arraigned them.

Since there was no love lost between FBI agents and the other feds (not to mention the sheriff's people or the Richmond cops), the best way to get a story fast was to go over to the marshal's office and tell them you knew something was up, but the FBI guys weren't releasing anything and you didn't have much time and had they heard anything?

One deputy U.S. marshal, who loathed the FBI agents because he felt they looked down on him, and who loved seeing his name in the paper, was the one to go to with your plea. (Which deputy to approach and which to avoid was part of the invaluable advice the veteran gave me.) I still marvel at how the deputy managed to get information to us without violating any federal regulations.

"Oh yeah, we got some guy in the lock-up," the deputy would

mention, "and he was arraigned last night. Maybe the commissioner will remember who it was he arraigned last night."

And sure enough, the U.S. commissioner, who relished seeing his name in the paper as much as the FBI agents hated seeing it before they were ready to break the big story from J. Edgar, would provide the details of this federal bust: what the charges were, what bail had been set, and any other circumstances on the record. Then he would listen happily as you picked up the phone in his office, called the *News Leader*, and began dictating your story.

Sometimes the deputies would tell me that they had a suspect in the holding cell behind the marshal's office, and if I wanted to talk to the fellow, I could. It was up to the suspect to answer my questions or not. So I'd walk to the cell and chat up some guy behind bars. Often the prisoner was so glad to have company—especially that of a young lady totally interested in what he had to say—that he'd give me all I needed to know, like his name and age and hometown and other vital statistics, where and why and when he got picked up, and everything else the FBI had on file but was not ready to dole out to the press.

Between my conversation with the prisoner and hints from the deputies and facts from the commissioner, I could dictate a detailed story to the paper and get on with the rest of the beat.

When the FBI finally came lumbering in with its made-in-Washington handout, usually hours after the first deadline, I always went down to get the release: first to encourage the agents to keep in touch by letting them think that what appeared in the newspaper came from them, and second to see if there was anything I had missed.

Usually the only thing missing from my story would be J. Edgar's pronouncements about his sterling department and its wondrous feats, a routine part of every handout composed at FBI headquarters. The main difference between a story based on the FBI account and my story was that the FBI story usually began: "FBI Director J. Edgar Hoover announced today that a suspect in the hijacking of a federal mail truck was arrested by agents of his bureau in Richmond, Va. . . ." My story usually started with the local commissioner's name. That made more sense for a local newspaper, anyway.

Beat reporters also had to be their own editors. All day long we sifted through enormous amounts of information from the offices and courts we covered, selecting and rejecting the stories we were going to give the paper. We never ignored handouts from government offices, but we knew the difference between a self-serving handout, which we threw away, and a handout with information important to the public, which went to the newspaper.

We were supposed to use our own judgment and seldom had to consult with the city editor, unless it was a question of whether there was enough space that day to run a story that was interesting but not important; or to advise him, if the paper was tight for space, whether a story could be held without fear of being scooped.

Covering the courts taught me how to listen totally to what was said. There was no such thing as bringing a tape recorder into a courtroom—it was absolutely forbidden during all of the years I covered courts. Using shorthand was not the best idea either, since you ended up taking down every word that was said, but never had a chance to develop an ear for the rhythms and quirks and nuances of the voices from the witness stand or from people you were interviewing.

Although no two people have the same speech patterns, you can read newspaper stories with lots of quotes in which each person quoted sounds like every other person in the story. This means that the reporter has not really listened, doesn't have the ear, and has imposed his own speech pattern on what he thinks he heard from the people he interviewed or heard testify. So they all sound like the writer.

In addition, with the ear, you can always tell that a lawyer is leading up to a highly important, maybe explosive question. You hear a change in the lawyer's voice, a subtle excitement that tips you off to pay careful attention, and you start taking down every question and answer, no matter how innocuous. Then when the big question, and the big answer, come, or if the witness starts shouting or bursts into tears, you have the Q and A that led up to it, and you can easily show your reader how this critical interrogation developed.

In Richmond, the FBI gave me my first—and for a long time, my only—experience in being treated as an adversary. At the time it was no more than sort of a good-natured game: getting a news story quicker than the FBI wanted us to have it. And we under-

stood it wasn't the fault of any individual agent; it was just part of
J. Edgar's dictatorship. He demanded, and he almost always got,
total control over not only every single agent in his army, but of
every bit of news that involved the FBI.

I still remember the anguish of Bill Foster, my replacement on
the Federal beat, who inadvertently got one of his FBI buddies into
trouble. In a weekly gossip column about doings on his beat, Bill,
who always wore bowties, wrote that while he was lunching with
an FBI friend, he told the agent that he too would look good in a
bowtie, and that he could bring him one from his collection. Bill
wrote that the agent said that would not be possible, for he had to
wear regular knotted ties according to regulations. Bill stuck this
in among the rest of the gossip as a moderately interesting little
item—that the FBI had restrictions about even the kind of ties their
agents wore. Innocuous, no?

No. The agent was called in by his superior and told that he had
committed a sin: he had revealed an internal FBI regulation to a
reporter! He had confided absolutely nothing of importance, but in
the Hoover mentality, revealing a little secret meant you might
reveal a big secret. So the agent was told that he would be watched
very carefully, and one more mistake would be his last.

We were so innocent in those days; we thought this was such a
weird invasion of a man's privacy to be told what kind of a neck-
tie he could wear and to be chastised for revealing such a bit of
nonsense. But we also thought J. Edgar was unique, that he confined this kind of control of private lives to the agents in his
bureaus, and that this paranoid interference did not extend to the
citizenry at large. All the time I worked in Richmond I was made
to believe that I was an important and respected representative of
the people, who had an inalienable right to know what was going
on in the courts and the FBI offices and all of the other places that
their taxes paid for.

It wasn't until the 1964 Republican convention in San
Francisco, however, that I actually learned what it was to be
treated like an enemy—as someone totally unwelcome, an
intruder who should be prevented from obtaining any information that was not spoon-fed.

Having been lucky enough not to have worked in Washington,
it was my first experience with people who disliked me on sight,
who had blind antipathy toward me merely because I represented

the press. Things got so bad that when I went to cover a session I would keep my notebook tucked away until after I was sitting somewhere in the back row, so I wouldn't have to put up with the looks of contempt from my fellow Americans. And the fact that I represented the *Daily News*, which was ramrod Republican on its editorial pages, made no difference. To those Republicans—ah, the foretaste they gave me of the Agnew attacks on the press—I might just as well have come straight from the newsroom of *Pravda*. As far as they were concerned, what they were doing at their convention was none of my or any other reporter's goddamn business.

The hostility toward the press at that convention peaked during an otherwise predictable speech by Dwight Eisenhower, who made a derogatory reference to "sensation-seeking columnists." The audience exploded into applause so tumultuous that it seemed to amaze Ike as much as it startled and dismayed me and my fellow reporters. I never forgot it. (Twenty years later, after a press conference, when President Reagan thought his mike was turned off, he turned off his smile and said about the reporters asking questions he didn't want to answer, "Sons of bitches!")

The Republicans in 1964 hated me just because I was a reporter at their convention. Mayor Daley's Chicago cops at the 1968 Democratic convention hated me just because I was a reporter watching bloody battles in their city. Ron Ziegler and other Nixon aides held the Washington press corps in absolute disdain. Despite all of this, I still believed that, as a reporter and a representative of the people, I was inviolate.

It never occurred to me that my telephone would be tapped or that my apartment would be placed under surveillance, as they were while I was covering the Pentagon Papers trial in Los Angeles. I thought Daniel Ellsberg was completely paranoid when he asked to use my apartment in Los Angeles for a pretrial press conference; according to him, his apartment was surely bugged. But I found out later that Dan was right.

Most of the out-of-town press corps at the Pentagon Papers trial rented apartments at a downtown complex named Bunker Hill, which at that time was almost vacant. We rented the furniture that we needed. It was more comfortable and less expensive than living in hotel rooms. Ellsberg and his lawyers also rented and furnished apartments there, since Bunker Hill was within walking distance of the federal courthouse where the case was being heard by U.S. District Judge Matt Byrne.

Throughout the trial we joked about being under surveillance. Linda Deutsch and I used to end our phone conversations with, "Are you listening, FBI honey?" Even so, I was truly astonished when, after the trial, Bill Farr of the *Los Angeles Times* told me he had figured out that my apartment had been under surveillance.

A friend of Bill's with access to intelligence dossiers informed him that the files indicated four occasions when Bill and Ellsberg had been together. Bill easily accounted for three of them: Dan visited Bill in jail (Bill went to jail rather than reveal the source of a story he wrote during the Charlie Manson trial), the two went to a book store after Bill was released, and they both spoke one night at an ACLU meeting.

He couldn't figure out the fourth incident until he recalled that both he and Dan had been among the guests in my apartment at a big party celebrating Bill's release from jail, to which I had invited the Ellsberg defense team as well as Bill's prosecution friends and other law-and-order buddies. So that meant my apartment was under surveillance, and explained why the apartment across the hall never seemed to have anyone permanent in it, only single men who never said good morning when I met them in the hall.

I also discovered after the trial that our phones were indeed bugged. Marty Arnold of the *New York Times* had complained to me during the trial about the clicking noises on his phone at Bunker Hill, and told me all our phones were tapped. He complained to the phone company. "Oh Marty," I said to him. "You're getting as crazy as Dan." Smart me. Crazy them.

So reporters were nothing sacred, and you didn't have to be a fist-in-the-air radical to have your rights violated by agents of the government. And then along came Watergate, and it was worse than I ever imagined: reporters on presidential "enemies lists" and other revelations of how mean-minded, vengeful, and intrusive were our leaders toward the press.

When I started covering the county, state, and federal offices and courts in Richmond, the officials I worked with, made me understand that as a member of the free press I was expected to ask questions and get answers.

I was given to understand that elected officials were obligated to give me answers so I could relay this information to the people who were paying their salaries.

I believed I was getting information for the people, who had no other way to find out about their city. I thought my job was to bring to the citizens, through the newspaper they depended on, facts that would make them aware and knowledgeable, or just stories that would make them laugh or cry.

And I discovered that in the courts, particularly, there were stories that were irresistible, because they were about people. Heroic, corrupt, honest, greedy people. Dedicated lawyers fighting for justice working side-by-side with shysters using the system to wheel and deal and circumvent the law.

The trials I covered in the U.S. District Court in Richmond involved every kind of a federal crime imaginable, including moonshining. This court had jurisdiction over the entire eastern district, so the federal agents brought moonshiners in from rural counties far afield from Richmond.

A family I will call the Obies of Louisa County were the ones I was most familiar with, and I remember one trial in U.S. District Court before Judge Robert Pollard which caused a big commotion at the courthouse.

The defendant, whom I will call Tony Obie, had a moonshining record, and the Alcohol Tax Unit agents—"revenuers"—had arrested him after they found a still hidden on his property. The agents had photos and other evidence. Of course, everybody in the courtroom, including the jurors, knew about the Obies. They had been in court many times.

Obie pleaded not guilty, insisting it was not his still. He admitted it was on Obie property, but swore he knew nothing about it until he was arrested. The jury retired to deliberate, and returned quite quickly: not guilty.

As Obie walked out of the courtroom a free man, I thought Judge Pollard would have a stroke. He sat there, glowering at the jurors until Obie was gone. Then, turning to Deputy Marshal James Braithwaite, he said icily, "Marshal, I don't want to see those jurors in that jury box in this courtroom again!" Then he marched into his chambers, every fold of his black robe quivering in outrage.

I trotted along with Braithwaite back to his office, talking about how ticked off Pollard was. A couple of the jurors, looking put out, joined us in Jim's office. Everybody knew each other in those days, and one of the jurors said to Braithwaite, "What's wrong with ole Pollard? What got him so fired up at us?"

The deputy stared at them, and then said, "What's wrong with ole Pollard? Why, he just didn't think a jury should cut loose a moonshiner like Obie when there was plenty of evidence to convict him. That's what's wrong with ole Pollard."

"You mean that little bitty still those revenuers said they found on Obie's land?" the juror asked. "Why, we all know Obie. We've sent him up before. We just figured Obie would never mess around with a piddlin' little still like that, nor would any of the Obies. He said it wasn't his, and it wasn't."

The jurors had decided that somebody else must have "borrowed" some of the Obie land to put up the little still on a sort of freelance basis, and that when Obie swore he didn't know anything about it, he was telling the truth. The overgrown Obie land could conceal lots of stills. In fact, the jurors declared, Obie probably had a trespassing case against the other guy, if he were ever found.

When Braithwaite reported this to Judge Pollard, the judge was somewhat mollified. There had been no skullduggery, just jurors trying to be fair and to deliver a good verdict. The jurors were allowed to serve in his court again.

Braithwaite and his sidekick, Deputy Marshal Hamner, along with Luther Irby, the federal probation officer, explained to me why moonshiners were different from ordinary lawbreakers.

These were Southerners who had been moonshiners for generations. They were churchgoing, hard-working, and otherwise lawabiding. They did a cash-only business, didn't trust banks, and lived dirt poor, although their rundown houses way out in the woods were stuffed with money.

Irby took me with him on some of his visits, telling me that these were stubborn Americans, real individualists: they believed the U.S. government had no right to make them take out licenses to make the moonshine—white mule—that their daddies and their granddaddies and their great-granddaddies had been making and selling on the land that had been theirs for generations.

Irby and the two deputies regaled me with wonderful stories about the kind of men who insisted on making illegal liquor. There was one moonshiner who came in to complain to the feds about "unfair competition." This gentleman sold the smoothest, most delicious white mule in the area, for he came from a line of moonshiners who had been making liquor for such a long time that they could let their new stuff age while selling the liquor that had been laid down years before. They took a lot of pride in their moonshine, and knowledgeable Virginians knew they were drinking the best when they got a bottle of white mule bearing the name of, well, let's call them the Jakes family. The deputies had all tasted the Jakes' product and said it really was as smooth as anything could be that had the kick of a mule.

One day Jakes came into the marshal's office in his bib overalls and straw hat, carrying with him a bottle in a brown paper bag which he plunked down in front of the deputies. He was one indignant moonshiner.

"Marshal," he said, "somebody is selling this rotgut and saying its mine, and I want him stopped! It is plain poison. It is so green it could kill you. And the guy who is making it is getting top dollar by telling everybody it comes from the Jakes."

Jakes wanted the marshals to taste the rotgut. They sniffed it and declined. They knew from its smell that a small taste might not be fatal, but would surely cause such a horrible hangover that death would seem appealing.

To Jakes it was a very simple problem. Somebody was using the proud family name to foist lethal moonshine upon an innocent public, and he was seeking government protection both for himself and for the unsuspecting citizens of Virginia. He wanted the other moonshiner enjoined by the federal government from selling his hooch under the Jakes name.

How do you explain to an enraged moonshiner that the marshals couldn't do anything for him? They explained that since both he and his competitor were breaking the law, the last place Jakes could get help was from the lawmen who were supposed be trying to put him out of business.

"You know, I kind of felt sorry for him," the deputy who told the story said to me. "He came all the way from his farm to ask for some help, just like any citizen should. And since we couldn't help him legally, the way he asked, I always wondered if maybe he got rid of the other guy some way not so legal. I don't even want to know."

On the Federal beat, covering trials in U.S. District Court and arguments in the Circuit Court of Appeals, I learned how the federal court system worked. But I think I actually learned the law from the Main Street beat and the state and county courts with wonderful names like Hustings Court and Court of Law and Equity. The most active one was Hustings, which was similar to Superior Court in Los Angeles or Supreme Court in New York.

Judge John Ingram of Hustings Court was one of my most consistent tutors, and the way he taught me was unusual, spontaneous, and effective. He used to let me use his telephone to dictate a story if I was on a deadline and it was a case of some importance. I'd be leaning across the desk, flipping through my notes and dictating something like, "Judge Ingram today granted in Hustings Court a writ of habeas corpus to . . ." when—fwap! the judge would smack me across the fanny with some papers to grab my attention. Appropriately startled, I would look up and he'd say, "That is a *petition* for a writ of habeas corpus I granted."

So I'd start the dictation over, and you can be sure that I never forgot that or any of the rest of the law he taught me. This was not harassment; we developed enormous respect for each other, and there came a time when I was so proficient that Ingram would sit there and beam at me as I dictated, nodding his head to show I was on course.

The *News Leader* expected me to explain to readers what a petition for a writ of habeas corpus was. My job was to break it down into layman's language and I depended on the judge to keep me accurate. When he explained it to me so that I understood it, I was able to write it so that everybody else could, too. That's how I learned to ask questions of lawyers and judges. I discovered that far from being annoyed by my questions, they enjoyed giving the information if it resulted in making the law understandable to the thousands of readers who read about a case or an appeal or a trial or an arrest.

Among the courts I covered on Main Street was Probate Court, where wills and estates are handled, and where I was introduced to unadulterated, nasty greed and watched how it fractured families and made hogs out of what appeared to be ladies and gentlemen. Probate did not have the daily urgency and news breaks of Hustings Court with its criminal cases, but it had its share of contested wills which made wonderful news stories. Since I was fascinated with anything that had to do with people, especially eccentric Southerners, I found it absorbing, if sometimes depressing, listening to these tales of families gone awry.

Over the years, one probate judge had seen more greed than I ever thought existed, and it took a lot of hard evidence for him to change a will. During a contested probate his court would be filled with witnesses trying to convince him. That's where I heard brothers and sisters fighting over money, sons and daughters saying heinous things about their own parents and each other, simply to get a bite of some juicy estate.

There were the relatives who came to tell the judge how dear old Uncle Hampton had lost all of his marbles before he died and should not be allowed to leave his millions to a cat and dog hospital when he had loving next of kin entitled to the money. The judge let the will stand after calling witnesses who testified that Uncle Hampton was a helluva smart old fella who said repeatedly, even on his death bed, that animals had been truer friends to him than his rotten, money-hungry relatives.

I remember the judge stating repeatedly in reaching a decision that a person's last will and testament was sacred, and that as a probate judge he was the only person who could protect and speak for a dead fellow being. Sometimes that meant he had to protect the dead person by not upholding a will, if he was convinced that some outsider had taken advantage of a senile old party and had pushed him into writing a will designed to disinherit truly beloved children. Mostly, however, it seemed that the wills were upheld as accurate reflections of what the deceased really wanted.

Were the judges just super great in Richmond? Well, lots of things were different in Richmond, so why not the judges? Where else would a judge keep a jury from coming in with its verdict until he could get word to me in another court to get downstairs in a hurry?

Judge Ingram's bailiff panted into the other court, signalling me to come with him in a hurry because a verdict had been reached in some big criminal case and the judge could delay the jury for just a little while.

On the last day I covered that beat, it was Judge Ingram who took the bench and, in open court, read into the record:

> The court notes with regret that our able reporter, Mrs. Theo Wilson, is leaving us for the City of Brotherly Love. Her fairness in

getting the facts, her desire to understand technicalities, so that even to a lawyer her articles make sense, but above all her ability to receive and treat matters in confidence makes us conscious of the great debt we owe Brooklyn. . . . Let the above be spread on the minutes of those invisible books which friends keep and read and no one else sees or understands.

Richmond was different in other ways, too. Where else, on Robert E. Lee's birthday, would the editor of a daily newspaper march into the news room, call out "Ladies and Gentlemen, please rise!" and recite from memory Lee's farewell to his troops?

That editor was Dr. Douglas Southall Freeman, the Pulitzer Prize-winning biographer and scholar, whose knowledge of the Civil War and the men who led it was monumental. Richmonders were very proud that an author of Dr. Freeman's fame was the editor of one of their newspapers. This admiration didn't stop them from telling stories about how confusing it was to read his editorials during World War II, in which Freeman would review and critique the great overseas battles.

"I swear, I wouldn't know whether we were fighting at Appomattox or the Ruhr," one lady told me. "Dr. Freeman would start out writing a commentary about a big battle that had just taken place in Europe. Then he'd compare the military action the Allies and the Nazis had taken to how General Lee and the Yankees had done it in one of their big battles, and by the time we all got through reading Dr. Freeman, none of us was sure if it was 1943 or 1863!"

When I left the *News Leader*, Dr. Freeman called me into his office to tell me goodbye. As I sat down, he called out to his secretary, "Bring in 'The Last Parade.'"

I was in great awe of him, and I thought that maybe he had a bunch of old Civil War vets on call to march through his office on demand for special occasions.

Instead, his secretary came in reverently carrying a large, thin, white book. She placed it on the desk and Dr. Freeman opened it, wrote in it, and gave it to me. Without knowing what it was, I thanked him fervently.

I wasn't fervent enough. The book was a limited edition, a special deluxe reprinting of an editorial Dr. Freeman had written for the *News Leader*, illustrated with magnificent photographs of the monuments of the Confederate leaders that decorate Monument

Avenue in Richmond. Printed on heavy paper, the pages were double thick, open on the sides and bottoms, and each photo was protected by onionskin. As noted on the flyleaf, the editorial had been published in the *News Leader* "of Friday, June twenty-fourth Nineteen hundred and thirty-two, the last day of the forty-second annual reunion of the United Confederate Veterans."

It was a newspaper editorial that deserved the elegant book in which it was preserved. How that man could write! He described Richmond during the Civil War, the end of the Civil War in Richmond, the city's recovery from "poverty and pain," the first parade past the monument erected to General Lee on Traveller, and the many reunions of veterans.

"Today the city has its last review," his editorial concluded. "The armies of the South will march our streets no more. It is the rearguard, engaged with death, that passes now. Who that remembers other days can face that truth and still withhold his tears? The dreams of youth have faded in the twilight of the years. The deeds that shook a continent belong in history. Farewell; sound taps! And then a generation new must face its battles in its turn, forever heartened by that heritage."

In his incredibly tiny but remarkably clear and distinctive handwriting, my editor had inscribed on the title page: "To Theo Wilson, with the admiration and thanks of Douglas Southall Freeman."

3

On the Road

Many of us who met in 1954 at the first Sam Sheppard trial in Cleveland stayed in touch for a long time. We kept each other advised of stories that could develop into future trials, and as often as possible arranged our schedules so that we could be on the road together, covering the same trials and staying at the same hotels.

One of the early regulars was Ray Brennan of the *Chicago Daily News,* who knew and wrote about all the big-time hoods in his city. Ray was a big burly Black Irishman, and, like most tough-talking, tough-acting reporters and editors I met in those days, had a marshmallow heart.

One of Ray's stories about an imprisoned gangster resulted in the prisoner's release, and as soon as the hood got out, he hot-footed it over to Ray's house to thank him. Soon after the gangster left, Ray heard shots outside and ran from his house to find his visitor dying in the street. Ray held him in his arms as he died, and years afterward was still tormented by the death: "I should have left it alone, Theo," he said. "The little guy was safer in the pen. Maybe he'd still be alive if I hadn't written that story."

And once when a famous gangster lay mortally wounded in a hospital emergency room, surrounded by Chicago cops telling him to come clean and give them information and the name of his assassin, the gangster croaked out, "Get me Ray Brennan." Ray was summoned, the room was cleared, and the mobster unburdened himself to the big reporter.

When we were at the Sheppard trial we used to go out to dinner in a big group every night, and every so often Ray would get the urge to drink wine out of my "slipper," as he called it.

He really did mean it as a charming after-dinner gesture, except that to get to my place at the table he'd walk on top of the table. The slipper he'd pour the wine into was usually an open-toed, sling-back pump.

We were together at the 1963 trial of Tilmer Eugene Thompson, a lawyer accused of hiring a man to kill his wife in their house in St. Paul, Minnesota. The hired killer did a horrible job on Carol Thompson, who staggered naked and bleeding with a knife blade broken off in her throat through the snow to a neighbor's house, where she collapsed on the doorstep.

The wife's dreadful death and the fact that the young lawyer-husband was accused of masterminding the killing to collect the hefty life insurance he had taken out on her was enough to bring most of the clique of national trial reporters together.

Through some strange legal thinking, the trial was granted a change of venue all the way across the river from St. Paul to Minneapolis. A change of venue is customarily granted so that the defendant gets the benefit of jurors who live at such a distance from the crime that they may not have been as exposed to or prejudiced by publicity as those at the original murder site. I have never figured out how the Thompson change of venue was supposed to have benefited the defendant, since it was like moving a trial from Manhattan across the Harlem River to the Bronx.

We all congregated at the same Minneapolis hotel, where one night Ray confided that he had met a young couple, deeply in love, who desperately needed a room, and he had offered them his. Maybe the lovers were too impoverished to pay for a room of their own, or maybe there was no room for them at the inn, but Ray now needed to bunk in with somebody. I told him it was nice that he was such a sweet sentimental slob, but it sure as hell wasn't going to be me, and the others with us gave a variety of reasons why they also couldn't share with him.

At this point Doc Quigg of UPI, who always was late meeting us because he had to write an overnighter (a story for the early editions of PM papers) sauntered in. Ray explained his situation.

"I'd let you use the other bed in my room," Doc said, "but I don't think you'll want to, because I snore." He went on to explain that his snoring was very loud, and he warned Ray that if he shared Doc's room "you won't get any sleep. You won't find it possible to sleep. You'll be up all night."

Ray said he didn't mind, but Doc was really concerned that he'd give Ray a sleepless night and tried to talk him out of it. Nevertheless, Ray insisted it would be fine; he was a very sound sleeper, he said, and he wasn't worried about Doc's snoring. So Doc agreed to let him share his room.

Early next morning we gathered as usual at the hotel coffee shop for breakfast before heading off to the Hennepin County Courthouse. Doc and Ray walked in.

Ray, bright-eyed and fresh-faced, was hanging onto Doc's arm, and as he approached us, we heard him say: "Sweetie, I want to buy you a nice breakfast. Okay, sweet-ums?"

"Get away from me you son of a bitch," Doc said. We all stared at him. Doc looked exhausted; behind the Ben Franklin glasses that were his trademark were pink rims around his blue eyes, and there were black circles under the pink lids.

As they were getting seated, Ray continued his dippy imitation of a satisfied lady the morning after, and Doc kept snarling at him.

Then, wearily sipping black coffee, Doc told us what had happened.

"I was really worried about Ray not getting any sleep, remember?" he asked us. "I didn't want to keep him up with my snoring, remember?"

"Well," Doc continued, glaring at Ray who was contentedly stowing away a huge breakfast and making goo-goo eyes at his ex-roommate, "I fell asleep. And I don't think I was asleep five minutes before this terrible screaming started. It woke me up, it would have woken the dead. It was awful. It was coming from Ray."

Doc said he got up and shook and shoved Ray, who continued the caterwauling until he finally awoke. He told Doc he was sorry, and Doc, who had learned to sleep anywhere under any conditions after covering WWII and the Korean War, fell back asleep.

"Next thing I know, Ray is screaming again," Doc said, and once more he had to wake him.

"And then," Doc said, "Ray told me he has this habit of screaming all night. Here I'm telling him I'm afraid my snoring will keep him up, and he forgets to tell me that he screams all night long. No wonder he wasn't worried about my snoring. With those screams you wouldn't hear an atom bomb in the same room with you."

Ray, said Doc, slept soundly and screamed piercingly all

night long, and poor Doc gave up trying to sleep and never closed an eye.

"Oh honey," said Ray, "I thought we had a swell night together."

Doc yawned all through the court session, and every time he did Ray would look over at him and wink and blow little kisses.

There was very little space in the Hennepin County Courthouse for the press. Doc got a broom closet to set up his typewriter, and Ray and I were in a small anteroom down the hall, facing each other across a table so narrow our typewriters were back-to-back.

It was lunchtime and both of us were pounding out the events of a fairly routine morning session. It was November 22, Doc's birthday, and we were planning to celebrate it that night at a restaurant with goofy gifts and a cake we had ordered.

Doc came in, calm as always. "You may as well stop writing," he told us. "The President's been shot in Dallas."

My whole body stiffened, as if to ward off the blow of those words. I remember Doc saying, "It looks bad" and leaving. Ray and I picked up our phones and called our offices, and both of us were told the same thing: Jack Kennedy had been shot, don't file anything more on the trial today, stand by.

I remember hearing Ray swearing. I had my head in my hands, staring down at my typewriter, and I remember hearing sobs. Ray was crying, just sitting there, letting the tears run down his face, crying and crying. Everybody remembers where they were when JFK was killed. I was in the Hennepin County Courthouse in Minneapolis, listening to one Irishman keen for another.

Doc never did celebrate his birthday with us that night. He left the trial to fly into Dallas, where reporters were converging from everywhere. Three hours after the shooting, his UPI colleague, Merriman Smith, witnessed the swearing-in of Lyndon B. Johnson and returned to Washington on Air Force One with the new President, the new First Lady, and Jackie Kennedy, in her blood-stained pink suit, sitting next to the casket that held her husband's body.

In Dallas the UPI wanted Doc to capture the mood of that stricken city and Doc did what he was best at; he walked all over Dallas looking at everything and talking to everybody and then wrote a story, sent worldwide, that started with a description of the place in the road where JFK was killed:

The flowers wilt now on the cool grass. Beside the gray pavement where the shots echoed, the wreaths lie on the green. And the ache lingers in the hearts of Dallas. The noise of bullets that entered bone and flesh is yesterday's. No longer heard, and yet, you think as you watch the throngs go by and linger at the spot and drop their wreaths of mourning and just look and look and no noise comes— you think: maybe they hear the way the sad poet did when he said, ". . . as I stand by the roadside, or on the pavement gray, I hear it in the deep heart's core."

Back in Minneapolis, the Thompson trial was recessed by the judge until after the funeral, and Ray and I and others who remained clung together, watching television endlessly. There was nothing else we wanted to do.

On Sunday, two days after the shooting, I was talking from my hotel room to my son in New York when he shouted into the phone: "Mom! Mom! He's shot him! Somebody just shot Oswald!"

As we were talking, Delph was watching the live TV coverage of Lee Harvey Oswald being brought through the police station and he saw Jack Ruby shoot him. I didn't see it that first time, but I saw it and saw it in the countless replays of that scene. With no trial to cover, no desire to do anything but grieve, we had time to watch everything that happened in Dallas and in Washington.

At the time I didn't know that I would be covering the Jack Ruby trial, and I didn't know until I went to that trial how indelibly those TV pictures were printed in my mind.

Besides Ray and Doc, Bob Considine and Dorothy Kilgallen had been at the first Sheppard trial.

It was there that Bob, who at that time had one of the most famous bylines in the business, taught me such wonderful things as the meaning of the words "grace under pressure"—even on a deadline, he would sign an autograph for somebody with a smile, or patiently answer a reporter's questions—and how to flavor a verdict story with the colorful phrases that had been used by the attorneys during the summations, and how to survive a long night of drinking by sticking with tall glasses of Scotch and water, heavy on the water.

Bob, whose column was called "On the Line With Considine," wrote books and features and magazine articles and sports events and space news (we saw each other a lot at Cape Canaveral when

we covered the first Mercury astronauts) and never stopped working except when he started playing, and he was a wonder at that.
He was one of the funniest and kindest men I met in the business.

He never said a dirty word, and when moved to anger his worst
expletive was "Drat!" His wife Millie was a very funny lady herself, but she did use the language without inhibitions, leading Bob
to once tell her, as they sailed past a boat marked *Falmouth, Me.*,
"Look Millie, they've named a boat after you."

As one of the Hearst star reporters, Bob traveled all over the
world, and at one time Millie was going to write a book about her
experiences as the partner left behind to cope with many kids (natural and adopted) and household crises while the husband is in
exotic places living on big expense accounts.

Millie never did write the book, but Bob was supportive, urging
her on and finally giving her a title so wonderful it should have
pushed her into immediate authorship: *Pop Goes, The Weasel!*

After the Sheppard case, Dorothy and I next met in Los Angeles,
during the first Dr. Bernard Finch-Carole Tregoff murder trial in
1960.

We didn't see very much of each other at either trial, because I
never went out to lunch, using the noon recess to file the morning
session, and on weekends, when the out-of-towners mainly got
together and played, she had to fly back to New York to keep her
commitments, which included her appearances on *What's My Line*,
the TV show that made her more famous than her newspaper
career.

I seldom ran into her in New York, either, because I was out
there doing hard news and she was not. I liked Dorothy, and I
loved her father, the indestructible Jim Kilgallen. He was one of the
last of the old-time all-around reporters, and I was told that he was
totally nuts about this daughter who had so successfully followed
in his footsteps.

Jimmy broke all records for longevity as a working reporter, and
Doc Quigg would do an annual birthday interview with him for
the UPI. At 93 Jimmy finally retired, telling Doc he was doing so
only because "my wife has been after me to retire since I was 90."

Everybody loved Jim. When Dorothy was found dead in her
Manhattan town house of an overdose of barbiturates and alcohol,
the rumor was that she left a suicide note but it was destroyed at
the behest of the first reporters on the scene, who wanted to spare

Jim, that good Catholic, the knowledge that his beloved daughter had killed herself and committed a mortal sin. It was a believable rumor because of the fondness old Jim inspired in other reporters, but we never found out if it was true.

Jim and his wife, Mae, first were told that Dorothy had died of a heart attack; later that she had accidentally taken too many sleeping pills.

To this day, we don't know if Dorothy died accidentally or intentionally. Some people believe she was murdered because she was investigating JFK's assassination and making discoveries.

Dorothy was a hard-working and conscientious reporter and a facile writer, and when I first met her she was already a seasoned Hearst star who could turn out the Hearst style of copy with color and flair.

I always felt kind of sorry for her, mainly because although she was making piles of money, she didn't seem to have the chance to enjoy it; she rubbed some of her colleagues the wrong way with her intense competitiveness, and some reporters apparently resented the fact that she had a butler and townhouse and rode around in limousines.

She also seemed very vulnerable. Once, at the Ambassador Hotel where we both stayed during the Finch trial, she showed me a bunch of flowers she had received from Johnny Ray, the singer, and from the way she preened and giggled I figured she was gaga about him. I couldn't believe it. Johnny Ray, for pete's sake!

She was among the first news reporters to become well-known through television, and although she wanted to remain one of the guys and horse around with the rest of us and be taken seriously as a reporter, her fame got in the way. Part of being a good reporter is to be anonymous, to stay out of the story so that you can better watch and study and listen to the principals. She couldn't do that, mostly because people wouldn't let her. She'd walk into a trial and the prosecutor would ask for her autograph for his wife or the judge would send out greetings.

The problem was that Dorothy's TV appearances had nothing to do with news or journalism or reporting. Lots of people didn't even know that she had been a good reporter. It was hard for journalists who only knew her from the TV game show or the gossip column to take her seriously when she showed up on a news story, and that must have bothered her. But Dorothy's biographer, Lee

Israel, believed that Dorothy actually was working on the biggest story of her life, the Jack Kennedy murder, and was killed because she was getting close to the truth.

Because Dorothy had to leave the Finch trial on weekends to fly to New York she sometimes missed stories, and it upset her, especially if she had to pick up the *News* on Sunday or Monday and read something I had dug up during the weekend recess.

But although she sometimes raised hell with others and had a reputation for being temperamental and demanding, we got along and had fun together; she told me that when she was not at a trial, she would read me in the *News* "like the Bible."

Bob Considine, who made a habit of being kind, was very protective of Dorothy, who unfortunately was often on the receiving end of undeserved criticisms ranging from her looks to her lifestyle. When we were in Dallas for the Jack Ruby trial, for instance, I remember getting a phone call from Bob in my hotel room, where I was waiting for him to finish a column so that we could go together to the Press Club.

The big Ruby trial press corps, which included lots of reporters from abroad, had been invited to a cocktail party there given by Texas newspaper publishers and their wives.

"Dorothy just called," Bob said. "She's at the party at the Press Club and she's been there a while. She says to come right away and rescue her, they're driving her nuts. She sounds like she's been drinking. I'll finish the column later."

We rushed to the Press Club, and started working our way through the mob over to where Dorothy was sitting, being introduced along the way to the publishers and their ladies who were hosting the event.

As we approached Dorothy, I saw her take a big gulp of vodka and then I heard an exchange and realized why poor Dottie was getting plastered so early and so quick.

One of the publisher's wives, carrying an empty glass and wearing a glittery cocktail dress, came over to Dorothy and in a thick Texas accent said, "Oh, Miz Kilgallen! Ah'm just so thrilled to meet you. Ah love your television program. You certainly are smaht on it."

"Thank you so much," said Dorothy, smiling uneasily as the wife came closer and peered into her face.

"And you know what?" the wife confided. "You're nothin' as

ugly as you look on television!"

Poor Dorothy! "This has been going on all night," she muttered to us, draining another glassful, and when she came up for air another sweet Texas belle was there.

"It's terrible why you-all are here," she was saying, "just terrible what happened."

I said: "Yes, it is terrible. To think a man so young should have been killed."

"Oh, I don't mean Jack Kennedy," the woman said, her voice vibrating with disdain as she said the dead President's name. "I mean it's just terrible that it had to happen here—in our wonderful Dallas!"

At that Dorothy and I both dove into our glasses. Considine grabbed our arms, whispered "Let's get out of here" and we escaped, making totally unintelligible but important-sounding excuses to our hosts for our premature departure.

It was also at Dallas that one of Jack Ruby's defense lawyers, huge Joe Tonahill, gave me the name "Squeaky" because of the way I entered the courtroom, with a leap and more of a squawk than a squeak. The reason was that the deputies were ordered to frisk all of us, along with the public, before we could enter the trial room. For some reason the ham-handed lady deputies assigned to body search the females loved to finish me off with a little extra love pinch of my bosoms, causing me to enter the trial room jumping and yipping. Judge Joe Brown used to come out of chambers early just to watch me erupt into his courtroom. It tickled him mightily.

It was during these disgusting friskings, to which we objected loudly and unsuccessfully, that columnist Inez Robb, that fragile and dainty blonde writer, had an unforgettable exchange with one of the most muscular and heavy-handed of the female deputies.

As the deputy was patting her down, Inez said: "If you're going to do this to me, I'd rather have one of the men deputies do it."

"That's against the law here," said the female deputy, still feeling up Inez.

"Indeed?" Inez queried through gritted teeth. "Well where I come from what you're doing to me is really against the law."

Because of all the bosom groping, I wanted to start one of my stories, "I dreamed I covered the Jack Ruby trial in my Maidenform bra."

In Dallas we became friends with Buck Marryat, the American Airlines public relations director who, like Bill Hipple of American Airlines in Los Angeles, was part of a breed of men now long gone from the world of journalism.

The airlines don't have such men now; great public relations reps who created solid friendships with newspaper reporters have disappeared, along with the other amenities of life. In Dallas Buck helped make life better for us out-of-towners, throwing parties, arranging outings, suggesting things for us to do during the weekends when the trial was in recess. It was people like Hipple and Marryat who you called when there was an emergency and you urgently and suddenly needed a flight. When JFK was killed, it was Hipple and Marryat who got desperate reporters onto airplanes—American's flights, of course—to fly into Dallas from all over the country.

Despite Buck's own charm and his wonderful parties, most of us wound up loathing Dallas, and after Ruby was convicted we left so fast that we didn't have our customary post-verdict party. Early in the morning, Buck met us at the airport to make sure we got VIP treatment on his airline. He also left a gift for me on the plane, and when we were airborne to New York, the stewardess presented me with a prettily decorated cake bearing this sentimental farewell: "Adios, you mother. . . ."

I wouldn't let anybody cut it because I knew there was one person who had to see it in all of its delicate splendor. When we landed in New York, a bunch of us shared a cab together back into Manhattan, and when I walked into the city room, I gave the cake to city editor Harry Nichols. He loved it, and we shared it in the city room while I regaled him and the other editors with Dallas stories.

Over the years, the group of trial reporters changed as we lost some regulars and gained others, but there always were enough of us locked together at any one trial to create our own unreal world.

During the Sirhan Sirhan trial in Los Angeles, we formed the Condor Hunt Club to find and preserve condors up in the mountains above Santa Barbara. We never even saw one of the endangered birds, but the club had regular meetings and field trips during the weekend recesses of the trial, and Virginia Berman, wife of the legendary defense attorney Emile Zola Berman, even ordered matchbooks printed up for us. Our main discovery was never to say the title of the club fast or drunk.

Emile Zola told us that in his first meeting with Sirhan Sirhan, he told the young defendant, "You don't have to call me Mr. Berman. You can call me by my first name."

"And you can call me by my first name," said Sirhan Sirhan.

Emile Zola had a fine New York accent, and the way he pronounced Sirhan's name it sounded like plastic wrap. "Saran Saran," he'd call out in court, cracking us up every time.

To be on the road at the right time so that you could meet up with your buddies took some calendar juggling, and sometimes I would have to miss a jury selection, which I hated doing since you can find out a lot of what the lawyers on both sides are planning from the questions they ask the veniremen.

This is in state courts, for in most federal courts the judge does all the questioning of prospective jurors. Jury selection goes faster this way, but I think the other way is fairer to the defendant. And watching an attorney like F. Lee Bailey, in his heyday, question prospects so that they all wound up loving him, was an experience.

When the Angela Davis murder trial started in California, after more than a year of pretrial activity, I was stuck in New York finishing up the wondrous tale of Clifford Irving and his forgery of the Howard Hughes "biography."

Irving had successfully duped publishers and others into believing he had pulled off one of the great feats of the time, claiming he had actually interviewed the hermit billionaire and had received permission to write his life story.

Irving would have succeeded if Hughes had maintained his legendary silence, but the eccentric recluse conducted an astonishing telephone interview with a group of reporters in Los Angeles who had known him before he went into seclusion, and they said it was Hughes himself denying he had ever met or spoken to Irving. The allegedly authorized biography was a hoax, Hughes told the reporters.

Before a Manhattan grand jury indicted Irving, the case became internationmal, with discoveries that Irving had stashed some of his fraudulent gains in Switzerland and revelations of Irving's extramarital love affair with the gorgeous Nina van Pallandt of Denmark, whom I called Irving's "Danish pastry."

Meanwhile, the Davis trial was starting in San Jose. It had

been moved on a change of venue from the San Francisco Bay area, where she had been charged with murder during the unsuccesful attempt to free prisoners at the Marin County Courthouse. Tony Burton was covering for the *News* while I was writing the Irving case, and from Burton and Linda Deutsch and Earl Caldwell of the *New York Times* I began receiving disquieting reports.

Security was so tight that it was like being in a POW camp. Lines had been drawn on the ground outside the courthouse, and reporters were warned not to cross them while talking with lawyers or other court personnel. Marijuana was found in a bin into which reporters and spectators had to dump their possessions before entering the courtroom, and Caldwell had been arrested and charged as the one who had brought it in. He was going to be tried in a lower court after Angela's trial ended.

After the Irving case ended with indictments against him and his wife, I flew out to San Jose and discovered things were really a mess, mainly because for months the reporters had been allowing the cops to make the rules.

The first day I was there, as I was filing the morning session during the lunch break, one of the security officers told me I had to stop writing and go with the rest of the reporters to be searched for the afternoon session. I told him we had another 40 minutes before the session started, and I had to finish filing; I assured him I could get there in plenty of time. The officer, who was wearing a gun, told me to get up right then, or I would not be allowed to leave the press room to get into the trial. He said the reporters had to be escorted and couldn't walk to the courtroom alone, and they wanted the frisking done in plenty of time.

I went with him, and then stood outside the locked trial room, fuming with the others for 30 precious minutes when I could have been filing the story to my newspaper.

That afternoon a group of us went to see the judge to ask for help, which he gave us. We also met with the security chief, in his office. He came to the meeting with a gun which he unstrapped and placed on the table in front of him. Among other things we asked for, besides dropping the armed escort, was the right for the wire services to have seats for two reporters at a session so they could cover for each other when one had to leave the courtroom to file on their many deadlines.

"After all, an AP reporter even rode with General Custer," said Linda Deutsch, trying to impress the officer with the history and importance of her organization.

"Yeah, and he had two horses," I chimed in.

Eventually, we got enough changes made so that we could cover the Davis trial properly, although the working conditions remained about the worst of any trial I have ever covered.

Edith Lederer, Linda Deutsch, and I led the delegations to the judge and security officer. All three of us were the same size, about 5'2", and a publisher who attended the trial for a couple of days to write a color story for his newspaper, became obsessed with our size.

"They are little, but they know!" his article trumpeted several times, as he described our exploits. After the story was published, Edie and Linda and I couldn't walk together anyplace—the press room, a restaurant, a party—without our colleagues standing and shouting together: "They are little, but they know!"

Earl Caldwell was acquitted of the marijuana charge at a non-jury trial which all of us attended after Davis case ended. At Angela's trial a great deal had been made of the fact that not one black juror was on her panel, and when she was found not guilty, some of us wrote leads beginning, "An all-white jury today acquitted Angela Davis. . . ." So when Earl, who is black, was acquitted, I suggested that he write this lead for his paper: "An all-white judge today acquitted Earl Caldwell. . . ." He thought not.

4

The *Confidential* Trial

The first case I ever covered in Los Angeles came to be known as the *Confidential* trial; two months in 1957 of strange goings-on during which film megastar Maureen O'Hara and singer-actress Dorothy Dandridge appeared before the jury to testify against the scandal magazine that was giving the Hollywood movie moguls severe heartburn.

Confidential magazine was the forerunner of today's supermarket newspapers. It was flashy, full of photos, and successful in a highly competitive field of sensational magazines purporting to give movie fans the inside dirt about Hollywood's royalty that respectable publications would not print. At a time when movie stars were protected by their studios from any hint of scandal, at a time when the marriage of a matinee idol was kept secret from his fans, when the kings and queens of Hollywood were truly untouchable and unknowable, *Confidential* catered to millions of moviegoers entranced by forbidden juicy gossip about the stars.

Compared to what is now standard fare in supermarket and TV tabloids, and to what some modern celebrities and superstars seem happy to reveal about themselves on talk shows and in tell-all books, however, the exposes of the old *Confidential* seem positively innocuous. These days we read with a yawn an item such as this in a respectable family newspaper like the *Los Angeles Times* (February 25, 1992): "Actor Jack Nicholson and girlfriend Rebecca Broussard announced Monday that they are the parents of an 8-pound, 6-ounce boy. . . . They also have a 20-month-old daughter, Lorraine Broussard-Nicholson." Who cared that Nicholson and his buddy Warren Beatty were bachelor fathers?

Or as Beatty himself put it, in a *Los Angeles Times* interview at about that time: "Before I came along, you could really get away with things; it was pre-TV, pre-proliferation of cable TV, pre-tabloids. In that time, the only outrageous outlet was something called *Confidential* magazine. Now we are all more in the fish bowl, but does it matter anymore? Who's watching the bowl? There is so much going on in the fish bowl—everybody is in the bowl, with a loss of privacy for everyone, not just celebrities."

In the 1950s, if a story about out-of-wedlock babies had been leaked to the public, the movie career of the unwed fathers would have been ruined. The stories about the stars that came out in *Confidential* were filled with innuendo and hints about alleged sexual peccadillos that wouldn't lift an eyebrow among today's readers. But in those times, the stories were considered so steamy that the publication developed a large following, and the studios became nervous. At the time of the trial, *Confidential* claimed the largest newsstand circulation in the country—four million issues bimonthly.

The titles of some of the articles published in 1956 and 1957 that were charged in the indictment with being either libelous or obscene give an idea of the dirt that was being dished:

- Robert Mitchum: The Nude Who Came to Dinner
- Mae West's Open Door Policy
- How Long Can Dick Powell Take It?
- Where Was Eddie Fisher When The Lights Went Out?
- Only the Birds and the Bees Saw What Dorothy Dandridge Did in the Woods
- That Rug Party in Mark Stevens' Office

Two *Confidential* articles were charged in the indictment with violation of California's Business and Professional Code: a March 1956 effort entitled "Beware the Newest Abortion Menace: The Pill That Ends Unwanted Pregnancy," and the January 1957 "Pega Palo—The Vine That Makes You Virile." In addition, the entire June 1957 issue of *Whisper* (a sister magazine) and the May 1955, May 1956, and September 1956 issues of *Confidential* were listed in the indictment as lewd and obscene.

The trial was being touted as one of the biggies of all time. In

New York, we heard that it had come about because the powerful Hollywood studios had been pushing the authorities to drive the scandal magazine out of business; it was even rumored that Mervyn LeRoy had raised a war chest of $350,000 to finance the battle. (The studios kept behind the scenes throughout the trial.) It was also rumored that a large cast of stars was going to take the stand to denounce the scandalmongers and to swear that the stories appearing in the magazine were untrue.

The headquarters of Robert Harrison, the 53-year-old owner of *Confidential, Whisper, and other scandal sheets—Titter, Wink, Flirt,* and *Eyeful,* was in Manhattan. But Harrison, along with his niece and her husband, Marjorie and Fred Meade, were indicted in Los Angeles because they operated Hollywood Research, the West Coast agency for Harrison's magazines. In all, the indictment named 11 persons (including Harrison's two sisters, his secretaries in Manhattan) and five corporations. They were charged with conspiracy to commit criminal libel, conspiracy to circulate lewd and obscene material, conspiracy to disseminate information about male rejuvenation, and conspiracy to publish material pertaining to abortions.

Uncle Bob, as Marjorie called Harrison, had made a lot of money from *Confidential,* and the Meades had made nice money with Uncle Bob. For 18 months they had run the L.A. office, hiring writers and paying tipsters for information about the film stars— actors' ex-wives, madams, prostitutes, bandleaders, interior decorators, governesses, bartenders, and even reputable journalists picking up easy money for information their own publications would never use. They were paid $150,000 for this work, but they never bargained to become defendants in a suit that was so important that the California Attorney General's office joined the Los Angeles District Attorney in its prosecution.

To defend the Confidentials, Uncle Bob hired some of the best legal eagles around. Arthur Crowley, a top Los Angeles criminal lawyer, and *Confidential's* New York attorneys, Jacob Rosenbaum and Albert DeStefano, made up the defense team. They were aided by legendary private eye Fred Otash.

The prosecutors were Assistant Attorney General Clarence Linn and Deputy District Attorney William Ritzi. Ritzi taught Sunday school, it was noted in newspaper reports.

Presiding in Los Angeles Superior Court was Judge Herbert V. Walker. Judge Walker was a genial old boy, but his nickname among court habitues was "The Phumpfer" because he had a tendency to mumble. The British writers especially could not understand the judge's phumpfering, and I was constantly reading them my notes from my little black notebook.

Walker had a busy calendar, and whenever there was a lull in the *Confidential* proceedings, he would have defendants from other cases brought in for arraignment or to set trial dates. You can imagine the surprise for the poor defendant in some little case who was schlepped into the courtroom to find it bursting with the press and eager onlookers. He had to be reassured that his minor infraction had not been elevated to a capital offense, and that we weren't there for him.

At some point, Judge Walker realized that the foreign press was bemused by this parade of defendants, and he decided to explain.

"Ladies and gentlemen of the press," he started out, leaning toward our rows."I suppose you are wondering why . . . ," and here he began his phumpf phumpf phumpf, earnestly declaiming unintelligibly for several minutes. When he got through, he leaned back, satisfied with a job well done. Then the Brit in front of me turned around and said briskly, "Well! That certainly clarified everything, didn't it, dear?"

Before the trial started on August 3, both sides proposed a deal—leniency for the Meades in return for an agreement from *Confidential* that it would no longer publish stories about the stars. Judge Walker denied the request.

The courtroom in the old Hall of Justice was packed for the trial, with citizens and the domestic and foreign press—including a large contingent representing the gossip-loving British—lured in the hope of seeing famous faces. I was astounded that during one recess, with the judge off the bench, a tie salesman paraded down the aisle, unabashedly hawking his wares from a tray suspended on straps around his neck. I had to explain to the foreign press that this was not a typical U.S. court happening. (Years later, during the Jack Ruby trial, I had more explaining to do. That Dallas courtroom, with its spittoons and pistol-packing prosecutors, also was not your usual U.S. court of law. Thanks to Melvin Belli, who defended Ruby, the spittoons were removed and the assistant prosecutor as well as the spectators were ordered by Judge Joe

Brown to park their guns at the courtroom door.)

Maureen O'Hara was scheduled as a prosecution witness to denounce *Confidential* for printing an article claiming that she and a male companion had been seen by an usher making out in Row 35 in Grauman's Chinese Theater. This is the movie house (now known as Mann's Chinese) famous throughout the world for the superstars' hand and footprints in the cement sidewalk in front. To make things even more scandalous, the movie was—gasp—*The Robe*, which had a religious theme. The gorgeous, red-haired, green-eyed star claimed heatedly she wasn't even in the country when the love-making allegedly occurred, and she had a passport to prove it. And her Irish was up because the magazine referred to her companion as "her Latin boyfriend." Everybody in Hollywood knew that the reference was to Enrique Parra, mentioned in a 1955 child custody battle between Maureen and her ex-husband.

In court, the March 1957 article, indicted as libelous, was read to the jurors. "It Was the Hottest Show in Town When Maureen O'Hara Cuddled in Row 35" was the title, followed by this sub-head: "Even the usher in Grauman's Theater was shocked when he turned his flashlight on Maureen and her Latin boyfriend."

"Escorted by a tall and handsome Latin American, she looked as dignified as a queen" to the theater manager, according to the article. "He got the shock of his life an hour later, though, when the usher in charge of Aisle C came rushing out to report there was a couple heating up the back of the theater as though it were mid-January. Easing down the aisle he saw the entwined twosome. It was Maureen and her south-of-the-border sweetie" surrounded by "a sea of empty seats." The love-making stopped when the pair was asked to leave.

Michael Mordaunt-Smith, *Confidential*'s editor in England, who had bought the O'Hara story, testified as a defense witness that he understood "practically an act of sexual intercourse" took place at Grauman's. Mordaunt-Smith was identified as the nephew of Lord Cranmore and Browne, of old Irish peerage. No wonder Maureen was all outraged Irish womanhood, with one of her own country-men trying to do her in, and him from a good family, too.

But before Maureen took the stand, there was so much conflict-ing testimony about Aisle C and whether the two were allegedly carrying on in Row 35 or Row 40, which was the last row in the section, that one juror requested that they be taken to the theater to see for themselves. Judge Walker agreed and arrangements were made for the panel to be taken by bus to Grauman's to view the rows in question. Next day the theater was opened at 10 A.M. and with the press, the defendants, the judge, the lawyers, the court reporter and other officials in attendance, the jurors solemnly marched up the aisles. As usual when accompanying a jury to a crime scene, we reporters stayed at a respectful distance. (I was so careful when I was covering trials that I used to get off an elevator in the courthouse if jurors were on it. The last thing I ever wanted to do was overhear something a juror had to say, or make a juror uneasy because a reporter was nearby. No mistrial was ever going to be my fault.)

As we stood in the darkened theater, we heard strange sounds and then running feet. We ran too, following the noise, and found the bailiff apparently wrestling with one of the male jurors. What he was actually doing was prying the juror—a very large fellow— out of a seat in Row 35.

The juror, who had bushy hair, an imposing mustache, and the wonderful name of LaGuerre Drouet, had gotten stuck attempting to determine if it was physically possible to do what *Confidential* claimed Maureen was doing with her beau. He had been squirming around with his arms in the air, as if he were cuddling a movie queen.

As we stood there trying not to fall down laughing, Drouet bellowed that he was merely trying to re-create the situation in the interest of justice. Drouet was the same juror who had made the original request to Judge Walker for the tour.

The jurors got back to the courtroom for the biggest day of the trial. As reporter Jack Jones wrote for the *Los Angeles Times:* "The stars finally came out to light up the *Confidential* magazine scandal trial yesterday as a quietly angry Maureen O'Hara and a solemn Dorothy Dandridge appeared to deny published stories about themselves. . . . Appearing as prosecution witnesses to attack defense allegations that spicy articles about Hollywood stars are true, the flame-haired actress from Dublin and the serene Miss Dandridge were the first to show up of a long list of personalities who have been named. Whether others will appear is a matter of question." (When Jack Jones was off the story for a few days, his place was taken by Jack Smith, who later became a beloved *L.A. Times* columnist. Many years after the trial, I learned from them that an irate reader wrote to the *Times* that when she saw the bylines "Jack Jones" and "Jack Smith," she knew that at least the paper had enough shame about covering the scandalous trial to let their reporters use fake names.)

No other stars showed up. In fact, the stars stayed away from the trial in droves, giving rise to the suspicion that maybe the dirt in the awful little magazine was closer to the real thing than anyone cared to admit. But the Misses O'Hara and Dandridge brightened up the story considerably. They shook hands in the courtroom and then each took the stand to tell the jurors that the articles written about them in *Confidential* were untrue.

Maureen admitted to Crowley that she had gone out socially with a Mexican gentleman at the time of the alleged movie visit in 1954, and that the gentleman was Enrique Parra. But when asked by Crowley if she had ever gone to Grauman's with Parra, her answer was an emphatic "Never!"

During a recess, O'Hara told some of the reporters who crowded around her that she had not been offered an acting job since the article appeared. She also confided sadly to them that her 13-year-old daughter "has been crying herself to sleep. . . . She told me, 'Mommy, I know that article is ridiculous because that isn't my Mommy, but it upsets me to see you upset.' And last night the child cried herself to sleep. The other children at school have talked about it."

Dandridge, the stunning black singer/actress, had sued *Confidential* for $2 million before the trial, claiming that the article about her was false and had jeopardized her career and her $250,000-a-year income. The article alleged that she and Daniel Terry, a white bandleader, had met for a torrid outdoor tryst in 1950 at Lake Tahoe during a two-week engagement there when she was singing with his band. On the witness stand, she testified that she had been told that it was Terry himself who had allegedly sold the story to the magazine. "I was never alone with Mr. Terry," she told the jurors. "I never took a walk in the woods with him, or alone. I never took a ride with him."

Then Dandridge gave testimony that says a lot about the 1950s. Decades later, it is shocking to read it; but at that time it was just another example of the fact that racial prejudice was not confined to the Deep South. The alleged tryst was impossible, the singer said, under cross-examination by Crowley, because of the "restrictions on Negroes" at the gambling resort. When Crowley asked if she had ever walked in the woods, or just taken a walk, she told the defense lawyer: "I wouldn't have done that . . . Lake Tahoe at that time was very prejudiced. Negroes were not permitted that freedom."

"Where did you spend your time?" Crowley asked.

"There was not much choice," Dandridge said. "I stayed in my suite most of the time. I worked nights and slept in the afternoon."

"Did you ever walk with Mr. Dan Terry?"

"No."

"You are positive?"

"Yes, I am positive."

"Do you remember taking a ride with Mr. Terry?"

"I couldn't have been seen with Mr. Terry in a prejudiced place like Lake Tahoe."

The trip to Grauman's and the appearance of the two beautiful witnesses was the kind of drama that gave the *Confidential* trial its special flavor. It overshadowed the more important issues of the case, such as the courtroom debates over the legal definitions of obscenity, libel, the prurient itch, and the rights and wrongs of abortion, which are just as much a matter of controversy today as they were in the 1950s.

Fighting the obscenity and libel charges, the defense lawyers told the jurors that Harrison retained a New York law firm for $100,000 a year to scrutinize *Confidential* for anything illegal (very much as the supermarket newspapers do today). They also claimed that the Post Office had examined every copy of the magazine for the preceding two years and had found nothing objectionable. This was an important point, for no publisher wanted to be caught violating postal regulations, which could result in federal prosecution; a conviction could force closure of the magazine.

The defense also made much of the "public service" articles that the magazine printed. They claimed that the article about the abortion pills was such a public service. Abortion was illegal at that time, and the *Confidential* lawyers said that the article named in the indictment was intended to save lives because unscrupulous criminal abortionists, who were responsible for the deaths of thousands of women, were recommending a pill that was not safe. The criminal doctors were supposedly doing this because prescribing the dangerous pill was less risky—for the doctors—than performing illegal abortions, for which they could be sent to prison. So the article was a public service, the defense claimed, and therefore was not in violation of California's Business and Professional Code.

Despite the lack of movie stars on the witness stand, the wrangling over such important social issues as these kept the trial front page news. Among the headline makers was perhaps the most interesting, if not the saddest, personality involved. It was Howard Rushmore, the former editor of *Confidential*, who testified against his ex-boss Harrison as one of the prosecution's most important witnesses. The 6'4" Rushmore, well known in New York and Washington, was the scion of an old-line American family. He became a Communist, and then turned on the party and for many years was the top anti-Red reporter for Hearst's *New York Journal-American*. He also served briefly as a special investigator for Senator Joseph McCarthy's Red-hunting committee.

A vitriolic man who obviously loathed what he had become, Rushmore accused Harrison of hiring call girls as tipsters; quoted the ex-wife of actor Bruce Cabot as telling him she had slept with men, including Clark Gable, to get information for the magazine; and named a number of well-known reporters and writers as being among those who furnished the magazine with dirt on the stars.

And although there was not much testimony *by* the stars, there was a lot said *about* them. One witness, a former Los Angeles newspaper reporter, testified he worked for Harrison briefly when he was unemployed, and was paid the grand sum of $300 to investigate a rumor that Joan Crawford was cruel to her children. It didn't check out, he told the jurors, and no story was written for the magazine. Decades later, of course, one of Joan Crawford's adopted daughters accused the late actress of heinous child abuse in a book that became a sensational bestseller.

That *Confidential* paid $300 for information sounds like pocket change in this age of five- and six-figure payouts to even the most unreliable sources. However, in the 1950s it was a princely sum.

The testimony of Marjorie Meade provides a benchmark. A prosecution witness had alleged that she had met him at Frascatti's, a Sunset Boulevard restaurant, and had offered him money to get information about Charles Laughton and his wife, Elsa Lanchester. Meade swore she had never been inside

Frascatti's at any time, including 2 P.M. September 16, 1955, when she had allegedly tried to buy scandal information. On that day, she testifed, she shopped at Helft's, an expensive hotel boutique, for an anniversary gift for her husband, and bought a shirt and tie—for a whopping $18.20.

She and a friend, Jackie O'Hara (no relation to the actress) went to the Polo Lounge at the Beverly Hills Hotel, the defendant continued, and while she sipped two sherries (she was on a diet) Jackie was served an order of poached eggs, bacon, toast, and coffee, a vodka gimlet and a vodka collins. The food came to $2.65, the beverages to $3.30, and with a $1 tip, the bill totalled $6.95. Mrs. Meade had paid for this with her Diner's Club card, and she brought her receipts to prove it.

Later Jackie took the stand to corroborate Meade's story, and took the trouble to explain that the only reason she had two drinks was that she didn't like the vodka gimlet when she got it, and so she ordered a vodka collins. Sure. Jackie described herself as a housewife; under cross-examination she admitted she had once been the girlfriend of Fred Otash, the private eye who worked for Harrison.

Confidential was my second major out-of-town trial. (Sam Sheppard's murder trial was the first.) The *News* wire service chief and the auditor, who made the out-of-town arrangements for political conventions and other big stories, went to L.A. in advance, and set me up in the then posh Ambassador Hotel. They arranged space for me in the old Hall of Justice press room, installing a big manual typewriter, a telephone, and a leased direct Western Union wire. They also got the best Western Union operator in town, Julius "Pearly" Pearlstein, to send my copy for me every day.

I didn't have much time to enjoy the Ambassador's elegant facilities, since I was sending copy seven days a week, including Sunday features, but one weekend I put on a bathing suit and went to the huge outdoor pool. As I lay there, half-asleep, a skinny man came over, kneeled down, and introduced himself as Walter Winchell of the *New York Mirror*. I had never met him, but I recognized the most famous gossip columnist in the country. Walter was a nonstop talker, and as he went on, I nodded off. When I came to, I was horrified, but Walter had just kept on talking and never noticed.

The next day I learned what a mammoth readership Walter had. It seems he wrote in his column that he had chatted with the *News'* crime reporter while she was showing off, as he put it, her "girlish figure." I was bombarded with telegrams and phone calls. I even got a wire over my courthouse machine from my managing editor, Bob Shand. He wanted to know, if I was working so hard, how I had the time, as he put it, "to show off my antlers" at the Ambassador pool.

My alleged helpmeet for the trial was Florabel Muir, the *News'* veteran Hollywood stringer, a tough warhorse who not only knew where all the bodies were buried but probably helped plant a few of them.

Florabel was beloved in New York by the old-time *News* editors because whenever a Hollywood scandal broke, she could come up with the information, which was difficult when the powerful movie studios were protecting their stars against adverse publicity. However, having to depend on Florabel to fill me in on testimony I missed when I was out filing a story was a disaster, because she didn't take very good notes. It was at this trial that I learned, the hard way, that if you need a backup, go only to the best reporter in the room.

She and her husband were more than hospitable. They took me out, almost killing me because their nights started late and my mornings started early. After a full day of taking notes and pounding out stories—one-half filed during lunch hour, the lead and the rest of the story at the end of the day to beat the three-hour time difference—I was becoming more and more fatigued. I also was getting paranoid, wondering if she was trying to cause my death or breakdown.

Fortunately, once the other reporters saw my copy and how thoroughly and fairly the *News* covered the case, they became best friends with me—fatherly, brotherly, loverly, protective. Florabel was not one of their favorite people, and they made sure that I did not have to rely on her when I needed a fill-in, especially after they learned that she failed to list for me her own name among the *Confidential* tipsters who had been announced from the witness stand. At one point, when I had to file something I didn't want Florabel to see, my buddies barricaded the press room door until I finished filing while Florabel yelled and threatened from the other side.

The case finally went to the jurors, who fought so bitterly that the marshals had to intervene when a couple of them threatened to throw another one out a window. On October 1, after two weeks of deliberation, the jurors advised Walker that they were hopelessly deadlocked, and the judge declared a mistrial. I had guessed they were never going to reach a verdict when, during the deliberations, I asked one of the deputies where the jurors were going to eat that night. He tipped me off about their divisions without breaking the rules: "Well, Theo, three of them want Chinese, two of them want Italian, two of them want to go for seafood, and the rest don't want to eat."

Our favorite juror, LaGuerre Drouet, also tipped us off that there was going to be a mistrial when he marched into the jury box on the last day carrying his belongings from the hotel room in unusual matching luggage—two big paper bags. After the jurors were dismissed, LaGuerre stayed behind to regale us with remarks about his fellow jurors that indicated he had been a lone wolf, and that there had been ugly dissension in the deliberation room.

I went home to New York, and did not return to Los Angeles for the second legal go-round. So with the rest of the nation, I read in the *News* how, on a motion by defense attorney Crowley, agreed to by the prosecutors, the felony conspiracy indictment against three of the five corporations and all 11 individuals, including Harrison and the Meades, was dismissed by Superior Court Judge H. Burton Noble on November 12, 1957. The next month, *Confidential* and *Whisper* were fined $5,000 each for conspiring to publish obscene matter. Nobody went to jail, which was a victory for the defense, and Harrison agreed to quit publishing scandal about the stars, a victory for the prosecution.

In Hollywood the studios and the movie stars were much relieved. The *Confidential* trial was history.

Very early Saturday morning, January 4, 1958, I was awakened by a call from the *News* city desk. While riding in a taxi in Manhattan on Friday night, Howard Rushmore had quarreled with his wife, Frances. In the cab, he shot her to death, and then killed himself with a bullet to his brain.

The Rushmore story was a page 1 banner in the Saturday editions: CONFIDENTIAL'S EX-BOSS SLAYS WIFE, SELF. Under it was a photograph of Frances—impish, pretty, smiling into the camera—next to a photograph of the death scene in the cab. There was Mrs. Rushmore sprawled across the back seat, her husband's head on her body, his left arm holding her almost protectively. The picture had been taken by *News* photographer Hy Rothman shortly after the frantic cab driver pulled up to a police station with the dead couple. The two photographs, plus two lengthy stories in the *News*, showed the speed and professionalism of my newspaper, decades before computers. The murder and suicide had occurred on *News* deadline time, after 7 P.M. on Friday night; the readers had every detail plus photos Saturday morning.

Saturday was my day off, but the editors were asking me to come into the office as quickly as possible. Our deadlines on Saturday for the Sunday paper were the earliest of the week, and the editors wanted me to write the feature about Rushmore to go along with the continuing news story because I had watched Rushmore at the *Confidential* trial and had listened to his lengthy testimony.

When I arrived at my desk, stacks of typed notes were waiting for me from reporters who had been assigned to get quotes and information from people who knew the dead couple. I did not have to spend hours working the phones, it had been done for me. All I had to do was read through the notes, organize everything, and write. I was done long before the early deadline.

> Howard Rushmore, a lanky, gaunt, sallow man with the face of Mephistopheles, was a professional turncoat on the skids when he made his last big public appearance in a Hollywood courtroom in the role he loved most—the role of a witness testifying to the world against something he said he hated. . . .
>
> Rushmore, who turned on his heritage as a "10th generation American" to become a Communist Party card-holder, who turned on the Commies to become a violent pro-McCarthyite and avowed anti-Red, used the Confidential trial to turn on the magazine he had once edited and on the publisher, Robert Harrison, who had paid him the highest salary he had ever earned in his life as a newspaperman and writer.

There were quotes from Clarence Linn, the deputy attorney general who engineered the *Confidential* trial and used Rushmore as an important witness. Linn said that when he last saw Rushmore, "he told me he had no permanent position, the magazine he had been working for had folded. . . . Rushmore thought he was a great man, but he knew he was slipping. He was a man with a super-ego. He was an unstable man."

There were quotes from *Confidential*'s defense attorney, Albert DeStefano, who said, "Rushmore once gave us his pledge, in a gentleman's agreement, that he would never hurt *Confidential*," because in 1956, when Rushmore was no longer with the magazine, *Confidential* took him off the hook by settling a $250,000 libel suit against him out of court. The pledge, said the lawyer, was violated almost immediately.

I wrote that Rushmore was a man suspected by everybody.

> He was dead in Hollywood, where he had made everybody, including the prosecution, angry by dropping names which nobody wanted mentioned. . . . Rushmore was dead in the newspaper world, too. He put the finger on many newspaper men and women, contending they were paid Confidential tipsters. Rushmore was suspect as an ex-Commie. He was suspect in the magazine publishing world, because of the knife job he did on *Confidential*. He had no place to go as a rabid anti-Red, because the witch-hunting was over.
>
> Yesterday, Rushmore's attorney, Martin Richmond, 40 Exchange Place, told the News that the ex-newspaperman, ex-editor, ex-Commie, ex-star of two sensational public appearances (the Un-American Activities Committee investigation in 1947, and the Confidential trial 10 years later) had become a lost man.

There were more quotes, and the Sunday article ended with: "Yesterday a close friend gave him the epitaph which seemed to characterize his recent life. 'The guy turned out to be an SOB,' the friend said. 'I don't think he knew what he was doing these last years. Yet—once he was a gentleman.'"

We decided to make the Rushmore story a two-part series, so on Sunday I came into the office again to write the conclusion. I was able to write quickly and smoothly, thanks to the mass of material accumulated for me by five staffers, Mike O'Neill, Lee Silver, Art Mulligan, Henry Machirella, and Bill Murtha, who had been working the phones across the country.

This second article dealt in depth with Rushmore's background, his life, and his marital problems, quoting from friends who explained that he loved his wife, Frances, and was crushed when she asked for a separation. I also went into detail on the life of the murdered wife, who was described by one old friend as "the best-looking girl in town" when she was growing up in Huntsville, Alabama.

> A lot of people started remembering things about Howard Rushmore yesterday. When a man winds up an often-spotty, some-times-spectacular career by blowing his brains out in a taxi after killing his wife, he becomes both a front-page headline and the sub-ject of post-mortem anecdotes.
> The epitaphs were as mixed-up as the man himself.
> He was charming—and chilling. He was interesting in casual conversation—and boring when he began his tirades. He was able to win jobs and influence friends—and invariably lost both.

I used a story from a fellow *News* reporter who had covered a trial attended by Rushmore, and had heard Rushmore happily relate that the woman committed suicide after being fired from her job under suspicion of being a Commie. "I was responsible for that," the reporter remembered Rushmore saying. "That's the sec-ond one I testified against that committed suicide." Yet, the same reporter said Rushmore could be "extremely charming. . . . When he heard that one of the out-of-town reporters had a birthday, he staged an impromptu party for him."

Attorney Roy Cohn, who had been a leader in the McCarthy witch hunts, refused to discuss the estrangement which led to Rushmore's public attacks against him, and said he thought Rushmore "had a mental quirk which resulted in his trying to hurt everyone he had ever worked for."

But close friends said that Rushmore pictured himself as a gen-tleman with a strong pride in his pioneer and Southern ancestry, too proud to beg for handouts. He never asked them for loans, even in the last six months when he was jobless.

Friends thought that Rushmore's unemployment was part of the problem that led to the murder/suicide, noting that, unlike her husband, Frances had been successful as a model, a newspaper writer, a magazine editor, and in public relations.

I let the sad man, Howard Rushmore, have the last word on the entire *Confidential* matter:

> Rushmore was able to apologize in public for every bad mis-

take he made in his life—except the last big one.

His most recent apology, probably among the last of his writings, appeared in the January issue of the Christian Herald. It was entitled "I Worked for *Confidential*" and it concluded with these remarks:

"I am not proud of the two years I spent at *Confidential*. I was an adult man, an experienced writer, a professional reporter, and I should have known better. I left Confidential forever two and one-half years ago. To Confidential's millions of readers I say this. My conscience is clear. I am out. Are you?"

5

Gag Orders and Other Pains in the Tush

For a long time, we trial reporters covered courts with the understanding that our very presence made the proceeding a public trial, one of a defendant's guaranteed constitutional rights.

We reporters were the public; we represented those millions of citizens out there whose taxes were paying the salaries of judges and prosecutors and public defenders, for the maintenance of courthouses, and for the cost of trials they could not attend personally but could read about each day in their newspapers. We were there to ensure a defendant's right to a public trial, and the public's right to know what was going on inside those courtrooms.

We were able to do this job without too much interference until, to our horror, we were confronted with burgeoning gag orders, closed hearings, locked courtrooms, all based on the undemocratic belief that the untrammeled presence of the press in itself could deprive the defendant of his other constitutional right—a fair trial.

There had been closures before: when I came to the *News* I met Julia McCarthy, who had covered the Gloria Vanderbilt custody case back in 1935. That trial, involving big money and big names, had been barred to the public and the press, but Julia had managed to get one front page story after the other anyway, along with exclusive photos of little Gloria and the millionaire Morgans and Vanderbilts embroiled in the custody war.

A salty-tongued, formidable, funny Irish lady, Julia regaled me

69

with the tales of how she became cozy with little Gloria's aunt, Gertrude Vanderbilt, who wanted custody of the hapless little heiress, and friendly with Gloria's young widowed mother, Gloria Morgan Vanderbilt, who was fighting to keep her child after she was accused by her sister-in-law of being an unfit parent.

Julia swore she got an ulcer in the service of the *News* from staying up talking and drinking each night first with one and then with the other of the embattled ladies, then staggering into the *News* to deliver her exclusive accounts of the secret courtroom sessions for the next day's editions.

Eventually Julia became the *News'* society editor, writing under the Nancy Randolph house byline, and since, in those days, we were a first class newspaper and spent money, she went where society editors are supposed to go—Palm Beach in the season, for instance. Julia also went to London for the *News* and probably was the only society editor in U.S. newspaper history who loathed British aristocracy, claiming that since the Brits rarely bathed and didn't have central plumbing, covering this unwashed society in any season was pure hell.

Julia liked me, thank God, probably because I wasn't scared of her and loved listening to every detail of her memories and to her outrageously acid gossip about society—real, cafe, and jet. Thanks to Julia, and to the scandalous stories about the upper crust that I was writing with court reporter Al Albelli, I never again looked upon our very rich, our very famous, and our very powerful with the reverence, much less the respect, usually accorded them. Both Julia and Al knew the closets where the skeletons were hidden. It was not a pretty picture, and after a while I began to feel that the weirdos we were writing about deserved the exposure; it was healthy for the public to know that wealth and pedigree need not be looked upon with unquestioning awe.

There were lots of Julia McCarthy stories: I unfortunately was not a witness when Julia stormed into the city room one Sunday morning and whacked Hugh Schuck, our quiet, white-haired, low-key wire desk (now national desk) editor over the head with that most dangerous of weapons, a rolled up Sunday *New York Times!* Hugh just put his hands over his head to prevent permanent brain damage and suffered the attack in silence while his deskmen, smart fellows, ran for their lives.

Abandoning Hugh may have seemed cowardly; it also made a

lot of sense to everybody who knew Julia, just as it made sense that Julia would have used a Sunday *Times,* our competition, instead of a Sunday *News* to make her point. I mean, you could break a toe just dropping a part of the Sunday *Times* on your foot. When it came to weight, anyway, the *Times* had no competition.

All of us, with the exception of Hugh, thought it was a helluva funny Julia story, typical of what went on in that office, and nobody in authority even mentioned it to her. These days, if anyone whomped an editor that way, they would probably be forced to take a drug or alcohol test.

Gag orders are instructions from judges forbidding attorneys to discuss an ongoing trial with reporters. It never has been proven that anything written in a newspaper about a trial in progress has influenced any jury member's vote, especially when the jurors are warned every day not to read newspaper stories about the case or listen to the TV or radio news, and also are forbidden to discuss the trial with anybody, including each other, outside the jury room.

Yet judges, generally the most insecure ones, still issue stringent gag orders in an attempt to prevent "prejudicial" information from getting into the papers which the jurors are supposedly not reading anyway.

The judges who impose gag orders say that they are doing it to ensure the defendant gets a fair trial. Well, let's take the Charlie Manson case, where a gag order resulted in a lengthy, totally unnecessary legal mess, and put a good reporter into jail years after the trial was over.

The Manson gag order was violated technically during the trial all the time, since we reporters often asked the trial lawyers questions to clarify our stories, and they answered us. But one particular incident became a cause celebre when Bill Farr, then with the *Los Angeles Herald-Examiner,* broke a story which had to have been corroborated for him by one of the prosecuting or defense attorneys.

In the judge's chambers, a witness had testified she had been told by Susan Atkins that Charlie Manson and the Family had plotted to kill other celebrities besides Sharon Tate, including Frank Sinatra. It was decided that this testimony was not to be given to the jury, but Farr found out about it and from a source he never revealed got a copy of the transcript with this witness's description of Susan's alleged revelation. It was full of gory details about what the Family intended to do when and if they got these alleged victims, and the *Herald-Examiner* broke Bill's exclusive story with huge Page 1 headlines.

Judge Charles Older called Bill into his office and asked him where he had gotten this information. Bill naturally refused to tell him, claiming the protection of the California shield law, which gives reporters the right to protect their sources.

That should have been the end of it.

Whether his gag orders were violated or not, Judge Older must have believed that Charlie Manson, Susan Atkins, Patricia Krenwinkle, and Leslie Van Houten had received an absolutely fair trial, because after the jury convicted them and recommended a death sentence, Older ordered that all four defendants be executed in the gas chamber. (The death sentences were changed to life sentences after the U.S. Supreme Court nullified all death sentences in 1971.) Obviously, Bill's sensational story had not impeded "justice."

After the Manson trial was over, Bill left the *Herald-Examiner* and took a job with the Los Angeles district attorney's office. Soon after he gave up his newspaper job, Bill was called by Judge Older, who told him that since he no longer was a reporter protected by the shield law, he had to reveal which lawyer had violated the gag order.

Bill refused. Thus started the needless contest between a judge's ego and a reporter's conscience that dragged through the courts for years, going all the way to the U.S. Supreme Court, putting Bill in jail for weeks, and finally ending when other judges ruled that to put a reporter in jail for contempt when he refused to name a source could be a life sentence, since Bill would rot before he would break his promise. Bill by then was on the staff of the *Los Angeles Times*. It was ruled that Bill should be released, and should not have to reveal his source, and he never did, not even in confidence to his best friends.

Being in jail almost made a radical out of Bill, the nicest law-and-order guy I ever knew. But he wasn't in there long enough to revolutionize him, only 47 days. Bill died of cancer too young, and I still miss him.

In 1953, when oleomargarine heir Minot "Mickey" Jelke was tried in New York City on vice charges, the presiding judge closed the trial in the name of public decency. He did this on his own motion, not at the request of either prosecution or defense.

Behind locked doors, Mickey was convicted on two counts of compulsory prostitution, but the conviction was overturned and a new trial was ordered by the New York State Court of Appeals, which held that Mickey was deprived of a fair trial because the judge barred the press and the public. At the young heir's second trial in 1955, open to press and public, he was convicted again.

The next time a trial went secret in New York City was in 1971, when Supreme Court Justice George Postel ordered the courtroom cleared of press and public and the records sealed until a verdict was reached in the extortion-conspiracy trial of mobster Carmine Persico, who was charged on a 37-count indictment stemming from an alleged loan-shark operation.

Persico's defense attorney, Maurice Edelbaum, made the request, stating he wanted either a mistrial or the exclusion of press and public because "of the comments of the press . . . and editorials that appeared in the *New York Times* and the *Daily News*," according to the story I wrote with reporter William Proctor, who was covering the case.

Claiming that the newspaper coverage was prejudicial, the defense lawyer said his client would "waive his First Amendment right to a public trial in order to insure his Sixth Amendment right to a fair trial." Besides closing the trial, the judge was also asked to seal the records until after the jury verdict and to order the lawyers on both sides not to discuss the case with the press or anybody else.

Persico had a mob nickname and a mob-related criminal record, neither of which the judge wanted mentioned in news accounts. At the start of the trial the judge warned reporters that he would hold them in contempt if they wrote about anything other than what transpired in the courtroom. He then met privately with some of them in his chambers and repeated the warnings, saying he would "throw them in the can" if they disobeyed his instructions.

The next day the judge's threats, in his own words, were used in news stories and there were editorials about the case. When the trial resumed, Judge Postel told the reporters, while the jurors were absent, that they had quoted his "idioms," that he found this "demeaning," and from now on he would talk to them only in court. Immediately after that, with the jurors still absent, Edelbaum made his motion.

The assistant district attorney, Samuel Yasgur, made a very strong objection. He asked the judge to sequester the jury rather than create "a secret trial," and said that barring the press and public "would set a precedent wherein anyone who is alleged to have any underworld connections, or anyone indeed who has a past criminal record, might then demand secret trials. The remedy lies not in a secret trial," the prosecutor argued, "but in keeping the jurors from being exposed" to newspaper publicity. He also reminded the judge that the jurors had been polled and had sworn they were following the court's instructions and "had read nothing about the trial."

The judge was not moved. Granting the defense requests, he issued a gag order and announced, "The courtroom is closed. Everybody out of the courtroom." As I reported, "To the court attendants, Postel then said, 'Don't let anybody in the courtroom during the course of this trial. The courtroom is closed.' The trial then proceeded in the absence of the press and public."

Between Mickey and the mobster came the U.S. Supreme Court decision in *Sheppard v. Maxwell* on June 6, 1966, a decision that was based on misleading information provided to the justices by F. Lee Bailey. The decision was misinterpreted by both the legal community and the public to the great detriment of the press and its right to cover public trials.

The decision granted Dr. Sam Sheppard a new trial on the plea by his defense counsel, Bailey, that Sheppard's first trial had been prejudiced by the publicity which surrounded the sensational 1954 case and by press excesses in the trial itself. To this day, it is thought that the trial reporters were disorderly at the Sheppard trial. They were not. Convicted of the murder of his pregnant wife, Marilyn, Sam had served 12 years before Bailey won him release from prison and a new trial scheduled for October 1966.

The Supreme Court decision resulted in the most stringent restrictions ever imposed on national trial reporters, before or since. Although it was the Cleveland newspapers, in particular the *Cleveland Press*, that had led a campaign to bring Sheppard to justice, the judge in charge of the new trial, Francis J. Talty, decided to eliminate all out-of-town coverage. Talty, who had been on the bench only two years, set aside only fourteen seats for the press:

one each for AP and UPI, two each for the *Cleveland Press* and the *Cleveland Plain Dealer,* and one each for Cleveland's five radio and three television stations.

Talty also forbade the news media to install telephones or teletype machines in the courthouse, making it impossible to set up a press room, banned cameras and tape recorders, ordered the courthouse grounds off limits to photographers, and banned newspaper and TV artists by prohibiting sketches and drawings by either newsmen or spectators. Reporters who were not accredited, he said, could sit in the spectator section and take notes, but they would be seated on a first-come first-served basis with the public, and were subject to strict regulations.

The judge's gag order extended even to county or courthouse employees and to witnesses. Nobody, including reporters, could enter or leave a trial session except during recesses or adjournment. Talty based these guidelines on a strict interpretation of the Supreme Court decision.

Doc Quigg of UPI and I called other reporters who had been with us during the first Sheppard trial. All of us were appalled at the allegations of bedlam in the trial courtroom. We knew that the late William Corrigan, Sheppard's defense lawyer at the first trial, had complained about "the carnival atmosphere" of the inquest into Marilyn Sheppard's murder, which took place three months before that trial started and before any out-of-town reporters came to Cleveland, but he had never made such accusations about the trial itself.

Sitting at my kitchen table in my apartment in Manhattan, Doc and I composed a 6 1/2-page letter to the U.S. Supreme Court and sent it to the justices on October 17, 1966. It was published in full in *Editor & Publisher,* articles about the our protest were sent over the wire services, and the *News* and the *New York Times* used stories about it. (Of course, the *News* article was a very long one, the *Times* article a very short one.)

The letter was signed by myself, and Doc, by Bob Considine of King Features; Ray Brennan, *Chicago Sun-Times;* Russell Harris, formerly the *Detroit News;* Margaret Parton, formerly the *New York Herald Tribune;* Ira H. Freeman, formerly the *New York Times;* Alvin Davis, formerly the *New York Post;* Jack Lotto, formerly International News Service. The Associated Press was not included, because Relman (Pat) Morin, the Pulitzer Prize-winning writer who had been with us at the first trial, was out of the country.

We tried to be tactful, for we knew we would have to work at the new trial in Cleveland. We would have to deal with Lee Bailey, who had won his appeal with allegations about courtroom behavior which we knew had never occurred and which, of course, he never saw. We told the Supreme Court that we were offering "an informal but heartfelt commentary" on one phase of the decision, because we felt "remiss in not speaking out at the time of the decision to express our shock at the court's comments on the state of decorum maintained in the courtroom" at the first trial.

> After recent consultation, we find that each of us had the same sense of incredulity, the feeling that "this part of the decision cannot be about the same trial I attended." Contrary to the statements about "disruptive influences in the courtroom" by the press, "constant commotion within the bar" and a noisy atmosphere, the courtroom was conducted in an admirable state of decorum.
>
> What we feel is a moral obligation to speak out in defense of a dead judge and in behalf of trial reporters everywhere. . . . This letter is about courtroom conduct only; we have no other issue to raise. We want to emphasize this, as we also want to emphasize that we do not believe the court was deliberately misled. We do believe that in the 12 years the Sheppard case shuttled among the courts, this one phase ballooned out of proportion to the facts.
>
> We were in the courtroom. So was the chief defense counsel, the late William J. Corrigan, whose affidavit in support of a motion for a new trial, made in 1954 when the trial was still quite fresh in his mind, never mentioned noise. . . . Mr. Corrigan also mentioned the movement of reporters in and out of the courtroom. To our certain knowledge, this leaving and entering, done by those whose deadlines require it, was accomplished with the utmost discretion, and in silence—and by relatively few, at infrequent intervals. This has been the common practice in federal and state courts in our memory, and the experience of some of us with courts goes back more than 30 years.
>
> Judge Blythin's courtroom was run with a decorum comparable with the best we have seen, both in well attended "big" trials and those that have little public interest. We do not presume to speak as other than reporters, but we do speak as reporters with many years of trial experience.

The letter noted that, as out-of-town trial reporters, we were not involved with the local politics or pretrial publicity in Cleveland which allegedly deprived Sheppard of a fair trial. "At the time of the trial, we never believed that the American press as a whole would be condemned 12 years later for local stories about revelations made by police, defense and prosecuting attorneys and the coroner in one city, in the Middle West—nor do we believe the Supreme Court, in this decision, intended this to happen."

In support of our point we quoted from *My Brother's Keeper*, by Sam's brother, Dr. Stephen Sheppard, who kept a daily diary of the trial. In the 31 pages of that book devoted to the trial itself, the author never mentioned the press disturbing the proceedings. We used quotes from other sources—including articles in the *Daily News*, the *New York Times*, and a pro-Sheppard book—indicating that Judge Blythin's courtroom was as quiet and orderly as could be. This was due in part to Blythin's tight but fair control, but also because we reporters were professionals. Our job was to take down testimony, and we were generally the first to straighten out any colleagues whose behavior was out of line. Furthermore, the out-of-town reporters were seated in the rear spectator rows. We never got close enough to the defendant to talk to him or otherwise bother him and his attorney, as the Supreme Court decision alleged. The court rule was that the press could not speak to the defendant, and we obeyed. We concluded our letter with these arguments:

> As reporters assigned to the Sheppard trial, as to so many before and after, we find we are being forced to defend the American press against charges of "trial by press" and "prejudicial pretrial publicity," although, as a whole, the American press was not involved; against charges that we were participants in a "Roman circus," in a "carnival atmosphere," although no such circumstances prevailed within the courtroom of the late Judge Blythin.
>
> We find there is a tendency to put the American press as a whole on trial now in the case of Sam Sheppard. We find we must defend ourselves and U.S. newspapers against certain allusions to the "press" in the Supreme Court decision which, in fact, are made only about one locality.
>
> . . . Of course, there is nothing that proscribes the press from reporting events that transpire in the courtroom. Unfortunately, the decision is being misinterpreted in some quarters.

We did not write it, but we all knew that if ever a case called for a change of venue and/or sequestration of a jury, the first

Sheppard trial was the one. Judge Blythin used neither judicial remedy.

There never was any doubt that I would go to Cleveland and cover the trial as best I could while fighting to get a seat there, and before I left, my editors did everything within their power to help me, with editorials, letters to Judge Talty, an editorial cartoon, and consultations with the *News* lawyers. I gave the lawyers extensive background as possible ammunition for their legal arguments. For instance, though I had filed 50,000 words during the first Sheppard trial, not one sentence published by the *News* was ever cited as prejudicial by the Sheppard appeals attorneys. Though I was barred from the courtroom, allowed in were representatives of two Cleveland radio stations named in the Supreme Court decision as among those which allowed prejudicial statements on the air, and representatives of the Cleveland newspaper cited over and over in the Supreme Court decision for publishing prejudicial pretrial editorials, cartoons, and news stories. And equipment such as cameras, lights, and tape recorders were banned from the entire courthouse. How then could TV and radio cover the story?

Another legal issue that I outlined for the *News'* lawyers involved Judge Talty's decision on which members of the press would be allowed in the press section. If he had set aside 14 seats for the press and said, "This is the press section—whoever gets there first gets a seat," there could be no charge of discrimination. But since he was in effect selecting who could sit in the press section, his action was a dangerous precedent. What if, for a controversial case during an election year, a judge could pack the press section with reporters from media outlets that were favorable to him? The potential abuses are legion.

So I had to go to Cleveland for two major reasons. One, it was an important trial that our readers needed to know about. We owed it to them to cover it as best we could. Two, I could not complain about reporters being hampered in their work unless I actually tried to cover the trial and proved I was hampered.

Doc Quigg of UPI and Art Everett of AP, both from the New York bureaus, covered the trial for the wire services, using the one local seat per wire allotted by Judge Talty. They had visions of me locked outside the courthouse, a pitiful homeless waif, waiting in the cold for crumbs of information from them as they left each session. Art wrote an hilarious piece likening me to the little match girl who had no place to go and froze to death selling her wares on the streets.

Since we were not allowed to work in the courthouse at all, the *News* and the two wire services jointly rented an empty basement several blocks from the courthouse where we installed our tables, telephones, and typewriters. The *News*, of course, set up its usual Western Union direct leased wire to New York, with Western Union's best local operator to man it. It was a gloomy, dank, rat-infested press room. The three of us had to race back and forth to the courthouse in all kinds of weather, me running the fastest because I had no reserved seat and had to stand with the spectators hoping to get inside. And the advantage of having reserved seats was negated for Doc and Art, since they were barred from leaving the courtroom except at recesses, which made it almost impossible for them to meet their constant deadlines.

Every morning during the first week, I got up hours early and went to the courthouse in the dark so that I would be among the first in line before the doors opened to get one of the seats available to the public. Standing with me was Jeanne King, who was a stringer for the *New York Post*, the UPI and AP backstop men, and a representative of the North American Newspaper Alliance.

Every night after I filed my story to the *News*, I went to see Judge Talty after court, sometimes accompanied by Jeanne. Staying as charming, as polite, and as low-key as possible, I would plead my case: "Judge, I had to get up at 5 A.M. today just to get a seat. I had to cut short my filing at the lunch hour just to be sure I got a seat for the afternoon session. My newspaper and I are truly dedicated to covering this trial, as you can see, so can't you help us by setting aside just a few more seats for the press?" I refrained from pointing out that some of the seats he had reserved for local radio and TV were empty (Who could blame them? If you can't get voices on tape and pictures on screen, why sit all day in the trial room?) and that he was not being bombarded by requests for seats from any other major newspapers. But I did keep reminding him that I was writing for millions of readers, thus making this a truly public trial, and that giving me a seat surely would neither disrupt the courtroom nor prejudice Sheppard's right to a fair trial.

I even went so far as to ask Talty, a bachelor, if he could recommend a good hairdresser, since both Jeanne and I needed shampoos and sets after standing outside in the windy dawn. Talty was good enough to give us the name of a salon his relatives used, and Jeanne and I went there on our first free morning. The owners were apparently dedicated to the ideal, "When in doubt, tease it out," and Jeanne and I came out of there looking as if we had been electrocuted—our sprayed, teased hair stood straight up off our heads and was so stiff that when we turned, our hairdos didn't. If we didn't originate the expression, "Don't fall down, you'll break your hair," we brought it to life.

But next day in court, we caught the judge's eye and pointed happily to our heads, nodding to show him our deep appreciation for his guidance. And during my after-court visitation, he told me that I looked swell. I wouldn't have looked that good if it weren't for him, I told him.

Finally, we got the good word from a deputy sheriff: for those reporters who had sweated out the first week standing in line with the public, reserved seats had been made available in the second row, near the door. No more threat of being locked out of a session because no seats were left. I promised the judge that I wouldn't tell anybody that he had made this possible, and we remained cordial throughout the trial.

Inside the courtroom, Talty ruled with an iron fist. We were under a stern injunction against talking, and if a reporter whispered a question to another reporter, he was immediately shushed by a deputy and threatened with eviction. One day Doc copied a diagram that a witness drew on a blackboard for the jurors, and a deputy confiscated his notebook. He had violated the judge's rule that "no sketches or drawings, by pen, pencil, or otherwise, shall be made within the courthouse premises"!

Outside the courtroom, when the jurors were taken to the murder scene, TV editors were asked to cooperate with the court by not filming the event. They agreed, and in return got the screwing of their lives. As I said in an FYI note to my editors: "They would have had the only, first, and best live TV so far—the jurors at the murder house, the jurors being shown the Houk house [Mayor Houk and his wife were neighbors, and Bailey kept hinting, though he never proved it, that they somehow were implicated], the jurors going down to the beach [where Sam said he pursued the intruder who he claimed killed Marilyn]. Since a still camera was allowed to shoot this, a TV camera should have tried. The least they could have done was go there with a crew, and if asked to leave, leave. They didn't even try."

Well, Sam was acquitted and we went off to other trials, where, depending on the judge, we were allowed to do our jobs or were again subjected to inane restrictions. Meanwhile, bar associations, newspaper groups, judges, publishers, lawyers, and reporters debated the problems of the free press/fair trial controversy.

Justice Tom Clark, author of the Supreme Court's *Sheppard* decision, was in Denver to address law school students during the second Sheppard trial. An enterprising *Denver Post* reporter asked him if he was aware that some prosecutors and police departments were refusing to give reporters details of criminal investigations, contending that the *Sheppard* decision barred them from doing so.

"Nothing we've said tells them what to do," Clark answered. No Supreme Court decisions, the justice said, prohibited police and district attorneys from discussing details of a crime before arrests were made, and he could not see how the rights of a free press interfered with the right to a fair trial. "The exercise of good common sense should be used by officers in disseminating pretrial information," said Clark.

Even some bar associations issued guidelines for the press, which we trial reporters considered extremely presumptuous. The lawyers writing them were essentially ignorant of the techniques, deadlines, wire service cycles, and needs of trial reporters. Some of us wondered how bar associations would react if reporters set out guidelines for how attorneys should run their cases and act in a courtroom.

When one of the Supreme Court justices stated that a trial was public if one member of the public was there, and that a reporter had no more standing in a courtroom than any member of the public, we were both angry and amused. Technically, he might have been right. But if there was no difference between reporters and the rest of the public, why didn't the Supreme Court simply hand down its opinions to any group of tourists who was visiting Washington instead of to the Supreme Court press corps? Perhaps these passersby could do just as good a job interpreting the opinions and disseminating them worldwide.

Almost immediately after the second Sheppard trial came the murder trial of Dr. Carl Coppolino, in Freehold, New Jersey, the trial that made Bailey really famous. Although the judge gave seats to the major newspapers, he also issued restrictions similar to those in Cleveland: "No one shall leave the courtroom except at recess"; "No photographic, television, or sound equipment, including tape recorders, will be permitted in or upon the courthouse grounds immediately surrounding the courthouse"; "No sketches may be made in open court"; "Nothing except that which occurs in open court, adduced only in evidence and in argument in open court, will be disseminated."

In December 1966, during jury selection for the Coppolino case, the ACLU released a report on the free press/fair trial debate, and the *News* ran it on the jump page of my Coppolino story:

> If there must be sanctions against anyone to prevent prejudicial pretrial publicity, let them be invoked against law enforcement officials, the bar and the courts rather than the press, the American Civil Liberties Union urged here yesterday.
>
> In a report capping an 18-month study, the ACLU opposed a recent recommendation of the American Bar Association that judges be permitted to cite the press in contempt for certain actions, such as publication of statements "calculated" to influence a a trial's outcome.
>
> Shunning citation of the press and placing the responsibility for protecting defendants from prejudicial publicity on law officials, lawyers and judges will, said the ACLU: "Avoid a direct collision between two rights deeply embedded in our constitutional system (freedom of the press and the right to a fair trial) and narrow the application of sanctions to those persons most intimately concerned with the administration of justice."

Eventually, it was ruled that while a judge could gag his court officers, he could not directly gag the press or cite them for contempt.

The next big trial was that of Albert DeSalvo, the "Boston Strangler," in Middlesex Superior Court in Cambridge, Massachusetts. Since Lee Bailey was the defense attorney and the case had attracted worldwide attention, I and other national trial reporters went up to cover it. To our great joy, we had the opportunity to work with Judge Cornelius J. Moynihan, a man who was so secure, so self-confident, and so comfortable with the press that he ran his large courtroom without imposing restrictions.

When the trial was over in February 1967, I couldn't resist sending a love letter to Judge Moynihan:

> It was sheer pleasure to come to your court and discover there was one judge, at least, who did not think it necessary to issue rules and regulations to the press, as some others have done since the Supreme Court decision in the Sam Sheppard case.
>
> Your courtroom was an example of absolute decorum, even though you allowed reporters and spectators to leave and enter the trial room at will. I think this is a tribute to your own ability to run your courtroom well. Some other judges seem to have panicked in recent months.
>
> I was most impressed by the fact that your orders were issued to the court officers—the defense and prosecuting attorneys, the sheriff and others—and not to the reporters and cameramen, in connection with interviews, photos and use of equipment.
>
> Your one request to the press from the bench, not to use the names and addresses of the women victims, was so reasonable that no one violated it, even though you made it plain in open court that this was a suggestion and not an order.
>
> The press corps at the DeSalvo trial was much larger than that at other major trials I have covered recently, yet your handling of this problem was the most intelligent and non-restrictive for both press and spectators.
>
> Again, I am grateful. Thank you for trusting the trial reporters to behave with decorum and quiet, and for allowing them to do their jobs without prohibitions.

It has been decades since the Supreme Court's *Sheppard* decision, but trial reporters are still fighting hindrances on fair coverage of trials.

In the Rodney King case in Los Angeles in 1992, the attorneys representing the four policemen accused of beating King after a high-speed chase won the right from an appellate court to move the trial out of the city, over the objections of the prosecutor, who said a fair trial was possible in Los Angeles. The appellate court granted the change of venue because, the justices said, the case had created "a political firestorm" in Los Angeles. This case, of course, had received international pretrial attention because the beating was captured on videotape and shown on television.

Superior Court Judge Stanley Weisberg, given a choice of venue, picked Ventura County, and the trial was moved to Simi Valley, a

45-minute drive from Los Angeles.

Simi Valley had a reputation as a predominantly white and insulated bedroom community where many policemen lived, and there were doubts at the outset about the wisdom of selecting that venue.

Early on during the trial, Judge Weisberg called the attorneys on both sides into his chambers and convinced them to quit talking to the press. A transcript of his conversation with the parties is, as Linda Deutsch of the AP wrote in her story about it, a "unique insight into the thinking of advocates and the court about media coverage of a high-profile trial."

The judge told the attorneys that he had seen television interviews between the lawyers and reporters. Then he asked them: "What is your thought about why you want to talk to the press? Is there some particular motivation or reason why anybody talks to the press? Other than the fact that the press asks you to talk to them, that you are responding to their request and trying to be nice by being responsive to tbe press, is there any other real reason to talk to them?"

The prosecutor said it was the policy of the district attorney's office to be responsive to the press, and some of the defense lawyers said they felt obligated to respond because "there has been so much negative publicity" and because "for the first time the media is having to deal with things in this case rather than a selective and stilted version of the videotape, together with myopic commentary by news media poeple."

"It is not to try the case in the media," one of the defense lawyers explained, "but it is . . . to demonstrate that I believe very sincerely in the innocence of these men, all of them, and I don't think you can do that if you just walk by and say 'no comment.'"

Another of the defense attorneys told the judge: "In my opinion there has been a good eleven months of heavy media coverage from the district attorney's office and the press which is ill disposed toward our clients" and so he had "very mixed feelings" about not talking with the press. Another defense attorney said he felt that the officers "have been brutalized in the media for a year . . . and I feel that the public . . . needs to see the facts and needs to know that there is another side to this case."

Judge Weisberg, although stating that "we've taken steps, great steps to insulate the jury from contact with the media" and he believed that the jurors were following his instructions to not read, watch, or listen to anything about the trial, still thought that the lawyers' interviews with the TV reporters and others should stop.

The attorneys accepted the voluntary gag order on condition that the judge make the announcement to the press in open court, and one of the defense attorneys predicted that when the press was told, "they will be all sad and they will have one big blitz about the First Amendment and it will be over."

"Okay," said the judge. "We are certainly not interfering with their right of free speech or the right of the press to report what they want."

Judge Weisberg then announced to the press that the court and the lawyers had agreed that there would be no further conversations between attorneys and the news media during the trial.

As the whole world knows, the jurors acquitted the four police officers, setting off the worst riots in Los Angeles history.

If nothing else, the acquittal proved one thing. Pretrial publicity, if it was as damaging and prejudicial for the cops as the defense lawyers made it out to be, certainly did not influence the jurors in Simi Valley. As for the gag rule, it obviously wasn't necessary at all. And it never is if you have experienced, professional trial reporters working with ethical, professional trial lawyers.

Unfortunately, as demonstrated at the O.J. Simpson trial, that is a big "if." Because of the actions of the lawyers in that case, and the general irresponsibility of the media, it seems to me that limited gag orders may become a hard necessity of trial life.

When you have lawyers manipulating stories by bellowing accusations and misinformation on national TV, and when you have gullible, hungry reporters buying everything the lawyers and scandal-mongers are selling outside the courtroom instead of sticking with the testimony actually heard by the jurors, they need to be reined in. The public must be allowed to see and read about what is happening inside the courtroom—it is their right. The antics at the O.J. trial have put that right in jeopardy. The gavel-to-gavel trial camera is being eliminated in more and more courtrooms, and the reporters who are trying to bring informed and accurate trial coverage to the public are being hampered by unnecessary restrictions. If limited gag orders will make it possible to bring cameras back into the trial room, and prevent the excesses of the O.J. trial outside the courtroom, so be it.

6

The Colonel's Lady

Now that checkbook journalism is encouraging victims and defendants and witnesses to tell their secrets on TV talk shows and in magazines and in supermarket tabloids for a price, it seems remarkable that nobody got to Marge Farber before or during the two murder trials of her one-time lover, Dr. Carl Coppolino. When Marge finally decided, after the conclusion of the second trial, to tell her story in more detail than she was able to do when she testified, she chose to tell it to me even though she and I had not exchanged a word during either trial. She never asked for money for her story, and none was ever paid.

Marge Farber was the mystery witness, the colonel's lady whose bizarre accusations against Carl Coppolino had convinced the states of New Jersey and Florida to take from their graves the bodies of Marge's husband and Carl's wife—and then charge Coppolino with the murders of both of them.

The dead husband was a retired, decorated Army colonel, buried in Arlington National Cemetery. The dead wife was a second-generation doctor, buried next to her mother in the family plot at St. Mary's Cemetery, Boonton, New Jersey. After the exhumations and autopsies, the authorities said that Lt. Col. William Farber was strangled and died of a broken cricoid (larynx) cartilage, even though his death certificate listed a heart attack as the cause of his demise at age 52; they said that Dr. Carmela Coppolino had been murdered with an overdose of an almost untraceable drug known as succinylcholine chloride, even though her death

86

certificate listed a heart attack as the cause of her demise at age 34.

And Marge Farber said that retired anesthesiologist Carl Coppolino, 18 years younger than she and her lover when they had been neighbors in an exclusive New Jersey township, was the one who had killed both her husband and his wife.

From the time the story broke in the summer of 1966, we got tantalizing hints of Marge's role in a case that was shaping up as a most incredible crime story. At first, all we knew was that a two-state probe into the 1963 death of William Farber in New Jersey and the 1965 death of Carmela Coppolino in Florida had resulted in murder charges against Carl Coppolino; we knew that the accused man had married a well-to-do divorcee only six weeks after Carmela's sudden death, and we knew that Colonel Farber's widow was among the witnesses who had been questioned.

We didn't find out until a little later that Marjorie Cullen Farber, a stunning, vivacious, witty woman who looked years younger than 52, was the one who had triggered the investigations and the exhumations that had resulted in the first degree murder indictments against her former lover.

When we discovered this, we were told she could not discuss her role in the upcoming trials. She was the star witness for Monmouth County prosecutor Vincent P. Keuper at the first trial scheduled for Freehold, N.J., the historic county seat, and so she was off limits. Unlike what undoubtedly would happen today, nobody from the press hounded her or offered her irresistibly big bucks to go public with her story.

Marge was not invisible, though. The *News* ran a pretrial interview with her in her Sarasota home, with photographs, and there was extensive coverage of the Florida preliminary hearing in which she admitted to having been "very intimate" with Coppolino. But she didn't tell our reporter or anybody else in the media the real story until the day she walked into the courthouse in Freehold and testified.

And what a story it was.

"COPPOLINO CASE GOES TO TRIAL: DA WILL ASK DEATH PENALTY" was the Page 1 copy for the advance story that I had written from Freehold for the editions of Monday, December 5, 1966. That was the day the trial was due to open with the selection of a jury that would hear charges that Coppolino had murdered

William Farber, his mistress's husband.

This "curtain raiser" alerted our readers to the start of a sensational and mysterious case, to involve them in the trial that would be unfolding in the subsequent weeks, and to give them background on the people they would be reading about as well as the legal events that had brought them to this day.

The lengthy article was decorated with photos of the widow Farber, of Colonel Farber, of Coppolino and his new wife, Mary, and of the opposing counsel: veteran prosecutor Vincent Keuper and rising defense attorney F. Lee Bailey, fresh from his victories in the Sam Sheppard case. I set the stage for my readers:

> At 33, the Boston defense attorney is about half the age of his chief opponent in the fight for Carl's life. Prosecutor Keuper, a rugged, distinguished looking court veteran, was admitted to the bar in 1926, seven years before Bailey was born. . . .
>
> In the few years he has been an attorney, Bailey has managed to build up an awesome reputation for brilliance and success. But Keuper has 40 years of practice behind him, he has been reelected to serve his third five-year term as county prosecutor—and he is on home ground.

Four days after this opener, with the jurors selected, Marge Farber was called to the witness stand. This was the long-awaited and dramatic highlight of the Coppolino case, and the *News* readers who paid their seven cents for the Saturday edition got the whole front page and three other pages devoted to the trial.

Half of the front page was the headline: "MRS. FARBER SOBS: DOC HYPNOTIZED HER FOR LOVE: 'WATCHED HIM' KILL HUSBAND." Below that was an extraordinary picture taken by *News* photographer Paul DeMaria. It was of Mary Coppolino, wife of the accused, walking past the table where the accuser, Marge Farber, and her lawyers were seated in the cocktail lounge of the Americana Hotel in Freehold. The photo showed that Carl's ex-mistress and his new wife looked enough alike to be brunette twins, with identical haircuts—short and with bangs. The women ignored each other.

The public could not see or hear Marge Farber on the stand, as they could today with televised trials, so the pictures and my words in the *News* provided the best images of her testimony. On Page 3, the main story began under this headline: "I TRIED TO

KILL HIM, THEN CALLED CARL; DOC HAD HER IN TRANCE
FOR LOVE OR MURDER, WIDOW TESTIFIES."

Swearing she was hypnotically entranced, under a strange magnetic spell that drove her into the arms of Dr. Carl Coppolino, a weeping Marjorie Farber twice today stood up in the witness chair to show Carl's jurors how, she said, her husband was strangled to death by her "jealous" one-time lover, as she stood by and watched.

Branded as a vindictive, venom-dripping woman, furious because Carl married somebody else after his first wife's death, Marjorie spent almost the entire day battling with defense attorney F. Lee Bailey, who made the accusations.

He told the jurors Marjorie wants Carl "so badly she would sit on his lap in the electric chair while somebody pulled the switch, just to make sure he dies."

Marge insisted she went to the authorities after the death of Dr. Carmela Coppolino, her ex-lover's first wife, because she felt toward Carmela "like a sister" and "was convinced Carmela's death was not natural."

The cross-examination came at the end of a day that started with powerful opening arguments by Keuper and Bailey, immediately followed by Marge's unexpected and enthralling eyewitness testimony for the state.

Questioned by Keuper, Marge described for the first time how she met the anesthesiologist when they were neighbors on Wallace Road, a street of handsome houses in the Fox Hill section of Middletown Township, N.J.

Carl's doctor wife worked in a medical research laboratory, Marge's husband worked for an insurance company in New York, and with both working spouses absent during the day, Marge and Carl, who was retired because of a heart condition, spent time together, becoming ever more neighborly. They became lovers, said Marge, after Carl offered to hypnotize her to help her quit smoking. According to Marge, the hypnosis somehow put her under Carl's spell, and "I saw him constantly, daily." She told the jurors they even traveled out of town together. Finally Carl gave her a drug which was supposed to be undetectable and to kill instantly, and instructed her to inject it into her husband's body; she insisted she tried but could not kill her husband, and she described how Carl allegedly did it, and how Carl got Carmela to sign the death certificate for the Colonel.

As a sidebar were excerpts from my story with quotes from Marge's testimony. Each quote was given a heading:

The Trance: Soon after being hypnotized by Carl "I had this terrific overwhelming feeling that I just had to get back to Wallace Road and see this Carl . . . When I went past his house he was sitting there in the driveway . . . and I just had to be with this man. . . I had to touch him. The next day I had this feeling of—it was just like a magnetic pull . . . I told him that I had a very strong feeling that I wanted to be close to him and the next thing I knew we were in each other's arms embracing, kissing each other. He said, 'Let's go down to your bedroom,' and I said, 'What about your heart condition?' And we did not go into the bedroom. The next day we became intimate. . ."

The Attempt: Coppolino had given Marge a syringe and a powder which the prosecution contended was succinylcholine chloride, a relaxant drug used by anesthesiologists, and Marge testified that she "had a terrible struggle. I paced the floors. I went upstairs and downstairs. I don't know how to describe this feeling. I was doing this thing. I couldn't stop myself . . . I had no control over what I was doing. I finally went into my husband's bedroom as if a large magnet had pulled me in there. He was asleep . . . and I bent over him with this syringe in my hand and I started to put it in his leg and I started to push the plunger down and I couldn't. I froze. I couldn't do it. He jumped up and I helped him into the bathroom . . . He fell on the floor. I tried to help him and I couldn't lift him because he was too heavy, so I called up Carl. He came over . . . Carl told me to get a plastic bag . . . He put it over Bill's head and started to suffocate Bill and Bill was nauseated, and I told him to stop it, leave him alone, and he did."

The Slaying: "He (Carl) was furious, absolutely furious. He said, 'That bastard's got to go, that man has got to go.' And he took out a syringe . . . I begged him to leave us alone. While I was telling him this he was filling the syringe with whatever he was taking out of a bottle. . . Carl said, 'He is a hard one to kill. He is taking a long time to die,' and then he pulled this pillow out from underneath my husband's head, and he put it over, just put it over him, and he leaned full weight right down on him, like this, and I just stood there and looked at him. He told me to wipe some blood off my husband's hand . . . He opened my husband's eye and he said, 'He's dead.'"

The trial testimony filled all of pages 3, 4, and 5. Another newspaper would have prescheduled a certain space for the story before getting the full day's information, and then would have lopped off copy to fit the scheduled space. The *News*, however, fulfilling its promise to bring its readers into the courtroom, ran every word I filed, included numerous photos from the photographers assigned to the trial, highlighted the most dramatic quotes, and used the lawyers' opening statements, which I had filed early, as a completely separate story: "Opening Drama: Demand for Chair, A Charge of Hoax."

All the important details of that day—the two opening arguments, Marge's direct examination, and the start of Bailey's cross-examination were in all editions of the *News* the next day because of a routine the desk and I had worked out over more than a decade of high-profile trials. During the noon recess I filed hundreds of words covering every facet of the morning session, which the copy desk read and held ready until the end of court that day. Then I filed hundreds more words, weaving both of the day's sessions together so the copy desk could easily and quickly edit the story, write the headlines, and get it out with photos and captions before our first edition deadline.

Every word of the testimony I took down myself in my small black notebook (tape recorders at that time being barred from courthouses). I typed, organized, and edited from that notebook, the Western Union operator transmitting page after page on our direct leased wire to the wire room and the editors on the seventh floor of the *News* building on 42nd Street. Comparing the carbons of what I typed with what was printed in the *News*, there were few or no changes to the original copy, and no cuts. I sent it, they did good things to it, and it ran.

I saved the editors time, too, because they didn't have to read the copy from the wire services—what they were getting from me twice a day was much more detailed than anything the wire service reporters were writing. In return, they sure made it easy for me, with no second-guessing, no space restraints, and the mutual respect that great working relationship promoted.

In that decade of high-profile trials, the Coppolino case was the first one I covered in the New York metropolitan area, and for the first time I saw people buying and reading the *News* while a trial was dominating the front pages. It was wonderful to be in my own home area with my newspaper being read everywhere I looked. As I went back and forth between the Americana Hotel and the courthouse, I watched people in the lobby, on the street, in the restaurants, leaning against buildings, all of them reading the *News*. Freehold was a small town, so the residents began to recognize the out-of-town reporters, and people came over to tell me how hooked they were on the case, that they couldn't wait to get the next installment every morning, that the trial had become better than a favorite soap opera.

There was a sizable press corps at the Coppolino trial, many of us reuniting after the second Sheppard trial. All of us were dealing with the restrictions on the press that had erupted because of the Supreme Court decision reopening the Sheppard case. "Free press versus fair trial" were the catchwords, and we of the press were fighting every day to prove that giving access to a responsible press does not impair a defendant's right to a fair trial, and that writing intelligently about a case before it goes to trial does not jeopardize a defendant's rights. The national trial reporters I worked with were intelligent and responsible, and all we wanted was to be able to do our jobs without the restraints nervous judges were starting to impose on us.

During the questioning of prospective jurors at this trial, Bailey attempted to show that massive pretrial publicity prejudiced Coppolino's right to a fair trial. Over and over he asked the prospects about the newspapers they read, usually singling out the *News* by name. Whenever a prospect who said he had read about the case but that it hadn't prejudiced him was accepted by both defense and prosecution, I trumpeted the fact in my story, driving home the argument that pretrial coverage of a case does not foreclose a defendant from getting unbiased jurors.

In Monmouth County, each prospective juror was questioned individually, out of the hearing of the other veniremen. If he passed all requirements, then the lawyers had to decide, right then, whether to accept the prospect or reject him by peremptory challenge. If accepted the juror was sworn immediately. For the Coppolino trial, fourteen jurors were sworn and seated, but no alternates were indicated. At the end of the trial, two jurors were picked at random to be alternates. Court officials told me that since none of the jurors knew who would be an alternate, this ensured that all of the jurors paid attention throughout the trial.

When the first juror was selected and sworn on the opening day, the Page 1 headline was "PICK 1ST JUROR IN DOC'S TRIAL." All of Page 3 was taken by photos of the trial, a banner headline reading: "1st Juror Chosen for Coppolino Trial, Reads Papers, But Isn't Biased; Seven Others Are Excused" and my story:

> A *Daily News* reader who works for the Good Humor Ice Cream Co. was sworn as a juror this afternoon in the Dr. Carl Coppolino murder trial here.
>
> James E. Jerram Jr., young, dark-haired and married, was accepted by defense attorney F. Lee Bailey and Monmouth County Prosecutor Vincent E. Keuper after he swore he has formed no opinion on the doctor's guilt or innocence, although he has read about the case "about a half dozen times."
>
> He said he gathered from the newspapers that there was a suspicion of "foul play" in the murders of retired Army Lt. Col. William E. Farber and Dr. Carmela Coppolino, wife of the defendant.
>
> But he assured Bailey that it did not prejudice him against Coppolino because he had read that the doctor was charged in two states with murder. The trial here is on the Farber case in which he is charged with strangling the colonel. . . . Jerram will be taken tonight to the Hitching Post Motel, where each juror will be locked up as soon as he is sworn.

(Many years later, another reporter quoted to me, word for word, this lead, telling me he never forgot it because he thought it was the funniest trial lead he had ever read. He didn't have a clue that we were then in the midst of a free press/fair trial war, which was why I stuck the guy's reading habits into the top of the story. After the trial an article appearing in the *Columbia Journalism Review* purportedly analyzing how the *News* "promoted" itself during the Coppolino trial by mentioning prospective jurors' reading habits. The writer could not have been a working reporter covering major trials, since he seemed blissfully unaware of the free press/fair trial battle. Thank God we didn't have his type as an editor at the *News* then.)

This first story explained the reasons that other jurors had been excused, and described the defendant as "pale faced, slender and nattily dressed today in a continental-cut, iridescent gabardine suit." Our readers learned that Judge Elvin M. Simmill had overruled motions by Bailey "to exclude as a juror any person who knew that Coppolino also has the Florida indictment hanging over him" and to "keep on the jury anyone who says he is against capital punishment," with Bailey unsuccessfully arguing that "if we question 1,000 who don't believe in capital punishment and we dig up 12 that do," it would not be fair to the defendant.

At the next day's session, Bailey asked every prospect but one what newspaper they read, and I wrote: "Many named the *News*, and Bailey (once popping a large wink at the *News* reporter in the front row) asked a series of questions to find out if the newspaper accounts had prejudiced the prospect. None of the *News* readers said they had been prejudiced."

Bailey kidded a lot with the jurors, and when one of them said he read "everything about the case in the *News*," the defense attorney told him, "There is some suspicion that the *Daily News* is controlled by a syndicate of prosecutors."

Bailey and I, of course, had become acquainted at the recent Sheppard trial. Despite the problems he caused us with the U.S. Supreme Court, I thought he was a superb attorney. His handling of jurors was brilliant, he was quick-witted, he had great courtroom style and a marvelous sense of humor. He thought I was a helluva reporter and that my trial coverage was complete, objective, and accurate. In fact, after comparing my *News* stories of the trial testimony with his own official transcript, he asked me only half-kiddingly if I was wired.

It bothered me that the press was under attack because of the Sheppard decision, but I understood that Bailey had a job to do— to protect his client with all the necessary motions and tactics— and he knew that I had a job to do, which was to inform the public. Of course, me doing my job kept him on the front pages of the country's largest newspaper, so we remained good natured during the jury selection.

As it turned out, Coppolino was not moved out of Freehold, his jurors acquitted him despite the massive publicity the trial received, despite the fact that Marge Farber gave eyewitness testimony accusing Carl of murdering her husband, and despite the fact that New York City's legendary medical examiner, Dr. Milton Helpern, told the jurors that Colonel Farber died a "violent death."

Helpern was famous. I wrote:

It took almost 10 minutes for the old courtroom pro to go

through his list of professional credits for Keuper, saying he has done 20,000 autopsies in his 35 years in the medical examiner's office—the last 12 of them as chief. The snowy-haired veteran medical examiner said his autopsy on the colonel's exhumed body showed a double fracture of the larynx (voice box), an injury which he said immediately established that his death was a homicide.

He showed Coppolino's 14 murder trial jurors the small ossified section he removed from the colonel's body. As some of the jurors stood up to look at it in his hand—a couple of the four women gulping—he pointed out to them a fracture through the cricoid cartilage, one inch below the Adam's apple, and another on the other side, five eighths of an inch away.

"You can put your hand here and feel the fracture, which I'm sure nobody wants to do," Helpern said. The jurors took his word for it.

He also told the jurors that Farber's heart "was normal in size and shape. There was no evidence . . . that this man ever suffered a heart ailment."

The last witness the jury heard was Coppolino himself, who followed seven other defense witnesses called by Bailey. The Page 1 line that day, Thursday, December 15, 1966, was: "Cool Coppolino Testifies—HE WAS A LOVER, NOT A KILLER."

Unruffled, relaxed, and in perfect control of the situation, Dr. Carl Coppolino brought his best bedside manner to the witness chair today to tell his murder trial jurors about the death of retired Lt. Col. William E. Farber, the man he is accused of strangling out of jealousy for the colonel's lady.

From his story the jurors were given a picture of a dedicated doctor, friend and neighbor, a man who used his medical skills to give emergency treatment to his mistress' husband, who pleaded with Marge and Bill Farber to call an ambulance and provide hospital care for a man apparently suffering a severe heart attack.

This was the first time since the case broke that the 34-year-old author, anesthesiologist and hypnotist has spoken, and his 90 minutes on the stand under direct and cross-examination were a dramatic ending to the trial testimony. . . .

Moving his long-fingered hands gracefully, leaning toward his jurors to explain a point, politely "correcting" the prosecutor who wants to send him to the chair, Coppolino gave testimony that contradicted Marge Farber on everything except that: They had been to bed together. He hypnotized her to help her quit smoking.

The next day, Friday, December 16, 1966, the *News'* huge Page 1 headline over a picture of a smiling Coppolino told it all: "NOT GUILTY, BUT NOT FREE: Doc Still Held for Trial in Fla."

> In 4 hours, 25 minutes today, a jury acquitted Dr. Carl Coppolino of a charge he murdered retired Army Lt. Col. William E. Farber, husband of his one-time mistress.
> The verdict, returned at 4:35 p.m., brought gasps from the packed courtroom, immediately shushed by guards.
> Carl's mother, Mrs. Anna Fiore Coppolino, who had waited in the courtroom—sometimes alone—reading her Bible and saying her rosary, collapsed in tears on the shoulder of one of defense attorney F. Lee Bailey's women investigators. Carl's wife, in tears, hugged and kissed him. Carl wept with both of them.
> The acquittal verdict, branding Marge Farber as the "hell-bent" spurned woman described by the defense, did not give the 34-year-old defendant his freedom. Despite an eloquent plea by Bailey, he was taken immediately to his jail cell, to be taken from there by plane to Sarasota, Fla., where he is charged with the murder of his first wife, Carmela.

The acquittal was Keuper's first defeat in 30 cases after 12 years as Monmouth County prosecutor, but he was a gentleman, and I quoted him as saying about Bailey, "He is brilliant young man."

Bailey's victory, coming immediately after his Sam Sheppard successes, catapulted him into megastardom as a lawyer. He invited everyone to a champagne victory party that night at the Americana, but a lot of us had a massive amount of copy to work on. I was sitting at the hotel dining room with some other reporters, finally ordering a very late dinner after wrapping up our stories, when Bailey suddenly appeared, picked me up, and ran upstairs with me to the champagne party, while the photographers chased us. He was, understandably, ecstatic.

The next time I saw Carl Coppolino was four months later in Naples, Florida, where his trial had been moved on a change of venue from Sarasota. Naples, on Florida's west coast, was then a wealthy but low-key tourist, fishing, and beach resort with only 5,000 permanent residents.

Marge Farber was again listed as a witness. In January 1967 a Monmouth County grand jury had refused to indict her in connection with her husband's death, and prosecutor Keuper declined to go into details of the proceedings. "This action ends it as far as New Jersey is concerned," said the prosecutor. "I close out my files, that's all." Keuper said he had turned over to the grand jurors all testimony, which obviously included Marge's confession that she made an attempt to kill her husband but lost her nerve.

In March 1967, lawyers for Coppolino in Sarasota voluntarily dismissed a $1,275,000 malicious prosecution suit against Marge Farber, in which her ex-lover had alleged that she had made false statements to law officers accusing him of killing her husband. No reason for the dismissal was given.

I filed the curtain raiser on April 2, 1967:

> My last glimpse of Dr. Carl Coppolino was on a bleak December morning last year in Freehold, N.J., when he was hustled from the Monmouth County jail into a waiting car for his return trip, under guard, to Florida. . . .
> Coppolino then was skinny, drawn and pale after months of living behind bars. As soon as he arrived in Florida he was set free in $15,000 bond, and today, when he arrived here from Sarasota for his second murder trial, he looked like a different man. The trial starts tomorrow.
> He was bronzed, he was back to his normal weight of 165 pounds . . . and in shorts and a sports jacket today, he appeared relaxed and affable as he lunched at the Golfing Buccaneer, a resort motel that advertises itself as being "planned for people who enjoy elegant comfort in an atmosphere of complete relaxation."

I had come down from New York with *News* photographer Dan Farrell, and most of the out-of-town press stayed at the Buccaneer, a modern, glass-walled motel (a big difference from the old-fashioned Americana in Freehold) so that we could relax together after the sessions, usually meeting in my room for drinks before heading out for dinner at the restaurants the townsfolk recommended to us.

I was fighting the flu and although I seldom go to a doctor I was advised that the motel had a physician who made house calls, so I broke down and called him to come see me.

This was a retirement town, and the doctor who tottered in to my room that night had been retired a very long time. He wore a baseball cap and a flowered shirt and shorts and briskly set about examining me, having me sit on a chair as he sat facing me on another chair with his back to the door. My motel room was on the ground floor, and I had left the door unlocked for the physician. As the ancient doctor leaned toward me, with my blouse pulled up so that he could listen to my breathing, Dan came to the door to make dinner plans. He could see only the back of the doctor's head and the natty shirt, and since the sporty-looking guy appeared to have his head pressed to my half-exposed bosom, poor embarrassed Danny figured I was into some kinky lovemaking with a stud townsman and fled. I looked up just as he disappeared. Realizing what Danny must have thought, I got a fit of giggles, totally confusing the old gentleman, who decided I was a terribly ticklish person and quit burrowing into my chest.

Covering a trial in a Florida resort in April wasn't half bad, and we had a remarkably happy crew considering that the press room was some distance from the courthouse and we had to run what seemed like miles back and forth during the trial.

Bailey mercifully did not dwell on the press and pretrial publicity. He now was one of the most famous criminal defense attorneys in the country, and having won an acquittal for his client in Freehold despite eyewitness testimony and damaging opinions from a heavyweight medical examiner, he must have been confident that he could waltz out of this second trial, where there was only circumstantial evidence.

If he could beat an experienced pro like Vincent Keuper, he must have figured, the battle with the small town southern prosecutor, Frank Schaub, would be no contest, especially since Judge Silvertooth had ruled that Schaub could not tell the jurors how similar were the facts surrounding the deaths of Colonel Farber and Carmela Coppolino.

Lee, an experienced flier, had his own Lear jet and loved piloting it to speeches and events nationwide, so he was not in the trial room every session as he had been in Freehold. Thus, he left some of the cross-examination of prosecution witnesses to his co-counsel, who were competent and hard-working.

I didn't pay too much attention to his absences until one day when Lee, who had been up north, stopped me on the way into court and asked me what in the world I had been writing. People up north seemed to think that Coppolino was going to be convicted, and since he had been in *News* territory, he could tell they were getting this impression from my stories.

What I was writing, of course, was exactly what the jurors were hearing in the trial room, and if my readers were thinking that the state was making a good case, so were the jurors. And if he were in the courtroom all the time like I was, I told Lee, maybe he'd think so too.

I think Lee didn't recognize that Schaub was getting lots of first class help from big guns like Helpern who had been upset with the Freehold acquittal and now had a second chance to prove that they had been right. Because the state was trying to prove that Carmela's death was from a drug injection, not strangulation, the medical testimony was even more important than before, and the parade of medical experts for the state was impressive.

The most dramatic testimony came from a New York anesthesiologist, who in 1964 had himself injected with succinylcholine chloride in a carefully controlled experiment during which he became "completely paralyzed (but) retained consciousness." An artificial breathing device was used to prevent death. The story for that day began:

> Carmela Coppolino died knowing she was being murdered and helpless to fight back, if her death was caused by an injection of succinylcholine, as charged by the state.
>
> Further, through questioning of New York anesthesiologist Dr. Valentine D. B. Mazzia today, Prosecutor Frank Schaub indicated that she might have been suffocated with a pillow to hasten her death.
>
> The state threw its biggest haymakers at Carmela's husband, former anesthesiologist Carl Coppolino, 34, who is charged with murdering her because he wanted to marry a well-to-do divorcee.
>
> From Mazzia the jury heard how a person dies from the drug . . . conscious and aware, but cannot move a muscle.
>
> From another New York doctor, Bert La Du Jr., they bombshelled the defense with testimony that evidence of the drug had been discovered in Carmela's left buttock, at the spot where Medical Examiner Milton Helpern said he found a needle point track . . .
>
> This testimony was a surprise because Helpern on the stand— apparently aware of this discovery—had never given it away under cross examination by chief defense attorney F. Lee Bailey.

Marge Farber's second appearance as a state witness against her former lover gave her a chance to repeat her denials that she had accused Carl of murder out of anger that he had married another woman when Carmela died. She told the jurors that on the

Coppolinos' ninth wedding anniversary, Carl told Carmela he no longer loved her. That was August 18, 1965. Ten days later Carmela was found dead.

Greed and his love of "the sweet life" were the reasons Carl murdered Carmela, prosecutor Schaub told the jurors, and he painted the defendant as a man who lived off his wife, his physician father-in-law, and money from insurance and disability policies, which he started collecting after retiring because of heart trouble. The prosecutor said that Carl murdered his wife so that he could marry Mary Gibson, whom he had met after he and Carmela moved to Sarasota.

Bailey's defense, which had been successful in New Jersey, was that there had been no murder because Carmela had died of natural causes; nobody knew for a fact exactly what had caused her death. But at this trial, in his closing, Bailey said he wanted the jurors to consider some possibilities. "The jury has no assurance," Bailey said, "that this woman did not dispose of her own life." Carmela was a doctor and could have injected herself, he said.

Carl did not testify at this trial, and he said it was his joint decision with Bailey, explaining to us outside the courtroom: "There was nothing more I could say. In Freehold there was an eyewitness who was lying and I had to speak. Here I have already said I didn't do it by my plea."

On Thursday, April 27, the all-male jury got the case, deliberated slightly more than three hours, and then were taken to their hotel. The next morning, after deliberating less than an hour, they had a verdict: Guilty.

> The "sweet life" ended today for Dr. Carl Coppolino.
>
> Speechless, looking stricken, he stood before his judge and heard himself sentenced to prison "for the remainder of your natural life" after his jurors convicted him as the killer of his 32-year-old wife, Carmela, mother of his two children. Shortly after being sentenced, Coppolino was taken to Sarasota County jail. . . .
>
> Coppolino's second wife, the former Mary Gibson, sat alone in a spectator seat directly behind her husband as the judge pronounced sentence. She was flushed, expressionless, dry-eyed.
>
> She heard each of the 12 jurors, standing in front of the jury box, give his name and say: "That's my verdict."
>
> It meant that the 12 men believed Prosecutor Frank Schaub when he accused the doctor of injecting Carmela on Aug. 28, 1965 with a lethal shot of the paralyzing drug, succinylcholine, to become

free to marry well-to-do divorcee Mary Gibson.

It meant they believed, as Schaub's witness testified, that Carmela died an agonizing death, knowing that she was being murdered, unable to move a muscle, unable to breathe, finally dying of suffocation.

It meant they believed Coppolini killed out of "greed," that he got rid of Carmela because neither she nor her retired father, Dr. Carmelo Musetto . . . could keep him in enough money to continue "the sweet life" he had enjoyed for years.

Schaub said Coppolino's luck ran out when he came to Sarasota.

And so it had. The life sentence was the maximum on second degree murder, which carries a minimum of 20 years. In Sarasota Judge Silvertooth denied defense motions to set aside the jury verdict and to declare Carl a pauper, which would have made the state bear the cost of an appeal. Carl was driven by deputies to Raiford State Prison, 250 miles away, where he served 12 years before he was paroled.

A month after the Naples trial, I was back in Florida with photographer Danny Farrell, this time in Sarasota to meet with Marge Farber and finally talk with the woman I had been writing about for so long.

What she told me made a three-part series for the newspaper, illustrated with photos of her and her children and her home on Longboat Key, near the house where Carmela died.

She told me about her feelings of "terrible despair" when Carl was acquitted of her husband's murder. "I was in shock. That was the worst, the very worst day of all."

Her reaction when he was convicted of Carmela's death? "I do not feel any guilt." She told me how she had to explain to her children what had happened between her and Carl, how she had to reveal the dreadful details of their father's death. "I told them everything, and they understood," she said.

She said when she looked at Carmela's corpse, she realized that if she had spoken up earlier about her husband's death, Carmela would not have died. And that, she said, was why she finally went to the authorities with her accusations.

The series ended with Marge telling me: "They say you should put your past behind you. I haven't been able to. It's been thrown back and thrown back at me. Maybe now I can do it. . . . What do I really want to do now? I'd like to rejoin the human race."

7

The Joy of Writing

Like the other top rewritemen at the *News*, Henry Lee could give sparkle to anything he wrote, no matter the pressure, no matter the subject. And only the *News*, with its lack of pomposity and love of the New York scene, would encourage Henry's sparkle by giving enormous space to stories that other newspapers did not find irresistible.

For instance: what do you do with the news out of Brooklyn that the dangerous but inept Gallo mob ("the gang that couldn't shoot straight") had saved six kids in an apartment house fire? Important it wasn't, but it made page 1 of the *News* on February 1, 1962, with a huge headline—"7 GALLOS RUB OUT FIRE, SAVE 6"—over a huge picture of the hoods with the kids, and a big story on page 3. And why wouldn't it, when it was written the way Henry wrote it?

> To the amazement of all South Brooklyn, especially themselves, the Gallo mob, generally considered the hillbilly hoodlums of the borough, were cast yesterday in a strange, blinding, new light.
>
> As heroes.
>
> Seven of them, headed by Larry Gallo, their temporary leader, bravely dashed through smoke and flame to rescue six small children from a third-floor apartment fire.
>
> Larry, acting boss since the mob was left fatherless by the imprisonment of Crazy Joe Gallo, swallowed so much smoke in his moment of heroism that he required medical treatment. His six companions escaped, singed but safe, the terrific heat failing to explode even one of their cartridges.

The story, written on deadline and under the double byline of reporter Joseph Kiernan and Henry Lee, quoted Albert (Kid Blast) Gallo as insisting: "We're not heroes. We only done what any red-blooded American boys would do."

Describing the rescue as "the Gallos' giddy flirtation with valor," Henry wrote that while some of the hoods "took the children downstairs, growling reassuringly to them," the others "with professional finesse" smashed windows, broke up the burning furniture to throw outside, and had the fire extinquished by the time the fire trucks arrived.

"Carried away by their day, the mob went even further," and raised money for the burned-out family by canvassing "startled storekeepers" in the neighborhood, Henry's story continued. There were other details, including a "cautious" commendation by one of the Brooklyn South top cops "who has made a sort of a hobby of arresting Galloites as often as possible" and the story ended this way: "Kid Blast had the last word. 'With our crummy run of bad luck,' he snorted, 'we'll probably be pinched for fighting the fire without a union card.'"

With this kind of news writing—you understand, all of the facts were absolutely accurate, as were the quotes, since good writers know that real quotes are always better than inventions—the *News* didn't need columnists. These news stories were better than columns; they were about real people, they weren't canned items from agents or flacks.

At the *News* we had the challenge of not only getting the information out fast, accurately, completely, and tightly, but of making the story as dramatic or as hilarious or as sad or as packed with information as possible, and it had to be readable.

Even when a rewriteman was being cute, he could be creative, as when Jimmy Davis, who wrote plays on the side and kept asking to be transferred off of rewrite and onto the entertainment pages, got ticked off because he was asked to do some dumb little story on a fire in Central Park.

To his amazement, the lead he sent over in a pique became immortal, because by nightfall all of us at the paper had called everybody we knew to share it. Jimmy's story started: "Fire broke out in an elm tree in Central Park yesterday, apparently caused by a squirrel smoking in bed."

It was Bob Sylvester, the *News'* long-time "Dream Street" columnist, who wrote a memorable description of a bad chanteuse: "She can't sing, but she's ugly." And then there was the dance recital that Bob covered and disliked intensely: "The frontiers of modern dance were advanced last night from wherever the hell they were before to wherever the hell they are today."

During most of my life in the business, I have found that reporters were each other's best and most appreciative audience. When an unforgettable lead didn't make the paper for one reason or another, it was kept alive by reporters who had seen it in the typewriter to be retold years later whenever someone did a column on newspaper writing. Ray Sprigle had one at the first trial of Sam Sheppard, who was charged with beating his wife to death. The autopsy pictures of Marilyn Sheppard were shown to the jurors soon after both sides had presented their opening arguments. As we left the trial room after the sorrowful display, white-haired Ray leaned over and said to me, "Wanna go out and have some liver, kid?" Then, in the crowded little press room, he sat at his typewriter and banged out this gem: "If Sam Sheppard doesn't burn after today's testimony, he's incombustible."

Those autopsy pictures were the first I ever saw. My initiation was unforgettable, since the photos of murdered Marilyn were huge, in color, displayed on a large screen in the darkened courtroom.

It was 1954. Never before, and never after to my knowledge, was such evidence allowed to be presented to a jury. The *News* editors recognized that courtroom history was being made, and my story was given Page 1 headlines and a big display starting on Page 3 and running several columns on the jump page.

> Cleveland, Nov. 4—Marilyn Sheppard's face in death, her forehead and skull bloody with gaping wounds, her eyes closed and swollen, her nose cut and broken, was shown today in a shocked and sickened courtroom.
>
> Her husband, accused of Marilyn's murder, deliberately sat out of view of the exhibit and wept.
>
> Marilyn's face was shown in color, enlarged to gruesome proportions, on seven slides thrown on the screen by the state to show how the pregnant young woman looked as she lay on an autopsy table in a coroner's morgue. The color pictures, measuring four feet by four feet, were made a few hours after she was murdered in her home July 4.

Unprecedented in criminal trial history, it was the state's opening move in its fight to send Dr. Sam Sheppard to the electric chair.
The defendant refused to look at the pictures. He moved
behind the screen and sat near a window at the side as the courtroom blinds were drawn and the screen was carried before the jury.
. . .
Though Sam Sheppard would not look at the slides, he could
not shut out the dry voice of Dr. Lester T. Adelson, the deputy coroner, describing wound after wound. They were numbered and there
were 35 of them.

Autopsy pictures like those of Marilyn Sheppard are not shown
to jurors anymore because the courts have ruled that the prejudicial effect of such evidence outweighs its probative value. There
was not one question from the *News* editors on my story, nor did
they cut any of the other details I sent; but then the *News* never was
timid about telling it like it was. It was the first New York City
paper to use the words *veneral disease* in an editorial, it was the
only one that showed the public a woman dying in the electric
chair, and if this sold papers, it also enlightened our readers.
Perhaps that awful picture of Ruth Snyder being electrocuted
helped lead to that period in the United States when capital punishment was banned, and maybe the story about Marilyn's horrible autopsy pictures helped defense attorneys in their successful
fight against such tactics.
When I covered trials I met writers who had made their reputa-
tions on big stories like wars. I didn't meet Homer Bigart until long
after he won two Pulitzer Prizes (in 1945 for World War II coverage and in 1951 for Korean War coverage as a reporter for the *New
York Herald Tribune*), but he attended a few trials with me after the
Trib folded and he went to the *New York Times*. He had a dry wit, a
stutter that disappeared when he sang, and a beautiful writing
style, which was not appreciated by his *Times* bosses. Homer was
seldom cranky, but he once showed me a beauty of a lead he had
written, and then told me that his editors had lopped it off and
started with his second paragraph.
They did this to a man who had written one of the legendary
leads about the end of World War II, from Hiroshima soon after the
bomb was dropped:

Japan, paying for her desperate throw of the dice at Pearl

Harbor, passed from the ranks of the major powers at 9:05 a.m. today when Foreign Minister Mamoru Shigemitsu signed the document of unconditional surrender.

If the memories of the bestialities of the Japanese prison camps were not so fresh in mind, one might have felt sorry for Shigemitsu as he hobbled on his wooden leg toward the green baize-covered table where the papers lay waiting.

After he was sent to cover the Vietnam War, Homer was one of the first newspapermen to conclude, based on his experiences in Korea, that our Vietnam involvement was a mistake.

Like everybody else I knew, I hated the Vietnam War and what it was doing to my son's generation. I hated what it was doing to this country and to all the Vietnamese people.

But when I was assigned in 1973 to cover the return of the first POWs at Travis Air Force Base in northern California, and saw them step off the plane, I could feel only pity for what they had suffered, and happiness that they were free and safe.

It was February 14. Waiting for the plane to arrive, I had sent a holding story for the *News'* early editions, but then the plane landed, the ex-POWs came off it, and I had to dictate a new beginning for all of the later editions:

> It was Valentine's Day and Christmas. It was Thanksgiving Day and the Fourth of July. It was home at last for 20 released prisoners of war who arrived today filled with such joy and gratitude that when one of them was asked to describe how he felt, he could only say:
> "I can't describe it, because I have nothing to compare it with."
> There were no bands, no speeches, no ceremonies for this first full planeload of released prisoners, and none were needed.
> The day was made glorious simply because of what happened.

Newspaper writers, at least in the old days, *kvelled* over each other's stories, and this was one of those leads that other reporters used to quote when they met me—the nicest compliment anybody in the business can give you.

News editor Mike O'Neill sent me kind words about how much the story had moved him, and he enclosed a copy of a note he had received from Pat McCormack of UPI in New York, who wrote that she had read about the POWs in four papers and on both wires, and that she thought ours was the one "that put the heart into this whole POW thing," and that the lead was "so great it had me spell-bound on the train."

The next day, when a second planeload arrived, I started the story by describing the senior officer who stepped out first:

> His pale face was aged beyond his years, his left foot in its highly polished boot was twisted painfully inward, but the Navy pilot stood ramrod straight in his immaculate khakis. . . . [He] quoted from a Greek poem 4,000 years old to tell his countrymen:
> "Nothing is so sweet as to return from the sea and listen to the raindrops on the rooftops of home."

There was no way that my hatred of the Vietnam War could make me write anything but compassionately about these men who had suffered in prison camps. What happened to me that day was described 20 years later by Laura Palmer, who said that when she was writing her book, *Shrapnel in the Heart*, about the mementoes left at the Vietnam War Memorial in Washington, she was finally able to separate the war from the warriors. She could hate the war, Laura told an interviewer, but she could not hate the Americans who had suffered there.

It took 20 years, though, before a lot of us quit making Vietnam veterans the victims of the bitterness we had felt toward the war itself, before we quit making them the victims of the anger and betrayal we felt toward the leaders who kept us in that war with the deceptions revealed in the Pentagon Papers.

After having worked for such formal, conservative papers as the *Richmond News Leader* and the *Philadephia Bulletin*, it was sheer joy to write for the *News*, which let you use any voice you wanted in your stories, including the language of the streets. It was wonderful to be able to call a police officer a "cop" if it fit the mood of the story.

When Tallulah Bankhead died in New York in 1968, I was assigned to the story. After it came out, one of Tallulah's friends telephoned to tell me that his greatest regret was that she couldn't read it, she would have loved it:

> Cabbies and cops called her by her first name, and adored her. She was a good dame, a nut about baseball and a rabid fan of the New York Giants when they were around.

She was a Southern belle who loathed professional Southerners, a magnificent actress who loved quoting terrible reviews about herself, and one of the few great ladies of the theater who was just as delightful off stage as she was on.

She was something special as an actress and something special as a personality, and a whole lot of people who never met her or even saw her on stage in her heyday were saddened that Tallulah Bankhead died yesterday.

Joseph Conrad once defined a writer's job as "above all, to make you see." Although most reporters probably never heard that line, and some editors probably never heard of Conrad, what we do every day is follow the great novelist's dictum.

A writer who could always "make you see" while being enchanting about anything he covered was H. D. (Doc) Quigg of UPI, whose assignments included World War II, the Korean War, and Admiral Byrd's expedition to the Antarctic, and whose interviews included everybody from Willie Sutton to Aristotle Onassis, with a few Presidents, bums, generals, judges, crooks, poets, and politicians thrown in.

Doc was assigned to cover the first lunar landing in the summer of 1969:

> You sat there and watched man step into his own dream. The silent footfall on the airless moon that was the leap of ages. You sat and saw a corner-turning in the human saga.
>
> Man left his footprints on the sands of space, and a great portion of the world sat and watched with you as the television eye stared at the audacity of the bootmarks of a civilian from Ohio and a colonel from New Jersey signing in on the register of the lunar soil.
>
> After a million years of dreaming, guessing, wondering, wishing, questing in the mind for the impossible visit, feeling the urge of the unknown sky above, humankind had gained a toehold on the heavens.

This was followed by Doc's description of Neil Armstrong and Buzz Aldrin in their first moments on the moon:

> . . . they were unbelievably eager, like kids in a schoolroom when the lesson is a stimulus. They hopped. They took their own pictures standing beside the Stars and Stripes. They romped, pranced in the elegant state of one-sixth gravity, invented a new

dance of sorts which may be named the lunar hop. They cavorted from nowhere into the middle of the television tube like men buoyed by attachment to a rubber band strung above them.

Reading this nearly two decades after it took place, anyone who remembers the landing—even those who don't—can see exactly how it was, lunar hop and all.

Three years earlier, in the summer of 1966, Doc had been sent to Austin, Texas where 25-year-old Charles Whitman had climbed to the top of the University of Texas bell tower with a shotgun and three rifles and killed people until he himself was shot to death by police.

Doc's roundup story several days after was headed with a quote from Thornton Wilder's *The Bridge of San Luis Rey:* "It Was A Very Hot Noon, That Fatal Noon." Like Wilder, Doc wrote about the oddities of fate that brought each of the victims to that particular place, to die at that particular time.

The story reads so effortlessly that you easily forget the enormous amount of legwork and investigation and patience that went into it. At least five other UPI staffers helped, although the distances, the heights, the sound of the chimes in the bell tower had all been measured, counted, timed by Doc. He had asked innumerable questions, pursued answers, had even gotten a weather report, and then had written a newspaper masterpiece:

> At high noon in Austin a man's shadow in early August on the University of Texas campus stands out only a foot and a half to the northwest, a little rounded thing that would shade a passing grasshopper but little else.
>
> The sun comes down just about straight. The Weather Bureau figures it's at least 110 degrees out in the sun on a day like last Monday, when the temperature stood at 98 degrees in the shade.
>
> A man taking sight with a gun does well to wear a stretch-type sweatband around his head to keep the salt sweat from his forehead out of his eyes. Charles Joseph Whitman wore one, and at high noon he was a busy man.

From where he stood on the observation deck, 231 feet above campus, Whitman could clearly see "the 12-story apartment building 10 blocks south, where, on the fifth floor, his mother lay dead by his hand. Now he had new business," Doc wrote.

He described the noon chimes, "16 notes, high and sweet" and after the chimes a long pause, "23 seconds if you held a wristwatch on it—time enough for a practiced man to reload three rifles and a shotgun." Then he told about those who were wounded and the 13 who died.

If you are a tower receptionist named Edna Elizabeth Townsley, it is your day off. But you are there in a twist of fate—a co-worker is on vacation and you are filling in. And you are lying, barely breathing, behind a couch near your observation-deck desk, dying—your head bashed in by a madman's gun butt and then pierced by a bullet.

If you are sweethearts at age 18 named Paul Sonntag and Claudia Rutt, you are walking hand-in-hand toward death—and you are here on the west mall by fate's tug: the swimming pool where he was a lifeguard, and where she always joined him, was closed for the day.

. . . A shot rang. Claudia wavered and fell. "Help me! Somebody help me!" she called. Paul bent over her. Another shot. He fell across her body. They died together there. On her finger was Paul's senior ring.

When I was preparing to go to London to cover Princess Anne's wedding in 1973, the desk asked me to do an advance story before I flew out, and our London bureau man, Henry Maule, sent me a lot of information.

The lead I wrote on that advance story was typical New York tongue-in-cheek, and I thought it would tickle only the *News* editors and our New York readers. To our astonishment, out-of-towners got a kick out of it, including the *Los Angeles Times*, which took the story off our wire and displayed it on Page 1. Nearly every reporter I knew on the West Coast cut it out and sent it to me. It wasn't until I moved to Los Angeles and became a daily *Times* reader that I realized what a departure such a story was for that paper at that time:

London, Nov. 11—Since the mother of the bride is one of the wealthiest women in the world and is marrying off an only daughter, there should be a wedding here Wednesday like you wouldn't believe.

Sitting on the bride's side alone will be 1,200 guests.

On the groom's side, as many guests as the family wants, since for this ceremony the royalty of Great Britain plans to use

Westminster Abbey, that spacious, 900-year-old, history-encrusted edifice where you don't even have to release swarms of white doves to impress the relatives.

Even when it's empty, the splendid abbey is enough to knock you out. As the setting for the wedding of Princess Anne Elizabeth Alice Louise, only daughter of Queen Elizabeth and the Duke of Edinburgh, to Capt. Mark Phillips, handsome son of Mr. and Mrs. Peter Phillips, of the sausage, pork pie and ice cream Phillipses, it should be a dynamite scene.

I went on with thousands of details about *the* wedding of the year, and ended in the same tone as I had begun:

> There will be a wedding breakfast after the ceremony, the new-lyweds will make the traditional balcony appearance at the palace to wave to the people, and in midafternoon, Capt. and Mrs. Phillips will be taken to a secret honeymoon site.
>
> The secrecy is something Queen Elizabeth demanded, because when she was married to Philip, newspaper reporters watched the bedroom window and reported to the world the exact moment the lights went out.

At that time, the *News* still had great appreciation and respect for its writers and the job they had to do, so they made life easier for me by flying me first class to London on Pan Am and putting me up at the Savoy.

In London, waiting for the wedding, I sent stories about the preparations. The *News*, as usual, imposed no space limits on me and ran everything I sent them, since we then had editors who could appreciate the fine art of giving readers accurate details without boring them to death.

I wrote about the crowds "milling around the palace all day, good-naturedly bundled up against the weather to enjoy a free show," and couldn't resist including some typical Brit wit from the queen:

> Along with the gaiety here, there is a certain amount of giddi-ness. The staid *Sunday Times* contained this news item:
> "The queen, who is is not given to hazarding jokes, has expressed over the royal wedding a thought that has occurred to many of her subjects: 'When they have children,' she has said, 'they are bound to have four legs.'"

This knee-slapper, I explained to readers, was a reference to the fact that "Anne and Mark are outstanding horse-persons, he being an Olympic finalist and she being the first member of royalty to win the European Cup championship."

The day before the wedding I sent a story about the remarkably joyous mood of the hundreds who shivered for hours in wind and cold to get a glimpse of Anne and the other royals coming to the Abbey for the final wedding rehearsal, and how they joked with everybody, including the equally relaxed helmeted bobbies on crowd control duty.

> Some of the spectators helpfully gave advice to the men decorating the entrances with scalloped canopies, trimmed in royal blue and gold, calling out little instructions like: "That gold tassel isn't hanging as pretty as the other one, mate," and "Watch it, you're getting finger marks on the white canvas there."
>
> And when a horse's hoofs were heard clattering on the stone, one old gentleman shouted in mock terror: "Don't tell me they're coming to the abbey on their horses!" It was a mounted cop, and he received a round of applause.

This story was updated later with an entirely different one describing a BBC interview with Anne and her fiance, during which Anne dominated the conversation. Her groom-to-be, barely able to get a word in and stuttering when he did, nevertheless delighted me with a great quote. I wrote that Captain Phillips "said it doesn't bother him that for the rest of his public life he must always walk behind the princess, it won't offend his male ego because 'in the home I'll keep my end up.'"

To show how kind we reporters can be, here is the question and Phillips' actual answer from the BBC transcript:

> *Interviewer:* Captain Phillips, Princess Anne in protocol must always precede you. D'you find that offends your male ego?
> *Phillips:* No. I mean, I think, no, not at all. I think the, I think where, where, where, where most of our life is, is in the home, I think, I think in, in the home I, I keep my end up. At least, I'd like to think I keep my end up well enough. [Laughter]

The day of the wedding itself was a rare day, brilliantly sunny. Thanks to the time difference, for once in my life on a big story I could take a little time to work on it.

I had gone to my reserved seat in the abbey dressed as instructed (day dress with hat), and on the dais I saw Princess Grace Kelly,
outshining everyone else with her pure beauty. I also watched a
handsome little boy cutting up while his mother the Queen shook
her head warningly at him. This turned out to be Andrew—Randy
Andy, as he came to be known when he was older—showing even
then signs of great charm, mischief, and personality, unlike the rest
of the royals.

The *News* ran a big Page 1 photo of the bridal couple, three more
pictures on Page 4, and devoted the entire centerfold to spectacu-
lar shots of the wedding. The paper turned over all of Page 4 to my
story, and continued it on a jump page:

> She spoke words used by brides for more than 300 years; she
> stood in a church where her ancestors have been crowned as kings
> and queens for nine centuries, and in this manner Anne Elizabeth
> Alice Louise Windsor, princess of the United Kingdom of Great
> Britain and Northern Ireland, married the man of her choice and of
> her heart today, and became a commoner's wife.
>
> To the obvious delight of an entire people, on a day so brilliant
> with sunshine that the city itself glittered, Princess Anne joyously
> swore to Capt. Mark Phillips that she would forever "love, cherish
> and obey" him, while he, in turn, promised her "with my body I
> (will) thee worship."

The day after the wedding, I described the newlyweds' departure on their honeymoon. This story ended:

> Today, with the wedding over, British newspapers agreed that
> the royal family had put on a terrific show. Some papers published
> color photographs of the marriage. The official Communist paper
> here, however, the *Morning Star,* brushed off the entire proceedings
> with a one-sentence story: "Traffic in London was disrupted yester-
> day when Anne Windsor married Mark Phillips in Westminster
> Abbey."

Ah, those wonderful little details that filled our stories, that our
readers loved because they made the *News* so special; those details
that in later years at the *News* some editors chopped from our copy,
edited with such heavy hands that our newspaper was emptied of
people and of color and of quotes, the stories so flattened that the
news may as well all have been written to formula by one very

competent, very dull hack.

The worst thing was writing a lead that was so good you would have won a bonus for it in the old days, only to have it smashed out of shape by an editor who just didn't get it—the type of editor who should never have been allowed inside the *News* city room.

When actress Louise Lasser, star of the hit TV show *Mary Hartman, Mary Hartman* was arrested in Beverly Hills in May 1976, I sent a story from Los Angeles with this lead:

> Louise Lasser Louise Lasser got busted got busted in Beverly Hills yesterday.
>
> The star of the TV comedy soap opera *Mary Hartman, Mary Hartman* was charged with creating a disturbance and with suspicion of possessing cocaine after police were called to a boutique where the actress was staging a sit-in.

The story was that Lasser was arrested for causing problems at the boutique in a dispute over how to pay for a purchase she had made. Then, after she was booked at the police station, she was booked a second time when a routine search of her purse turned up a white powder which lab tests proved to be cocaine.

I thought the lead was pretty good, especially since I had written it very quickly so as to make our earliest editions in New York. And of course it was absolutely accurate, since she was twice booked and therefore "was busted was busted."

But to my disgust, the next day the turgid lead of my article read: "Louise Lasser, star of the TV comedy soap opera *Mary Hartman, Mary Hartman* was under investigation today by the Beverly Hills district attorney's office on suspicion of illegal possession of cocaine." Snore. Yawn. Barf.

When I called the desk and asked why a perfectly good and typical *News* lead had been rewritten into a really bad one, the editor, who had never been around during our glory days, got all peevish and said, "Well, we just couldn't use it the way you sent it." He couldn't explain why.

All the other newspapers and newsmagazines were using the double wording. Finally, two days later, when it was no longer accurate, the *News* used this headline over my follow-up story: "MARY HARTMAN, MARY HARTMAN IS ARRAIGNED ARRAIGNED." It was a poor copy of what my editor "just couldn't use" for the first story, and it made no sense. She was arraigned only once.

I think it was over that innocuous Mary Hartman story that I realized, without seeing marketing diagrams, demographics, gloom-and-doom reports from Chicago, and other signs, that the *News* was on the skids. There have been many complicated reasons given for the downfall of the tabloid that for decades had the greatest circulation and most loyal readership in the United States, but I suggest that when the writers weren't allowed to speak to the readers anymore, the paper was doomed. With editors who were not sophisticated enough to understand what the *News* was all about, what our audience was interested in, the paper couldn't keep the old readers and couldn't win new ones. When readers are used to sparkle, they will leave if you bore them to death.

And what sparkle there was in the great days! Take this January 1959 gem headlined, "HER RHYME SAYS HE HAD NO REASON," which would have been a nothing little story if it weren't for the writing:

> *My heart is lonely when you're away*
> *It's like a sea in a raging storm*
> *But darling when you are near I can truly say*
> *My heart is light, happy and warm.*
>
> (From the collected [by an attorney] poems of Mrs. Grace Dworkin.)
>
> The exquisite stanza reproduced above was written by Mrs. Dworkin in the summer of 1953. It was a season vividly remembered by her, she said in Supreme Court yesterday, because her husband had taken to bouncing her around and throwing chairs at her.
>
> "Then why did you write this poetry to him?" demanded her husband's lawyer.
>
> "You can love a heel, even," replied Mrs. Dworkin.

The story was under the byline of Al Albelli, our court reporter. Al was a great legman, but he didn't write, and since this story bore only the single byline I am not sure who wrote it, maybe Henry Lee or maybe me or somebody else on the rewrite battery. It was typical work for our rewrite battery.

At the same time, over another Albelli story about a divorce involving a magazine editor as the other man, one of our inspired headline writers created this: "SAYS WIFE MADE TIME WITH A NEWSWEEK MAN."

"GOT $933 AN HOUR TO SPOT REDS UNDER BED FOR MAT-

TRESS OUTFIT" was the headline on an October 1957 story by Paul Healy of our Washington Bureau, which picked up Paul's tone nicely:

> Senate rackets probers today revealed that "union buster" Nathan W. Shefferman paid a self-styled "Communust extermina-tor" $2,800 in 1953 for one three-hour chore, or approximately $933 an hour, to spot Commies at the Englander mattress plant in Brooklyn.
>
> The exterminator, Mike Katz, said he found no Commies under the mattresses, but the prober noted that the company nonetheless footed the Shefferman bill.
>
> Katz, a pudgy witness who boasted of goon-like tactics in union activities on the West Coast, noisily took the stand after he had fallen asleep in the audience and had to be awakened personal-ly by committee counsel Robert Kennedy.

How could anyone resist reading this story?

As is evident from Henry Lee's story about the Gallo brothers, the *News* was into Mafia mob stories as a fact of New York life, treating the thugs with the same cynical disdain reserved for crooked politicians, and we had reporters who knew as much about the hoods as the cops did.

So when big-time gangster Albert Anastasia was knocked off in a hotel barber shop in October 1957, the *News* was on top of the story, and on the day of Anastasia's funeral we had two big stories and a box on Page 3.

One story gave the details of Anastasia's last rites under the headline "ANASTASIA, THE GUN, IS BURIED WITH 'HONEST MAN'S SIMPLICITY.'" The story, with Joseph Kiernan's byline and probably written by Henry Lee, informed our readers: "With unexpected simplicity which would have befitted an honest man, Albert Anastasia, the gun of old Murder Inc., was buried yesterday in Brooklyn. Mourners, flowers, crowds were at an austere mini-mum, and except for the immediate family, there wasn't a wet eye in the borough as the gravediggers' best friend himself received their last ministrations."

Next to this was the main story, which concerned Anastasia's henchman, Anthony (Cappy) Coppola, with the double byline of Anthony Marino, the reporter who covered Murder Inc., and Henry Lee, who did the writing:

Less than six hours after beating a vagrancy rap that had held him overnight in $50,000 bail, Anthony (Cappy) Coppola, the dumpy little lobbygow who never was more than a few feet from Albert Anastasia till the master hood needed him most, was held again late yesterday in $50,000 bail in General Sessions—this time as a material witness in Anastasia's barbershop murder.

An outraged figure in expensive but rumpled tweeds, with a three-day grayish stubble on his face, the 48-year-old Coppola denied the honor pressed on him by Assistant District Attorney Alexander Herman.

"If this man walks out," Herman told Judge Abraham Geller, "it may very well be the beginning of open warfare by the hoodlums in this city."

Indignantly, Coppola, who has been described variously as chauffeur, bodyguard and messenger for Anastasia, insisted that he had neither a fear nor a foe in the world. . . .

Going to the other side of the law, I once had to do a story in August 1962 on "Operation Decoy"—cops who put on women's clothes and patrolled areas where women had been mugged and raped. With pictures to illustrate it, the story started:

Wearing lipsticks in smashing shades like "plum blossom" and "pink lady," tastefully attired in things like white tennis sneakers, black stockings with runs, droopy dresses and skin tight orange capri pants, some of the Police Department's Tactical Patrol Force let the press in yesterday on the way they prepare for their female roles in Operation Decoy. . . .

Easily the pinup queen was John Hughes, whose blue blouse was remarkably filled out with his kid's pink balloons. He shoved them inside the tight blouse, and after some delicate maneuvering, managed to get them comfortable.

Hughes looked kind of exciting in a matronly sort of way, with pastel pink lipstick—applied for him by Patrolwoman Caryl Collins—baggy black slacks, a beige jacket, a knit hat decorated with sequins yet, large earrings and a straw purse, with his gun tucked neatly into the waistband.

Voted the sexiest and most likely to succeed in attracting a possible rapist was Noel Haeara, whose model wife, Barbara, had decked him out in her own tangerine stretch pants. . . . He also wore her open-toed black sandals, a black turtleneck sweater, a tangerine chiffon scarf over his fake curls. . . .

To nobody's surprise, the decoys obligingly arrested two alleged purse snatchers soon after they went on patrol, giving us a Page 1 line over the photo of the skirt brigade, and my description of the cops getting dressed ran side-by-side on Page 3 with a news story about the two busts that had been made.

That kind of a story was fun to write. Others were harder to cover.

Hurricane Carla was one of the hard ones. I flew out in one of the *News* planes to cover it in September 1961, but we had plane trouble and by the time we were over Texas, the hurricane had gone.

But we were the first plane to land in Palacios, where the eye of of the storm had struck, and we flew over Galveston, where a tidal wave had followed the hurricane, and for two days I wrote about the return of the refugees, the sad homecoming of those who had fled and returned to find nothing left:

> The evacuees of Galveston began their terrible homecoming today. They found their city—one of the most cruelly punished by hurricane, tornado, flood and tidal waves in this area—filthy with mud, water and wreckage, and foul with the smell of rot.
>
> But they were luckier than some who ran for their lives before the threat of Hurricane Carla. They have a city to return to. . . .

Planes were forbidden to fly over the desolate Gulf Coast area except for emergencies, but the *News* plane not only did it, we were forced by bad weather to land in Galveston. There I wrote about "hangars . . . alive with rattlesnakes," a huge food market that had been turned into "a reeking, water-filled cavern," the conditions at a hotel with "no water, no lights, no electricity."

In the plane, "we flew for hours over stretches of land so flooded that it was impossible to tell where the gulf or bay ended and the ground started. The destruction has not yet even been reported from some of the towns we saw, since they are completely isolated, without communication, and without any signs of human life in some sections."

The next day, we bulled our way into a landing at Palacios—we told the authorities our communications were out and we couldn't hear their orders not to land—and there I came upon a man who had just returned to his homestead. Photographer Paul Bernius caught the picture, which ran on Page 1, and my lead was:

"Weeping as he stood in the mud, a young airport worker mopped at his eyes with a ragged shirt he had just picked out of the dirt, pointed to a pile of smashed bricks and glass, and said: 'That was my house.'"

That one sobbing man summed up all of the heartbreak of the hurricane. The *News* won an award for the two stories. And I never forgot them.

8

Oh Lawdy!
How They Could Love!

Their story seemed straight out of a soap opera, and so seemed
their names: Candace Weatherby Mossler . . . Melvin Lane
Powers . . . Jacques Mossler. Candace and Melvin, known as
Candy and Mel to *News* readers and all of the reporters gathered
in Miami, were the codefendants at a murder trial that had all
the soap opera buzzwords: incest, adultery, money, greed, passion, hatred.

The government claimed that Candy and Mel were lovers, and
that they had conspired to kill Jacques Mossler, Candy's husband.
Since Candy was Mel's aunt and nearly twice his age, and since the
murdered man was a self-made millionaire much older than his
wife, and since Mel and Candy were Southern WASPs while
Jacques was a Rumanian Jewish immigrant, the elements were
irresistible.

They even looked as if they came out of Central Casting. Mel,
the younger man, was actually Candy's nephew—her sister's son.
He was a big ol' southern boy, 6'3", broad, with full black hair,
thick brows, dark eyes, and a sensual mouth. A beautiful man in
his mid-twenties. Candy, the young widow, was 39 or 45, depending on the source. She was a tiny, fragile Georgia belle—fine-
boned, blonde, blue-eyed, soft-spoken. Inside, however, was a
tough, clear-eyed, calculating woman. And Jacques—poor old
Jacques—was a Jew from Rumania, short and pudgy, who had

come to this country and had made a fortune. He was 69 when he was murdered.

But this was no soap opera. A man had been murdered savagely. His widow and her nephew were charged with the murder, and if convicted, they could be sent to the electric chair.

Jacques's half-naked body was found by Candy and their children about 4:30 A.M. on June 30, 1964, in the Mosslers' apartment at Governor's Lodge, Key Biscayne. Mossler's financial holdings included three banks in Miami, and the family came to Key Biscayne regularly for the winter season from their mansion in Houston.

The body was on the floor, an orange blanket covering the horrible wounds. Jacques's skull had been fractured, and he had been stabbed 39 times. No murder weapon was on the premises (and none was ever found), but the neighbors recalled that at 1:30 A.M. they had heard thumping, screams, and the barking of the Mossler dog, Rocky. Jacques had been home alone; Candy had had a migraine attack, and had gone with her children to a hospital emergency room.

Within the week, Mel was arrested in Houston. As soon as he was picked up, Aunt Candy hired Percy Foreman to defend him. Foreman was the most famous criminal lawyer in Texas, having become a legend in that homicidal state with his success in saving murder defendants from prison and Death Row.

Percy was 6'4", a dominating presence with the noble head of a Roman senator and a voice like a great church organ. He could use that voice to beseech, to argue, to skewer with sarcasm, to poke fun, and to show righteous anger; he could mesmerize a jury.

There were many stories about Percy. Some were about his brilliant arguments in court. For instance, one of his murder clients supposedly had shot another man in the back. Percy didn't contest the shooting, but he got his client off the murder rap by using medical testimony to prove that the dead man had had a fatal heart attack before the bullet entered his body.

There was the woman who telephoned the great man to ask if he would defend her on a charge of murdering her husband. Percy said he'd have to discuss it with her, and asked when she had made herself a widow. "Oh, I haven't killed him yet, Mr.

Foreman," the woman was reported to have replied. "I first wanted to make sure that you'd defend me."

Foreman didn't come cheap, but if you didn't have cash, he
would take payment in other items, negotiable or not. Word was
that he had a warehouse stocked with artwork, furniture, cars, and
appliances, and a strongbox filled with mortgages, deeds, bills of
sale, and jewelry. This was corroborated at least in part at the
Mossler trial when Percy made a pretrial attempt to have Mel
declared a pauper so that the state would have to pick up $5,700 in
travel expenses for Mel's witnesses.

Mel swore he had no assets, but Assistant State's Attorney
Arthur Huttoe introduced a document, dated July 6, 1964, showing that Candy had hired Foreman to defend her nephew for a fee
"not to exceed $200,000"; also, that she had given Percy, as a down
payment on his retainer, the following: "one blue white diamond
leaf design—$5,200. One blue white diamond sunburst—$5,000.
One blue white flower design brooch—$2,000. One emerald cut
blue white diamond ring—$20,000. One canary tear drop diamond
pin—$12,500. One yellow gold diamond watch—$1,000." When
Huttoe got Mel to admit he had deeded a $120,000 piece of prop-
erty to Percy, the circuit judge groaned and refused Percy's motion.

Candy herself was arrested in 1965 on charges that she was the
brains behind the murder and Mel was the brawn. For her defense,
she hired Houston attorneys Clyde Woody and Marian Rosen.
Because it is always wise to have a hometown lawyer on your side,
she also hired two well-known Miami criminal attorneys, Harvey
St. Jean and Henry Carr. They were fine lawyers, but Percy ran the
show for the entire defense. Nobody knows what Candy finally
paid Percy, although it was rumored to be more than half a million
dollars. It was worth it.

Before the trial opened, the newspapers and newsmagazines had
been filled with tantalizing tidbits about the personalities
involved. There was the allegedly incestuous affair between aunt
and nephew, and details about the vicious murder of the millionaire husband. There was interesting background about the Mossler
family, which included ten children: four grown daughters from
Jacques's first marriage, two dazzlingly blonde children by
Candy's previous marriage, and four adopted teenagers. The four
youngest had been adopted by the couple in 1956, when they

ranged in age from three to seven. They had been left homeless in Chicago when their father, a deranged war veteran, killed their mother. The father had taken the three-year-old hostage after the murder and the manhunt and eventual rescue of the child made headlines while the Mosslers were in Chicago. After the father was committed to a mental hospital, Candy and Jacques adopted the children.

Some of my colleagues, such as Stan Redding of the *Houston Chronicle*, Gene Miller of the *Miami Herald*, and UPI Miami Bureau Chief Andy Taylor, kept me informed on the progress of the pre-trial litigation. We had covered many trials together, and they all knew that this one was going to be a blockbuster. The *News* editors jumped on the story, too, and on Sunday, January 15, 1966—the day before jury selection was scheduled to open in the Dade County Courthouse—I was checking into Miami's Dupont Plaza Hotel. Also there were the other out-of-town press, the out-of-town lawyers, and the two defendants, both free on $50,000 bail each.

Before I flew down to Miami, my New York City pals gave me farewell parties, presenting me with sympathy cards on my "being forced by cruel editors to leave the slush of New York's winter wonderland for the brain-deadening sunshine of Florida's beaches." I even got a scarlet-mesh-and-black-lace bikini from one of the more outrageous members of the crew. While they pretended to grumble and kvetch, they were really being remarkably supportive, as befits a family of friends who exulted in each other's good fortune and admired each other's work.

As soon as I got to the Dupont, I learned from the reporters who had already gathered that Candy was arriving at the airport. We drove out together to meet her, and to our delight she obliged us by holding an impromptu interview, declaring her innocence and her faith in the good people of Dade County, which made for a nice Monday story. This set the pace of the Mossler trial; there was never a dull moment inside or outside the courtroom.

The press corps included a lot of reporters I had covered trials with before. Besides Gene Miller (who later won two Pulitzer Prizes) with his trademark bowtie and dark-rimmed eyeglasses, there was Doc Quigg of UPI, flown down from New York to work with Andy Taylor; Jim Bishop of Hearst, the dandy of the corps, famous for his best-selling book on Jesus Christ; Ben Funk, the AP

bureau chief of Miami; Stan Redding with his larger-than-life stories about the Texas Rangers; and Tom Cope of the Ft. Pierce,
Florida *News* Tribune, who in one of his stories called me a
"nuclear-powered pixie."

The new friends included Milt Sosin, who was asked by Judge
George E. Schulz to set up the press room for us, and Marge
Crumbach of the *Houston Post*, who had been on the case practically since the day of the murder. Marge suffered the trial
reporter's nightmare. Late one night when the jury was deliberating, she called Doc and me to say she was in agony with abdomi-
nal pain. We rushed her to the hospital for emergency surgery—
the very next day the verdict came in and Marge, immobilized at
the hospital, could not cover it for her newspaper.

Judge Schulz made it possible for the press to do a very difficult
job without unneccessary restrictions. Schulz, a thin-faced, silver-
haired, scholarly man, was the best kind of judge for a high-profile
case: low key, secure, in total control of his courtroom. He did not
feel threatened by the large press corps and issued no gag orders.
We met with him to offer suggestions and to receive ground rules;
for example, he asked us not to use the jurors' names, and we did-
n't, although we gave our readers other details about every one of
them.

Schulz gave us press tables where we could see the jurors, the
witnesses and the codefendants, and gave us quiet access in and
out of the trial room at all times through an unused chamber. Such
access is a must for wire service reporters who have deadlines all
day.

There were no restrictions on us outside the courtroom, except
of course not to talk to jurors. Schulz believed reporters trying to
write stories dealing with the law should be able to ask questions
of him and of the lawyers on both sides, and the stories I filed
included legal explanations of what was going on as well as the
complete details of every session.

The out-of-towners stayed at the Dupont until Stan Redding
discovered the Taj Apartments a few blocks from the courthouse,
and a lot cheaper than the hotel. We all moved in, turning the Taj
into a giant house party.

The neighborhood was on the seedy side, but the apartments
were spotless. They had kitchens and living rooms and were fully
furnished—for $8.24 a day. There was a pool on the roof, where we

converged during those rare hours when we were not cooped up in the courthouse. The others kept warning me to keep moving lest the vultures who lived on the roof of the nearby courthouse swoop down and fly off with me, mistaking me for lunch. I didn't think this would happen, but there really were vultures atop the court-house. I moved around a lot on those chaises.

Across the street from the Taj was a bar which I went into only in daylight, and only with one of my burly buddies. Its jukebox had a remarkable country song on it entitled "Oh Those Crystal Chandeliers," and we learned all the words to it and sang it togeth-er. Years later, we could still recall every stanza.

But a song we wrote ourselves, to the tune of "Frankie and Johnnie Were Lovers," became the Mossler anthem. Reporters write songs about politicians for the famous Gridiron dinner-show presented each year in Washington, they write songs on campaign trips, and they write songs about the trials they cover. Of all the trial songs written through the years, the Mossler creation remains the longest and the best, filled with references to the witnesses and events that we reporters and others at the trial would understand. The *News* readers, who were getting all the details in the paper, would have understood also.

"Candace and Melvin were lovers" we warbled to the tune of "Frankie and Johnnie," "Oh, Lawdy how they could love", we continued, when we sang it in public. But when we were alone we sang: "Candace and Melvin were lovers, Oh Lawdy how they could scarf, Used an orange blanket for a cover, While Rocky went arf! arf! Mel loved his candy, the box was always handy."

The Mossler trial was extraordinary for several reasons, and one of them was that it became a classic example of how an experi-enced defense attorney wins a case so sensational that the pretrial publicity, including overwhelmingly incriminating evidence against the defendant, seems to guarantee a guilty verdict. The allegations about Candy and Mel's love affair had come from the government to explain why the couple had been arrested and brought to trial for Jacques's murder, and had been given extensive publicity before the trial started.

But Percy Foreman took the offensive away from the govern-ment as soon as he began to question prospective jurors. Repeatedly, he asked them: "If you were satisfied there had been adultery, fornication, an incestuous relationship beyond a reasonable doubt, but were not satisfied that the prosecution proved homicide, would you convict them of murder?"

The prospects had no choice but to maintain that they were too intelligent to confuse incest with homicide, and having gotten a jury of twelve men who were able to swear they knew the difference, Percy then put on a defense in which he attacked not only the victim but the accusers—the Miami cops, the Texas lawmen, the Florida prosecutors, the Texas and Florida investigators, the prosecution witnesses, and even some members of the dead man's family.

The chief prosecutor, Arthur Huttoe, in his opening statement, accused Candy of trying to hire "for many thousands of dollars a person whom she knew had a criminal record, to kill Jacques Mossler."

He said that a year before the murder, Houston officers were called to throw Mel out of the Mossler home and at that time Mel told the financier: "I'll come back anytime I want to come back. You can't keep me out. And you, Mr. Mossler, will regret this the longest day of your life."

Huttoe also told the jurors that the government would bring witnesses who would swear that several hours before the murder Mel came into the Stuft Shirt Lounge, near the bridge leading to Key Biscayne, ordered a drink and asked for a large empty coke bottle, and that after the neighbors heard screams and Rocky's barks, a man with dark hair was seen running from the apartment and driving away in a white Chevrolet Impala similar to the one Candy had left the apartment in that afternoon.

The prosecutor said Candy received several phone calls from a man while she was at the hospital and after her husband was dead. He said that when Candy and her children returned to the apartment, the landlady heard one of them say, "Mom, we're not to tell? You don't want us to tell?" and 15 minutes later, after the body had been discovered, the kids were on the patio getting Cokes from a machine, acting as if nothing had happened. When the police and doctors arrived, Huttoe claimed, there were no tears from Candy.

The killing, Huttoe insisted, was the result of a conspiracy between Mel and Candy. "The motive for this murder," he told the jurors, "was a personal hatred of the deceased by Melvin Lane Powers and a sordid, illicit love affair between the deceased's wife and her sister's son."

And then there was the money.

Mossler's estate had a gross value in excess of $200 million and a net value of about $22 million. His will left half of it to Candy, and the other half divided amongst Mossler's four daughters by his first wife, Candy's son and daughter by her first husband, and the four adopted children. Jacques's daughters were not talking to their stepmother and were invisible during the trial, but the six others were with Candy, who rented two apartments for them after moving out of the Dupont.

Percy Foreman was an imposing figure as he made his opening statement. In it, he began his attack by describing Jacques as everything from an "insatiable" sex pervert to a "ruthless pirate" hated by thousands within and outside his huge financial empire.

The jurors listened, fascinated, as Percy told them that a lot of people wanted Jacques Mossler dead: "We believe the evidence in this case will convince this jury that if each of the 39 separate wounds inflicted on Jacques Mossler had been done by 39 different people, that there still would be at least three times that many people in the state of Florida or in the Mossler empire with actual justification to do this, for any one of a great many different reasons."

According to the defense lawyer, Mossler had "laid himself open to blackmail, to possible homicide, at very frequent intervals. The evidence will show that except for the shoe fetish, there is not a fetish in *Psychopathia Sexualis* [the famous Kraft-Ebbing book] he did not indulge in. Jacques Mossler had them all . . . transvestism, homosexuality, voyeurism, masochism, sadism."

Percy also claimed there were dozens of auto dealers in Miami "who were ruined by the machinations of Jacques Mossler or believed they were," thousands of "infuriated" people whose cars had been repossessed by Mossler or his hirelings, and many disgruntled former employes.

Most of these allegations were neither raised by Percy again nor proven during the trial. But never mind—Percy had placed the doubt in the jury's mind.

Candy was very quick and very smart. Before the trial, she was asked about love letters sent to Mel that the state claimed it possessed. They were signed "C. Mossler," and started "My Darling. . . ."

"Oh, pooh," said Candy. "I call everybody darling."

And what about the contents of the letters, which included phrases like "I love you . . . I miss you"? Goodness, said Candy, she wrote to her nephew like any loving aunt would.

During the first days of the trial, Candy held little talks with reporters in the corridors outside the trial room, and every word out of her mouth was perfect for her defense. The prosecutors eventually objected, and Judge Schulz advised the reporters not to talk to Candy in the trial room or the courthouse. Outside the courthouse, however, there were no restrictions.

Percy recognized Candy's acumen and let her talk where she pleased, but he forbade his own client Mel, who was duller, to talk to any reporters. The only reporter Mel spoke to the whole time was me. He would loom up behind me, pat my shoulder, and with a booming "Good morning, Mrs. Wilson," send me a foot in the air. That was it. Every morning.

Except for the brief, impromptu exchanges with the press those first few days during jury selection, Candy gave no formal interviews. But Candy's lawyers and Percy had been reading my stories in the *News*, and when I asked if I could sit down with Candy for a real one-on-one talk, they agreed. We met at defense attorney Marian Rosen's apartment at the Dupont on Friday night so that I could file the interview early Saturday for the Sunday paper. When I got there, Candy was holding her infant grandson, her daughter Rita's baby, and was surrounded by her attorneys and children.

Candy was small and Candy was fragile, but inside Candy was a high-speed calculator. Sitting there with her in that big pleasant living room, the baby on the floor playing with the photographer's cases, the attorneys and children chatting on the other side of the room, I asked her if she had some idea, some theory why her husband was murdered. In that soft, breathy voice, enhanced by a touch of Southern drawl, she said:

"My husband, unfortunately, very unfortunately, just picked up strangers. The children and I would walk into the apartment and the house would be full of strangers. They were young men, mostly, and they'd just clear out as soon as we walked in . . . He'd just pick them up, sailors and young men, on the beach and in bars, in restaurants, on the highways."

(From the day Jacques was murdered, Candy had claimed that

he could have been done in by a homosexual lover or by someone he had picked up at the beach. The first homicide officers on the scene had mentioned that the ferocity and number of the stab wounds could be indicative of the kind of murder committed by homosexuals. In fact, early on the police arrested, and then released, a suspect who was gay. The defense made a big point out of that, implying that the cops might have had the real killer, but let him go.)

Then she amazed me. Having dropped her not so subtle hints about her dead husband's alleged penchant for young men (something never proven at the trial) she went on with something new: "I think he'd be living today if the doctors hadn't told him in Houston he might have lung cancer. He always told me he had six months to live."

She told me, earnest and rueful, that Jacques had gone through a series of tests in Houston 18 months before he was killed, "and being the kind of man he was, he demanded that the doctors tell him what they suspected and they told him. And he refused, just refused to go back to them. He said every man has a right to die the way he chooses, and well, he always wanted to die with his boots on."

Unhappily, Jacques died wearing only an undershirt. And if there was any medical evidence that he was dying of lung cancer, it was never brought before the jury.

Then she called over one of the four adopted children, kissed him, and asked him to tell me about his father. The 14-year-old boy immediately launched into a description of how Jacques flashed "hundred dollar bills, even when it was just to buy hamburgers at the Royal Castle"; how he'd go up to people, mostly men, and tell them he owned banks and invite them up to the apartment, and how nervous it made the boy when his father would pick up strangers while driving on the highway.

"That's my little man," Candy said proudly as the boy finished, and patted him on the head. The interview went on, with Candy confiding to me how generous Jacques was to her during their sixteen-year marriage, and how she could always talk to him, even though he was short-tempered.

Since she had been in court for the week of jury selection listening to the lawyers go on about "adultery, fornication, and incest," I asked her how she felt hearing all this about her and Mel.

"I wasn't perfect," said Candy, giving me my lead for the story. "My husband wasn't perfect. But it was our personal life, just like you have one, just like everyone has one." Adultery, fornication, incest? Well, says Candy, nobody's perfect!

And how did she feel hearing her attorney Clyde Woody hint to the prospective jurors about "certain unusual conduct on the part of the deceased, amounting to acts of perversion"?

"The wife is the last to know," sighed Candy, giving me my end.

The Mossler trial was extraordinary in other ways. There seemed never to be a dull session, and nobody could predict or even imagine the kind of testimony that would come off the witness stand.

On one day, the defense attorneys would be at war with each other, and my story would be filled with their legal shenanigans. The next day, a prosecution witness would treat the unsuspecting jurors, judge, reporters, and public to testimony so graphic that it left nearly everyone open-mouthed. It became a constant challenge for those of us writing for family newspapers.

Edward Bart Diehl was the first prosecution witness to establish the state's accusations that Mel and Aunt Candy were lovers. Diehl, a pallid, sunken-eyed ex-convict, told the jurors that in 1962, two years before the murder, he and his wife were caretakers on Jacques's ranch near Galveston, Texas. It was there he met the boss's wife and her nephew. Candy and Mel used a trailer at the ranch, and, said Diehl, his wife used to clean it up and "it was always a mess . . . beds rumpled up right in the middle of the day."

Speaking in a low, emotionless voice, Diehl said that Mel had discussed the affair with him.   "He said he had a very good thing going there for him. He said he could wear good clothes and drive a good car, and all he had to do was scarf her."

Heads shot up from notebooks at the press tables. Prosecutor Huttoe asked his witness what he meant by that. "To eat her box," explained Diehl. "That is all he would have to do," Diehl went on, "and he could get anything he wanted."

I looked over at Candy, who kept a stony face. Mel, however, slid his eyes around, caught my glance, and smiled sheepishly.

In the story I filed, I had to substitute dots for Diehl's actual words and added the explanation that the witness used "a gutter phrase." But my editors would be dying of curiosity, so at the end of the filing I appended this note: "FYI—the term Diehl used about

Mel and Candy was that Mel would 'scarf' her. His explanation: 'to eat her box.' Regards, Theo."

The really important testimony from Diehl that day was his statement that when Mel and Candy were at the ranch, they told him they knew about his police record and offered him $10,000 to kill Mossler or get someone else to do it.

Then there was the unforgettable testimony of handyman Earl Martin, who said he worked at Mel's trailer sales office. Earl was an important prosecution witness who swore that in 1963 Mel offered him "quick money" to kill Candy's husband.

Taking Earl's testimony down was a challenge. He had a thick black southern accent, he spoke rapidly, and he also peppered his language with phrases our newspapers could never print. He described one conversation when Mel had picked up a letter opener: "He sitting at his desk and he shake his hair all over his head, and he say if he had his way, and nobody would know about it, he'd take that knife and jug and jug and jug him 'til he dead." Asked to explain what *jug* meant, he demonstrated with violent stabbing motions how Mel "jugged" at the desk with the letter opener. It was Martin who further enlarged our vocabulary by telling us that a "dirch" was a knife or a dagger.

Martin said he had seen Candy at Mel's office, kissing and hugging Mel in her blue Lincoln Continental. Then he told about the day when Mel was running short of money and the electricity was cut off. "I asked him how he was gonna get the lights back on and he asked me had I ever . . . ," and here he used gutter talk worse than Diehl's to describe oral sex. The handyman said he never had, and then went into graphic detail from Mel, who told him that when he needed a shave and he did the act, he could "get anything he wanted from a woman."

"So we left and went home, and the next morning the lights was on," said Martin, as the jurors and the rest of the courtroom gaped. "And I asked him, 'Did you do it?' and he said 'yeah.'"

Mel then told the handyman to listen in on an extension while he called Aunt Candy and asked her, "What do I love to do most, baby?" and her answer proved to the handyman that Mel had told the truth.

> Martin he squealed on old Melvin,
> Said that he carried a dirch,
> Talked about huggin' and juggin'

Usin' words you can't say in church,
Mel needed a shave
And made Candy a slave.

There was one thing Mel was good at,
Turning his Aunt Candy on,
Martin said 'Man, do you do dat?'
And the next day the lights was on,
Mel was her dandy,
And he turned on Candy.
(To the tune of "Frankie and Johnny")

Then there was the court session when the two prosecutors, Richard Gerstein and Arthur Huttoe, read for the jurors a taped telephone conversation between Candy and a longtime Mossler household employee, Roscoe Brown. The conversation indicated that Candy was trying to influence Roscoe to give answers to the investigators that she thought would be helpful to her.

The two prosecutors stood at opposite ends of the jury box and began reading, Gerstein taking Candy's part, Huttoe answering as Brown. They didn't try to imitate Candy's breathy drawl or Roscoe's black accent, but it came through. It was almost impossible for the jurors to remain straight-faced, and the rest of us didn't do too well, either, even though we were sitting directly under the cool gaze of Judge Schulz.

Candy was gently trying to persuade her employee that his memory was faulty about certain things he had told the police, and Brown (who knew the conversation was being taped) very politely was telling Candy that he was just going to continue to tell the truth as he remembered it.

Candy/Gerstein: "It would be awful nice if you don't let them put words in your mouth. It would be awful nice if you don't let them say you remember something you don't remember, and it would be awful nice if you don't let them coax you to say you did what you didn't do."

Brown/Huttoe: "Well, yes. Well, I tell you. I wouldn't say anything wrong . . . I'd just tell the truth."

Candy/Gerstein: "We are going to form a Mossler Enterprises and if you would like to work with us in Houston, I would be asking you first. So you kind of think about it, all right?"

Brown/Huttoe: "Sure."

Richard and Arthur were end men
Put on a big minstrel show
Candace was played by Gerstein
Roscoe Brown was Art Huttoe
They had a ball
On that long distance call.

There was more. Arthur Grimsley was another of the state's star witnesses, a mail-order minister who was brought from the Arkansas State Penitentiary to swear that in 1962 Mel propositioned him to kidnap and kill "an old mooch"—Jacques Mossler.

Grimsley never got around to doing the deed, but he gave a detailed account of his meeting with Mel at Grimsley's home in Truman, Arkansas, and said that Mel told him he was living with a relative in Houston, they loved each other, but she was married to the old mooch and "they wanted him killed."

They went drinking together in Grimsley's Cadillac, and Mel indicated that if Grimsley got rid of the old mooch, Grimsley "would get enough money to have two of these Cadillacs paid for. And I told him I was interested." The convict, who was serving time for burglary and grand larceny, said he confessed this to a prison chaplain after Mel was arrested because he had "accepted Christ as my Saviour and have been studying the Bible" and had received a certificate of ordination.

Foreman, an ordained Baptist deacon, started his cross-examination by booming, "Are you now a student of the Holy Writ? . . . Do you know an individual in the Bible called Ananais? . . . . He was the biggest liar of all time, does that help you?"

Grimsley swore repeatedly that he recalled the dates he met Mel, between June 15 and 17, 1962, because it was right after he had checked his own father out of a tuberculosis sanitarium, and he knew that date was June 14.

Two days later the defense asked for a mistrial: Grimsley, they charged, was a liar and perjurer, because they had evidence that on June 15 and 16, 1962 Mel was in a Houston hospital for four operations: tonsillectomy, face-sanding, correction of protruding ears—and a circumcision. As this last bit of information was announced from the witness stand by the physician called by the defense to read the hospital records, I couldn't resist looking up from my notebook to stare at Mel. He caught my eye, shrugged, and gave me that big sheepish grin. "What was this," I whispered to the reporter next to me, "Candy's beautification program?"

The doctor said that it would have been impossible for Mel to have left the hospital, since four different operations were performed, and he also told the jurors that because of the plastic surgery to his ears, Mel's head was wrapped in a huge bandage helmet.

Grimsley was brought back by the prosecutors to recant, and to swear that he erred only in the dates. He insisted that he had met Mel and been given the kidnap-and-kill proposition, but it had taken place in March instead of June.

After this recantation, Percy stood, glared at Grimsley, and in his most deaconly voice thundered: "Parson Grimsley, do you feel now that a great weight has been taken off your shoulders? Parson Grimsley, do you now have a New Testament?" He was interrupted with objections from the prosecutors. One of the objections upheld by the judge was to Foreman calling the witness "Parson," to which Percy responded by sarcastically prefacing every question with "*Mister* Grimsley," adding greatly to the hapless witness's discomfiture.

Judge Schulz refused to grant a mistrial but ordered Grimsley's testimony stricken. With this stunning victory, the defense rested.

> The Parson said, "I've known some baddies,
> Got Mel some bootleg hooch,
> When he came up with two Caddies
> I said, 'You nephew of a mooch!'
> Never mind Ananais
> What did you say the pay is?"

> Old Percy Foreman was hell-bent
> Sent Grimsley to the Pearly Gates
> Perce said: "You got a new testament?"
> "Yes suh! I gotta change my dates."
> Arthur Grimsley got religion
> Mel got a circumcision.

One day at the trial I learned that Jacques's brother had come to the trial but did not want to talk to the press. Usually at a criminal trial, the victim's family is present and willing to answer questions, but in the Mossler case not one relative or close friend of the deceased had come forward to defend him from the attacks and allegations the jurors had heard. It was important for me to talk to this man.

It was a half-day session, and I didn't have to file my story immediately after leaving, so I followed the brother out of the courthouse. He was a frightened, timid soul. I identified myself and said that if he felt he wanted to defend his brother, I would write what he said—and only what he said. The next day, my story in the *News* started this way:

> "I don't want the public to feel a dog has been killed and nobody cares. I want them to know there is a family, and we are concerned.
> "It isn't that I want to take revenge—but it isn't a dog that was killed. Forgive me . . ." and Samuel Marcu Moscovitz, the 76-year-old brother of murdered Jacques Mossler, walked away today, weeping.

Samuel, a civil engineer, was a gentle, scholarly man with fluffy gray hair. He had come from Tel Aviv to watch the trial of his sister-in-law and her nephew. I described for the readers the testimony the brother had heard that morning, and then continued the brother's conversation with me. I asked him if he had seen Candace. "Yes. She came over to me, and she said, 'Oh Marcu, how are you? I'm glad to see you!' and she wanted to shake hands with me. And I said, 'Oh no, please, I'm not pleased to see you.' . . . He shook his head and clasped his hands to show how he had reacted."

Moscovitz explained that he had been reluctant to say anything at first because he was afraid he might not be allowed into the courtroom anymore. But he wanted people to know that Jacques had a concerned family. He showed me copies of checks totaling nearly $30,000 which Jacques had sent his brother over the last three years and which had been distributed to the Chaim Weizman Institute, the Hebrew University, and Haifa Technical College.

Moscovitz told me he had gone into debt to come to the trial. "Yesterday somebody came over to me," he continued, "and said they were so surprised to know Mossler had a brother. He said he didn't know he even had a family!" He explained that he and a sister and Jacques were the entire family, but there also were Mossler nieces and nephews deeply affected by the murder.

Percy Foreman was the only defense attorney I ever saw who maneuvered a criminal trial so that he would be the last attorney to speak to the jurors before they began deliberations. This was stunning because the final argument is the most cherished privilege of the prosecution. It gives them the chance not only to rebut everything the defense lawyers said in their summation, but also to send the jurors into the deliberation room with pleas for conviction ringing in their ears. The prosecution gets this advantage because they have the tougher job. They have to prove guilt.

(You may also note that the prosecution team sits closer to the jury. The defendant not only sits the farthest from the jurors, but in olden days he was often brought into court in shackles and prison garb. The laws governing courts come from the government doing the prosecution, and the old rules were like the rules of war: dehumanize the defendant (enemy), and you make it easier to convict (kill) him. Defense attorneys finally prevailed upon the courts to end these practices as somewhat prejudicial to the defendant's right to a presumption of innocence.)

Percy won the right to make the final summation because, under Florida law, if a defense attorney calls no witnesses and introduces no exhibits, he can give the final closing argument.

Percy represented only Mel, although he was the lead defense counsel. Throughout the trial, only Candy's lawyers called witnesses, including those beneficial to Mel, although the witnesses were questioned by all the defense lawyers, including Percy. Thus, Percy met the requirements of the Florida law, and Judge Schulz, over many objections from the prosecutors, allowed Percy to be the last attorney to talk to the jurors. It was a magnificent closing lasting four hours and fifty-eight minutes, and I never quit writing.

I have no idea how many papers we sold every day during the Mossler trial, but since the *Post* used only a stringer, the *New York Times* sent nobody (the last time they made that mistake), and TV was decades away from discovering the drama of real-life trials, the *News* we had practically the entire New York metropolitan morning readership to ourselves.

Because of the enormous interest in the Mossler trial, the *News* began an unusual promotion campaign that ended up being featured in *Editor & Publisher*. As the trade paper pointed out, "The most unique aspect of the promotion of the *News'* trial coverage is that the codefendant in the case is featured in the film."

A Florida company had been hired by the *News* to shoot interviews between me and Candy (with the blessing of the defense attorneys) as well as shots of me in the press room talking about the case. The *News'* promotion chief and the head of the *News'* advertising agency spent two days in Miami directing it. Besides flooding TV stations with pictures of me and Candy and using numerous radio spots and house ads, the *News* placed 1,000 huge posters of me interviewing Candy in the subways and on *News* trucks. At the top of the poster was "CANDY MOSSLER MURDER TRIAL." Superimposed on a shot of me interviewing Candy was the advice: "FOLLOW THEO WILSON EVERY DAY." At the bottom of the poster: "NEW YORK DAILY NEWS."

On March 6, 1966, Candy and Mel were acquitted, so early that I was able to make all five editions of the *News*. The story started: "A weeping, ecstatic, trembling Candace Mossler, acquitted with her nephew Melvin Lane Powers, of her husband's murder, fell in love with the whole world today and showed it. She kissed and hugged everybody she could reach, including the jurors who saved her from the electric chair, her attorneys, her relatives, strangers in the street—and her alleged incestuous lover, Mel."

After describing the courtroom scene, I wrote: "It was a Hollywood style ending to one of the most sensational and lurid murder trials of our time because only the day before the jurors had advised the judge they were at such a wide breach they could not agree on anything and it was feared that the case would end in a mistrial. Yet at 10:37 A.M., the next day, they sent out word there was a verdict."

The *News* story gave our readers every detail of the pronouncement of the verdict, the excitement that surrounded it, and the press conference that followed it, when Candy answered all the questions until Stan Redding said: "Mel, all we've ever heard you say is 'Good morning, Mrs. Wilson.' Do you have something to tell us?" At long last, Mel spoke, saying he was very happy, wanted to thank everybody, and was going back to Houston. There were no plans to get married, Candy was quick to tell us.

Because I was up in the press room writing the verdict story, I couldn't watch them drive away from the courthouse, but Pete Hamill and Lewis Lapham came up and filled me in, and gave me the anecdote I used to end one part of the story. As they got into Clyde Woody's bronze Cadillac convertible, I wrote, "Candy reached out, kissing everybody including a little girl about 10, who pressed up to her.

"The girl's mother yanked her away.

"'Leslie, that's nauseating!' the mother said."

Later that day, when I saw Percy, I asked him if he was going to Candy and Mel's victory celebration. The big lawyer stared at me. "Theo," he said, "I can defend these people. But that doesn't mean I have to socialize with them."

At the acquittal party, Candy's children paraded happily around the room with one of the huge Mossler murder trial posters that had been sent from New York, getting everybody's signatures on it for me. It was bizarre, just like the whole Mossler case.

About three years after the trial, Candy came to New York on business and sent word through Marian Rosen that she wanted to see me. We met at her Park Avenue hotel suite, she posed for the *News* photographer with her grandson, now 3 1/2, and in my story the next day I wrote that all Candy wanted to talk about besides her six children was her real estate and banking empire and her multimillion-dollar company, Candace Mossler Enterprises.

"She's a little skinnier now," I started the story, "because of recent major surgery and complications that nearly killed her, but otherwise it's the same Candace Mossler—the pale blonde hair hanging shoulder length, the delicate hands, the Georgia accent and the rush of sentences punctuated with 'Golly sakes!' and 'She's a love!' and 'Bless his heart!'

"Even when she is talking about the snubs and the strangers demanding money and the 'thrill seekers' who still come by busloads to gawk at her Houston, Tex. mansion, Candy doesn't talk mean."

I had never thought of the Candy and Mel saga as a love story, not with all the testimony from witnesses who painted Mel as a kiss-and-tell braggart who would discuss with anybody his intimate relations with his aunt. But trust Candy to put a romantic spin on the trial, which she referred to as "that regrettable circumstance in Florida." I had interrupted her financial discourse, thinking that what she was saying would be riveting only to a *Wall*

Street Journal reporter, to ask how she and the children had adjusted after returning to Texas. She said she had had to build an eight-foot-high stone fence around Willowick, her estate in Houston's exclusive River Oaks area, because of the gawkers who came to take photos, and a security guard was a permanent member of the household staff.

"They'd still like to waltz in here, the thrill seekers," she said. "They come up, three buses of these people from Kansas City and Philadelphia or whatever, and the driver gives them this spiel." She held her hand up in front of her mouth, pretending she was talking into a microphone: "Here is where Candace Mossler lives. Her nephew, Melvin Powers, goes in and out of here quite frequently, we understand. These are the only two people in history who did not turn, one upon the other, when both were accused of murder. One did not let the other down to save his own life. These two were different, their love was so great they stood up at their trial, to live together or die together. Now, next we see. . . ."

Now that she had mentioned Mel, I felt free to ask about him: Were she and Mel married or engaged?

"After what we went through it sounds ridiculous to talk about being engaged," said Candy. So then, did they see each other? "I don't want to talk about it," said Candy. Period.

She discussed the children some more: "I always know where my children are. My children aren't in the streets. I don't want to be a fussy parent, and so I have provided adequate facilities for them at home and that's where other parents find their children."

The adequate facilities included a pool and a 30-by-40-foot theater living room in a new east wing where the kids could make a movie screen slide down a wall and show movies. There also was a new west wing with beautiful quarters for the housekeepers. Candy didn't know how many rooms Willowick now had, but she thought that one of her children had counted and told her there were 62. There were eight kitchens and 16 bathrooms.

The conversation returned to Candy's business life, and Marian Rosen told me about Candy's philanthropies and financial deals, including the recent purchase of a bank holding company in Miami which had pushed her banks' total assets to more than $100 million.

So what did she want, to be the biggest banker in the world? No, she was tired of living on planes. Then what was it she wanted most of all?

"She looked startled, as if nobody had ever asked her this before.

"After a while she said:

"I'd like to be happy like everybody else."

I never saw Candy again. A few years later I read that she had married and that her third husband had suffered a mysterious fall in 1972 trying to climb into an upper floor window of Willowbrook. He had permanent brain damage and they were divorced.

On October 26, 1976, Candy died suddenly in her sleep in Miami, of all places. A final autopsy report was not released until five months later, after chemical and microscopic tests were completed. At that time, Gene Miller of the *Miami Herald* wrote a long story about Candy's life and death, and in it reported that the cause of death was given as pulmonary congestion and edema consistent with multiple sedatives. That meant, Gene wrote, "the sum total of sedatives caused her to sleep too deeply so that she could not maintain an adequate airway in the particular position she was."

The medical examiner and chief deputy who conducted the autopsy in Miami reported "the entire buttocks was almost rock hard," and according to Gene "neither physician had ever seen such an extreme scarring of muscle and fat. . . . Candace Mossler, they concluded, had been injected in the buttocks—again and again and again. Thousands of times . . . Perhaps 10,000 times . . . over the years."

According to Gene: "She was addicted to Demerol, the pathologists declared . . . Candace Mossler, it seems, died a junkie."

9

In Nic's City Room

From the mid-1950s on I worked on the East Coast, first in Philadelphia and then back home, for good, in New York City. Unless you lived in New York in the 1950s and 1960s, you cannot understand how well the city worked then, when a woman alone could take subways everywhere, day or night, as I did, and run into nothing more threatening than a few preaching crazies; when graffiti was almost unknown on the A train I took every day from uptown Manhattan down to the famous *News* building on 42nd Street; when *homeless* was an adjective, not a noun in a city that was raffish and exciting but never dangerous and depressing. And I took all that for granted.

Because I had grown up with it, I didn't realize how remarkable the *New York Daily News* was, not only to have survived the intense competition from papers like the *World* and the *Herald* and the *Sun* in the country's largest city, but to become the country's largest newspaper and retain that status for more than half a century.

To work on the *News* from the 1950s to the early 1970s was to be part of the city's heart and soul. This was the newspaper that lived in an elegant art deco building with prestigious tenants and a lobby (featuring a revolving globe) that was one of Manhattan's popular tourist attractions, especially during Christmas when the ground floor was transformed into a holiday wonderland. This was the newspaper with two airplanes, whose reporters traveled to assignments first class, that spoke to New Yorkers as no other has done, before or since.

This was the newspaper that had a readership more irascible, vocal, and loyal than any other. It was a love-hate relationship between the readers and us: the first letter I ever received at the *News* started, "Dear Mr. Wilson, you jerk! If you *News* guys had a brain in your heads . . . ," and ended, "With sincere regards, your friend."

The *News* was an elegant tabloid, unlike the awful *Graphic*—the sleaze predecessor to the supermarket drek of modern time and which folded because smart New Yorkers wouldn't buy it. The other tabloid, the *New York Mirror*, tried awfully hard, but the sons of William Randolph Hearst who ran it and the Hearst afternoon newspaper, the *Journal-American*, did not have for these papers the passion *News* founder Joe Patterson lavished on his paper. Both the *Mirror* and the *Journal-American* had big circulations and dedicated, talented staffs, but they were squeezed dry and finally closed down. The *Mirror* building, only a few blocks away from our exquisite home, was in such poor shape it should have been condemned.

The Hearst papers never were in our league. Nor was the *New York Post*, which, before Rupert Murdoch turned it into a clone of his London trash, was a small, respected, cranky, but very literate voice in New York. Recently, when the *Post* nearly folded, newcomers to the business described it as "sassy" and quoted the brassy Murdoch-era headlines, but the *Post* held its place in New York because it spoke to the liberal, earnest, intellectual, and wannabe-intellectual readers. One of the jokes of the newspaper business was that half the *Post*'s staff was writing the great American novel and the other half was in therapy.

The *Times*, of course, was the paper of record. It had a modest circulation and was beloved of journalism professors who had never worked on newspapers, but so far as New York was concerned, it could have been published in Washington or Boston. It wasn't until the 1970s that one of the honchos at the *Times* finally instructed the staffers that what happened in New York would no longer be considered "second class news." We had always known their attitude—we used to say that the *Times* had a bureau in Bangladesh but didn't have anybody who knew how to get to the Bronx. We also said that New Yorkers bought the *Times* because they had to, but they bought the *News* because they wanted to; no paper in New York has ever come close to the more than 4 million

Sunday buyers and 2 1/2 million daily buyers of the *News*.

If you worked for the *News* in Washington, you were overwhelmed by the *Times*. But if you worked for the *News* in New York, you were part of a powerhouse. When *News* reporters marched in on a story in New York City, the *Times* guys, only half-jokingly, would say: "We give up, the big guns are here." We knew that the *Times* was riddled with the kind of internal politics from which the *News* was free. We did not discover until later, until a lawsuit was filed by its women reporters, that women at the *Times* were considered second class citizens.

I returned to my native city and began to work for the *News* after nearly a year on the *Philadelphia Bulletin*. As always, my moves—from Virginia to Pennsylvania to New York—had been dictated by my husband's ambition to work as a news commentator for a national network in New York, and I had followed as he had gone from Richmond to Philadelphia to Manhattan and ultimately to NBC-TV. These days it seems strange that I wasn't concerned about giving up my own work or thought of it as a career, but just followed Bob where his career took him. It was what wives did in those days, and I blithely followed him with our son.

At each newspaper I went to I immediately became involved in what to me was the heart of the business—covering and writing the hard news assigned by the city desk or rewriting the hard news from the legmen. On weekends I wrote long features and color pieces and interviews. At each newspaper I made many happy friendships, the editors encouraged me to write stories the way I wanted to, and although I loathed change and hated saying goodbye, I never thought twice about whether a move was or wasn't good for my career, but just left when Bob got a new job in another place.

At the *Philadelphia Bulletin*, where I was hired after a short stint at the Philadelphia AP bureau, I had a wonderful time writing news and features and working as the only female on the rewrite battery. My early days at the *Bulletin* were typical. When I first sat down at the rewrite desk some of the guys were friendly, some acted disinterested (I knew from past experience that they were just waiting to see if I knew what the hell I was doing there). Some, like George Staab, were upset. George was the husky, rumpled, tough-talking labor news reporter who sat directly behind me. Unlike the others, he was noisy about his upset.

There had never been a woman on rewrite before, and George, without addressing me directly, loudly made queries about whether there would now be lace curtains on the city room windows and whether we'd be serving tea and decorating our desks with potted plants. George had a big mouth and used terrible gutter language but I had met his kind before—blusterers on the outside, puppies on the inside—and I let it ride a couple of days. Then, one morning, as I sat down and George began some anti-female bellowing, I turned squarely around in my chair and stared at him. I looked like a little kid in those days, even though I was a mother, and I used a little kid voice for the occasion.

"George?" I said.

"Whaddya want?" he rumbled.

"Go fuck yourself." Then I smiled at him and turned back to my typewriter.

Fifteen minutes later he shambled over to my desk. "Kid, wanna go to lunch with me and some of the troops later?" We went to lunch then and nearly every day after that. Staab (I never called him George again) became one of my dearest buddies. He carried me around with him like a watchfob, and he loved telling everybody how I had, as he put it, won him over. He also dearly loved to tell about me and the surly bartender at the bar across from City Hall.

All the ward heelers and beat reporters hung out at this spot. I had been in there several raucous times with Staab and some of the reporters, and didn't even know that the bartender had noticed me. I guess he got the message that I was all right.

One day, I got to the tavern before everyone else. As I took a stool at the bar to wait for my friends, a beefy, red-nosed customer—probably another politician's brother-in-law—drunkenly and disapprovingly eyed me up and down. Finally, pointing to the "No Women Allowed at the Bar" sign over my head, he yelled to the bartender, "Hey, what's she doing sitting here?"

The bartender looked to where the man was pointing, and then slowly turned and fixed him with a glare. "Whatsamatter with you?" he growled. "She ain't smoking."

When I left the *Bulletin* in December 1951 after about a year, the editors and reporters threw a huge party for me at the Pen and

Pencil Club and gave me a farewell gift: a small Seth Thomas clock on which was engraved: "Her copy is always on time." (The clock has never needed repair, and is still ticking in my living room today.) After the presentation, one of the reporters took me aside and suggested I go out to the club's public bar. I went out and there was Staab, holding a drink and crying so hard his shoulders were shaking. I put my arms around him and cried too.

Neither Harry Nichols, the city editor, nor Robert Shand, then the managing editor, who became the two most important influences on me as a reporter, had anything to do with my getting on the *News* staff in 1952. Dick Clarke, then the executive editor, hired me. In fact, Shand was out of town when I went up to see Mr. Clarke about getting a job there.

Mr. Clarke (I have never called him by his first name) admitted he had been curious to meet me because of a letter he had received from my former boss at the *Philadelphia Bulletin*, Walter Lister. "To tell you the truth," he confessed to me when I met him, "I don't really have an opening for you here. I just wanted to see if you had two heads or something."

When I left Philly, Walter had told me he would send letters of recommendation to the editors he knew in New York, where he had once run the *Post*. The letters he sent created a real commotion because nobody could believe that Lister would actually say all these nice things about a rewrite/reporter, and especially about a female! When I worked for Lister he was a very mellow and courteous gentleman. I didn't know that he had left behind him in New York a reputation as a tough, demanding editor who thought nothing of firing staffers right before Christmas, or any other holiday for that matter.

After I did some Sunday features on assignment for Mr. Clarke (while also working some rewrite at the *Post*) Clarke hired me to work on the Sunday *News* writing features for Ama Barker, the Sunday editor. But the understanding was that I would go on the cityside as soon as possible.

I never knew what Shand thought when he returned to find a new hire—a woman yet—in the editorial department. But he was a pro and a decent guy: instead of getting miffed at Clarke and taking it out on me, he waited to see what I could do. After he found out, he would send me anywhere, anytime, on any kind of big assignment: space shots, political conventions, hurricanes, a trip abroad with Jackie Kennedy, big-name trials.

In fact, I was never told Nichols and Shand and Clarke said to each other about me, but one day in April 1952 I got an assignment from the city desk. I had to go to a nearby Connecticut town where a young boy was ill and unable to walk. Photographer Tom Gallagher drove with me in a *News* car, and we spent a couple of hours with the little boy.

My story started: "Up in the Connecticut dairy country, in a little place you probably never heard of, lives a 4-year-old named Allan Matthew Stout, who is the loneliest kid in town.

"Allan has never walked in his life," I continued. "What's worse, he never will."

I wrote that although he was so cute and healthy-looking that he once had won third prize in a baby contest, he had been diagnosed with muscular dystrophy.

"Because his family has no car, no television set and no opportunity to get out, the little boy's life is confined to three rooms." Allan's invalid father was his principal pal and the family, including an older brother, lived on the mother's $48-a-week wages.

"The little boy never complains but he asks over and over why Santa Claus or the Easter Bunny or somebody doesn't write him a letter. Every day he waits for the mailman, Frank Ozimek, and every day he's disappointed. When the *News* was there, Ozimek brought a mail ad. Allan's father pretended it was a letter for the little boy, who clutched it, held it while he ate and fell asleep with it."

The story was way back in the paper, but it ran an entire column and three of Tom's pictures were used in the centerfold. The day it came out, the *News* was bombarded by calls from readers offering not only to write letters, but money and toys and prayers for, as some of them called him, "da sick little kid."

Right after that, I was called into the city room and told I was working for Harry Nichols. It turned out that the story was my audition for Nic, who wanted to see how I could handle a spot story. From then on I worked for Nic, who sometimes loaned me to Floyd Barger, then the telegraph desk editor, and his successor, Sid Feingold, for out-of-town assignments; and sometimes to Shand, who took me to national political conventions as part of a big *News* team that he headed personally.

No two men could have had backgrounds more dissimilar than Robert Gordon Shand, the son of a Lynn, Massachusetts shipbuilder, and Harry Ward Nichols, the son of a Brooklyn watchmaker. Shand attended the Naval Academy, graduated from MIT, and served as a Navy lieutenant in World War I. Nic started high school, became a $3-a-week office boy for the old *New York American* at 15, and at 19 was a full-fledged reporter. His World War I service was spent in France as an Army sergeant major. But the one thing Nic and Shand had in common was a passion for the newspaper business. Neither one of them had a journalism degree, but what a professional team they made inside our city room!

Shand had thought he wanted to be a naval architect, but he got hooked on the newspaper business, and before he became the *News* executive editor, he had been reporter and sports writer and rewriteman and copy editor and makeup editor and Sunday editor and day city editor and managing editor. He knew what he was doing; and more important, he knew what you were doing on a story. Working for him was total joy.

Nic had never wanted to be anything but a newspaperman. He came to the *News* in 1924 and was broken in by some great city editors before he took over the desk in 1946.

Nic didn't dislike having women in the news room; women critics and columnists and feature writers and reporters had been brought to the *News* from its earliest days by the founder, Captain Joe Patterson. Staff reporters like Grace Robinson, Julia McCarthy, Norma Abrams, and Doris Fleeson had covered hard news before me, although none of them had worked the rewrite battery like I did. When I came to the *News*, it had a high-level woman editor, Ama Barker, who ran the Sunday *News* when no other newspaper in New York had a woman in such a position.

I wish I had known Captain Patterson, because he was one publisher who seemed to care more about what his readers wanted than what his rich and powerful friends thought. He was legendary for watching and listening to the people in the subways and in restaurants like the Automat to learn what they were talking about, what interested them. What he learned he used in his newspaper.

Patterson and Bertie McCormick, owner of the *Chicago Tribune*, were first cousins, and the *News* and the *Trib* were financially interlocked. McCormick, who described his *Tribune* as "the

World's Greatest Newspaper"—providing the call letters for the Chicago radio station WGN—never quite understood why the *News* was the largest circulation newspaper in the United States. He never quite approved of it, either, nor of New York City, which was the antithesis of his own conservative, Midwestern heartland city.

Nic looked as if he got his job as city editor through Central Casting. He resembled Jimmy Walker, New York City's Roaring Twenties mayor—fine-boned, feline, dapper. He spoke pure New York City and he wore a fedora pushed to the back of his head; you could set your watch at the time he walked into the city room every weekday morning.

He hated perfume, phonies, excuses, flattery (it embarrassed him), jerks, and anybody who put on airs. He was not a writer, but he recognized instantly and appreciated greatly the special talent it took to take facts and put them together fast with accuracy, style, and color. With one look at a lead, he would know that the story was going to grab every reader, even if it was only about an impoverished old lady pleading with a judge not to let authorities take her dogs to the pound and to certain death:

> An unkempt, ragged, barelegged, 65-year-old woman, with a heart as big as a St. Bernard, fell to her knees yesterday before Magistrate Walter J. Bayer and begged so piteously not to be separated from Queenie and Skipper and Princess Butterfly and Prince Friendly and the rest of her 49 dogs that the judge gave her four days to try to work a miracle.

Nic immediately decided this story was going to be played big up front, and he was right. The next day the *News* operators went nuts trying to handle all the calls from readers wanting to help the old lady keep her dogs in what was described as her welfare "muh-tel." That the editors also decided to put on the front page a heart-rending photo of the poor lady on her knees before the judge didn't hurt the story, either.

I didn't realize until after he was gone what a quality this instant recognition was in an editor, especially in one who made no pretense of being a litterateur. Nic scared the hell out of most of his staff. He was so taciturn that when he actually opened his mouth and addressed you, you were struck deaf from sheer excitement. This was a problem, for when Nic gave an assignment, he talked softly and out of the side of his mouth, like a tout slipping you a hot tip at the racetrack.

He was the quintessential New Yorker—his Brooklyn birthplace, his accent, his disdain for anything outside the metropolitan area, his amused cynicism around politicians, his refusal to be impressed by authority. Once the police reporter brought the new police commissioner—an Ivy League preppie-type—into the city room to be introduced around. Loud enough for the commissioner to hear, Nic snarled to his troops, "Watch your wallets while this guy is around."

From a street address he could tell whether a homicide was big news, mediocre news, or no news—and so did all of his police reporters. Nic knew New York City so thoroughly, and was so aware of exactly where his staff was every minute, that when a story broke in any part of his metropolis, which included New Jersey and Connecticut, he could send the nearest reporter and photographer to the scene without looking at a map or at the daily assignment schedule.

He knew that a subway could get you into some sections faster than any car, and that in other sections the only safe way to travel was in a marked *News* car. In those days, a police car might get into trouble in a tough neighborhood, but never a *News* car; the paper's devoted readers would crowd around the car the way they swarm around a TV crew these days.

He was unflappable. On the first day back after one of our longest union strikes in 1962-1963, I brought a Groucho Marx nose, mustache, and spectacles. When Nic summoned me to the desk I slipped them on and stood next to him, leaning over in a Groucho crouch waiting for a reaction.

Nic remained absorbed in the papers in front of him, saying nothing while his assistants almost choked trying to stifle their laughter. When I couldn't stand it anymore, I said, "Nic, do you think I've changed since the strike?"

Nic's eyes flicked at me for a second, and then back to his papers. "Sure. Your tits are bigger."

One Halloween, the reporters and rewritemen sitting directly around the city desk all brought in masks and costume hats, and right before Nic was due at the city desk—always at 9:59:30 A.M.— we put them on and waited for him.

Out came Nic from his office, and marched right past us as we pretended to type and talk on the phone wearing our fake hairy claws and weird hats and masks. He never changed his expression. When he sat down and we all turned to look at him, his only words were, "You never looked better."

You didn't cross Nic. You didn't lie to Nic. And in return, while you were out busting your butt on a breaking story, you could take it for granted that Nic knew exactly where you were, that he understood you were working under extreme pressure, and that he had everything organized to handle your story back at the city room. If you couldn't get back and had to telephone in right on deadline, somebody would be waiting to take your dictation.

The drill would go like this: "Okay, Theo, we're all set, Nic says the slug [the identifying name of the story] is 'riot,' start right in," and I'd begin dictating at top speed. The wonderfully fast typist had already familiarized himself with enough background so he didn't have to interrupt the dictation to ask about spelling. (The men in the wire room were so proficient that they could read while they typed, and would read back to me a garbled sentence I had dictated, correcting it before it was taken to the city desk.)

When Nic was running things, if you came panting into the city room with your story, a copyboy would be standing next to your desk waiting to run your story, page by page or a couple of paragraphs at a time, to Nic and his assistants at the city desk. The editors who would read it, check it for questions, then move it over to a fast and famous copy desk, where it would be polished and given a headline. You could handle the deadline duress—with the presses waiting for your story—so much easier because Nic was in control.

The copyboy would say to you quietly: "Nic says to send it over to him in short takes, a graf or two grafs at a time. Nic says not to worry, take your time, you got about two minutes." You'd look over at the desk and Nic would grin and you would just shake your head, roll a book of copy paper and carbons into the big manual typewriter, and beat the story out. The copyboy would be running between your desk and Nic's, tearing apart the dupes and putting a copy on your spike for you so that you could keep writing, nobody second-guessing, nobody saying how long or short to keep it because Nic figured his writers knew best what to put in a story and when to end it—a fact that later editors never accepted.

The "books" we used in our big typewriters were usually five attached pages of copypaper and carbons. One copy remained on our own spikes and the others were distributed among the city desk, the copy desk, and the news desk. When I was out of town on an assignment, the wire room ran my copy to the telegraph (or national) desk and to the news desk. It was at the copy desk that the editing was done, and it was at the news desk that it was determined where in the newspaper stories would be placed.

Newspapers were male-dominated, and Nic, like most newsmen of those days, probably never gave much thought to the dearth of women in his news room. Once somebody asked him: "Does it it bother you having Theo in here?" He gave the question a moment's thought. "Nah," he said. "Now I know where all the guys are when I need them. They're at her desk." That was Nic's idea of a compliment.

Sometimes he'd send one of his assistants—Moe Kivel or Ted Dibble—to tell the guys to get off my desk, to go sit at their own typewriters and look like they were earning their paychecks. He didn't ordinarily care what his reporters did when they weren't out on a story, but he did it when the publisher telephoned to say he was coming through to show off the newsroom to some big shot from Chicago. The publisher learned the hard way to call first to warn Nic, to avoid a repeat of an occasion when the VIPs had walked into a typical hilarious goof-off event in the city room. It had all started when a reporter had arrived earlier wearing a WWI pilot's helmet and a long white aviator's scarf—who remembers why, maybe he got it from some flack pushing a war movie. Everybody loved the helmet and scarf, we all tried them on, and since it was a slow day and we were mostly waiting to go to lunch, one thing led to another and we began re-enacting WWI, having dogfights with copy paper airplanes, yelling "ack-ack-ack" and "Curse you, Red Baron!"

It got fairly elaborate. Men were ducking under desks to avoid antiaircraft fire; reporter Josie DiLorenzo was pretending to be Florence Nightingale, wearing a white paper towel on her head with a red-ink cross on it. I had been taken as a spy who insisted on babbling war secrets so that I wouldn't be shot like Mata Hari; my captors were yelling at me, "Shut up already with your secrets! We don't wanna hear them!"

As soon as we spotted our bewildered publisher and his

guests trying to duck bombing runs by paper airplanes, we stopped all the nuttiness. But getting the high sign from Nic to go to lunch, we all yelled "Heil!" and goose-stepped out of the news room in single file past the VIPs, our right hands held up in salute. God knows what Nic told the publisher, or if he even bothered to explain.

Reporters and writers weren't the only ones who carried on in the city room. The scholarly, seemingly staid copy desk people had their fun, too.

The old horseshoe-shaped copy desk had big pastepots and scissors for each of the copyreaders who sat around the rim in those days of cut-and-paste editing. The pastepots were on top of the desks—how many screams of anguish I heard from copyreaders who absentmindedly stuck their paste brushes into their coffee cups! The scissors were attached by 2 1/2-foot chains fastened inside the ten rim drawers of the desk. When visitors were taken through the city room and approached the copy desk, as copyreader Paul Saffron recalled in a 1979 *Quill* article, the "rimsters wrapped the chains around their arms like phylacteries, rattled them, groaned and writhed in mock agony."

The steel desk had ten inside and ten perimeter drawers, seven outer and five inner legs, a "battleship" linoleum top, and a swivel chair for the slotman that raised him six inches above his crew.

The head of the copy desk, who assigned the stories for editing and headlining to the various assistants, was known on all newspapers as the "slotman" because he presided over the desk from the slot of the horseshoe. The *News*'s famous slotman, Bill Murphy, "and a team of 14 copyreaders carried on a tradition of writing outrageously witty heads that came to be known as the brightest and most imaginative in the country during the 1950s by trade papers, serious analytical magazines, and journalism schools," Saffron wrote in his article.

"In preparation for electronic publishing, the storied copy desk was cut into little pieces and junked last year," his article continued. "It had been the traditional massive steel horseshoe seen in movies about newspapers. It had been built by an iron house from plans by the paper's head carpenter."

Nic was already at the *News* when this custom-built desk was installed in 1930, and it was still there when he left. When it was destroyed, it was nearly 50 years old. It would have been nice if somebody had thought to preserve it as a part of newspaper history.

At the *News*, the idea was to take your job—not yourself—seriously. Even if you were writing the biggest story of the day, you were never allowed to get pretentious. Tony Burton, one of the talented writer/reporters who sat near me, used to come over to my desk as I was pounding away on deadline, lift my copy off the spike, start to read, and then pretend to be put to sleep from a glance at the lead. He would stand there snoring until I would look up and threaten him with death or worse. Then, in his beautiful British accent, he would say, "Actually, that's a rather good lead, Theo. Carry on," and run to his seat as I threw things at him.

We were our own best fans and critics. We were devoted to each other, and we were devoted to the *News*. When one of us was writing a story that was particularly funny or dramatic or well-worded, we not only stood in line to read it off the spike, but called our buddies at AP or UPI or other newspapers to read it to them. Our friends at other newspapers would frequently tell us that what we had at the *News*, particularly our closeness with each other and our respect for Nic and Shand, did not exist in any other city room.

We didn't realize until later that Nic was unique as a city editor. He absolutely refused to make us look busy when we weren't; he was so secure as a city editor he saw no need to keep us occupied with "make work" when we could spend the time better gossiping, trying to pay bills, quietly doing a little freelance for some extra money. (The unwritten rule for freelance was that you could sell anything you wanted as long as it did not compete with the *News*. Nic even thought it was okay for me to work for huge amounts of money on my free time at the *Enquirer*, when it was still being published by Gene Pope over in New Jersey. The only restriction was that my name could not be used in the paper, and I was there strictly for rewrite; I neither interviewed people nor went out on any story.) When there was a crunch of fast-breaking news, when he needed us, Nic knew we would be there, would work with no thought of hours or food, would break our backs for him and for the *News*.

As taciturn as Nic was, he enjoyed reporters' get-togethers and never missed the annual Christmas dinner party put on by the Newspaper Reporters Association of New York, to which everybody brought toys for poor children.

One year's Christmas party became a legend among *News* staffers. After drinks and dinner at the hotel ballroom, some of us were invited to a suite upstairs that had been reserved for an after-dinner cocktail party for association officers, editors and their wives, and other special guests.

Nic and I went up together, and were the first ones there. Nic noted that the party hadn't been very lively up to that point, and he thought it was going to get even stuffier when the VIPs joined us. Moved as much by the scotch as by the challenge I felt as a reporter-host to keep an editor-guest happy, I suggested that we startle the VIPs by removing the lower part of our clothes. When the others appeared, we would just sit there talking to each other as if everything was normal. This appealed to Nic's sense of humor.

I was wearing a black lace-trimmed petticoat and black panty-hose under my skirt, so I didn't risk revealing anything. Nic took off his pants, disclosing voluminous boxer shorts covered by his dress shirt and jacket, knee-high black socks held up by garters on rather elegant if extremely skinny legs, and highly polished black shoes. With his fedora and bowtie and shorts and no pants, and with my earrings, necklace, fancy top, petticoat, and no skirt, we looked terrific as we waited for the first guests to arrive.

The first person to enter was a very young waiter pushing a portable bar filled for the party. He took one look at us, gulped, made a U-turn with the bar, and fled.

Meanwhile, Bill Federici arrived. Being a young reporter at the *News*, he was scared to death of Nic, and when he walked in on us he didn't know where to look or what to say. He tried to be cool, and planted himself in front of us like there was nothing wrong.

Nic said, "Take your pants off, too." Bill gulped and did, still trying to look cool but figuring we had both gone crazy. Other people were now walking in, and nobody dared say a thing. Jim Antone, copy desk head at *Women's Wear Daily*, came in with his wife Mary. For years after, she would laugh uproariously when remembering her initial shock, and then how it became funnier and funnier as Nic and I sat there looking nonchalant while the crowd gathered.

Another *News* reporter came in, and when Nic said, "Take your pants off," this one got so nervous he forgot to remove his shoes first. He was hopping around with his pants stuck around his ankles when the hotel detective arrived along with some other reporters. (The young waiter had reported the "orgy" to the manager.)

Looking at their faces, I began laughing so hard I couldn't talk. Nic, however, sat there staring at everybody, and finally growled, "Will you get the booze back in here, for chrissakes?" We put our clothes back on, but Nic never cracked a smile.

In Nic's city room, we could make all the noise we wanted to, horse around, play games, make jokes, gossip with each other for hours—until there was news to get and to write.

Unlike what goes on in the movies, or when it's amateur hour at newspapers where editors shout orders and carry on, when a big story broke at the *News* it always became quiet. Like on March 1, 1962, the day we got hit with three Page 1 stories at the same time.

The seven Mercury astronauts, led by John Glenn, the country's newest space hero, were coming to New York for a huge tickertape parade. On that day, the city's bus drivers were scheduled to take a strike vote, threatening to throw the city's transportation system into disarray. We were prepared.

But then came the horrible and unexpected third headliner: a Los Angeles-bound jet fell into Jamaica Bay right after takeoff at what was then Idlewild (now Kennedy) International Airport, killing all 95 aboard.

I was not working in the city room that day because I had been assigned to accompany Jackie Kennedy to India and Pakistan, the first trip ever made by a First Lady to those countries, and I was running around Manhattan getting shots and visas and clothes for the three-week trip. When I walked into the usually raucous city room between appointments that day it was so quiet I knew that something tremendous had happened.

Reporters were working the telephones, rewritemen with their headphones in place were typing nonstop, the copyboys were all over the place, Nic—looking calm as always—and his assistants were bent over piles of copy and talking on telephones. Bob Shand, walking back into his office, waved at me. Nobody was yelling, nobody was panicky; the professionals were at work.

The reporter sitting next to me said: "A plane just fell into the water at International and everybody's dead."

"Oh my God!" I said.

"And the bus drivers took the vote. They're striking."

"Oh my God!" I said.

"And the cops are saying that the Glenn parade is the biggest ever and the crowds are going crazy." He went on to tell me that reporters everywhere had been calling Nic to offer help, including those who had the day off, "and you know Nic. He's telling most of them to quit tying up his telephone lines and go play golf."

Before I could squeeze out another "Oh my God!" Nic strolled over and said, "You hear what's going on?" I nodded, and he said, "Did you get the yellow fever shot? You okay?" I nodded again, and he said, "Everything's under control. Don't hang around here unless you want to," and he returned to his desk.

This was why we felt such loyalty to this prickly man and why he was such a great city editor; in the midst of all that turmoil and pressure, with three giant stories breaking at the same time, he was aware that I had come into his city room and took the time to tell me it was all right to keep going on with my travel preparations.

That night, the *News* came out with a marvelous front page. Shand, who created our Page 1 lines, didn't have the leeway of the *Times* editors, who had large pages with many columns to work with. Given the tabloid-sized front page, the way he handled this three-headed hydra was masterful. The front-page headline for the March 2 first edition was "DEATH, TRIUMPH & A BUS STRIKE." For the final edition, there was a different Page 1: "IN ONE DAY: 95 Die in Jet; Busmen Strike; Millions Share Glenn Triumph."

There was a huge photograph under these lines showing Glenn being applauded at a Broadway show he attended after his ticker-tape parade, and on either side of the caption below the picture were two boxes, which evened off the beautiful, clean makeup that was so typical of the *News* then. The boxes read: "Glenn's Day Here, 5 Full Pages of Pictures, see Pages A, B, C, D and 33, stories on page 3" and "Airliner Crash, 2 Pages of Pictures, see Page 30 and Back Page, story on Page 2."

This was 1962, the *News* cost five cents, and for that nickel our millions of readers got the best photographic coverage in the city and the kind of high-pressure deadline writing and reporting that has disappeared.

The air tragedy, written by Henry Lee, the top rewriteman in New York, crammed facts from the legmen into every colorful sentence. Reporter Gerald Kessler shared the byline with Henry, but obviously many reporters fed information to him under Nic's direction, because the completed story was a marvel of facts, color, interviews with officials, names of the dead passengers, and quotes from relatives.

The main astronaut parade story, under the byline of Joseph Cassidy and Arthur Mulligan, started:

> New York's millions roared their welcome to Astronaut John H. Glenn Jr. yesterday in an outburst of enthusiasm and acclaim never before equaled even in this city of traditional tributes to heroes.
>
> From the Battery to City Hall and from City Hall to 50th St. they jammed windows and sidewalks along the parade route and broke through police barricades to surround Glenn's open car and those of his six fellow astronauts. . . .
>
> Observers said that never before, not for Col. Charles Lindbergh in 1927, for Gen. Eisenhower in 1945 or for Gen. MacArthur in 1951 had there ever been a greater turnout.

To illustrate these lengthy stories, the *News* ran more than 50 photographs in that final edition. And the captions were as colorful as the main stories. Under a tremendous shot of the plane disaster was this caption: "In the Shallow Water—Deep Tragedy. Bits of wreckage, tiny fragments of a once magnificent airliner, jut from the shallows of Jamaica Bay as firemen wade through the frigid, muddy water in search of the human wreckage of yesterday's crash. . . ."

As for the bus strike, the story by labor editor Jack Turcott started: "The second strike in two months hit the Fifth Ave. Coach Lines, America's biggest privately owned urban bus combine, late yesterday, halting 2,278 buses that carry more than 1 1/2 million riders a day on 107 routes in Manhattan, the Bronx, Queens and Westchester. The strike was the union's answer to layoffs by the company's new management." Three photos illustrated that story.

What we had, all in one day, was the worst plane disaster in U.S. history, the biggest tickertape parade in New York City history, and a strike on the biggest private bus line in the country. All of this, plus the city's regular news, was handled by one city desk with one city editor, one photo editor, and their assistants. There was no such thing then at the *News* as a metropolitan editor. There was a copy desk run by copy chief Bill Murphy; there was a tele-graph desk (now known as the national desk) which handled all of the wire copy and everything outside the metropolitan area; there was a news editor; and there was a managing editor, Shand, and some assistants. That was it.

I worked with Nic and Shand every day, but I didn't see much of Mr. Clarke, and I still don't know how I got him to eat lunch with me at the rinky-dink restaurant-bar behind the *News* which we named Louie's East. Mr. Clarke was rather formal, and having married an English lady after his first wife died, he became more so, wearing British-cut suits and carrying a furled umbrella at all times.

Louie's East was hardly his kind of hangout—it was filled with guys from the composing room—and although I went there a lot at night for drinks with reporters from all over the city, it was not one of my regular lunch spots. But on this day it was pouring, I was going to lunch, I saw Clarke unsuccessfully trying to find a cab, and I suggested we make a dash through the downpour to Louie's.

Louie's never closed for repairs—even after it was nearly gutted by a fire—and when Mr. Clarke and I ran in from the rain, it was being replastered or repainted or something. Betty Chitjian, my favorite waitress in the whole world, wiped some debris off a table so we could sit down.

I explained to Mr. Clarke that it wasn't always this messy, and while he went to make a phone call I asked Betty to give us extra special service, explaining to her that Clarke was "the top man at the *News.*" Betty went right back to the kitchen and repeated what I told her to the chef. In his undershirt, stirring a big pot of stew, he asked in awe, "Who, da foreman?"

Betty was from Armenia and her accent was a challenge. She was always inviting me and my buddies to meet her in New Jersey at an inn whose name sounded suspiciously like "The White Swine." After lots of figuring, we finally determined that she was talking about "The White Swan." After we ordered, Mr. Clarke pointed out that he didn't have any utensils. As Betty was leaving the table, she shouted over her shoulder, "Okay, I'll get you a fuckin' knife!" Everybody in the place turned to look. I hastily explained to Mr. Clarke that Betty was simply telling him that she would get him a fork and knife.

A couple of minutes later, she brought out our food. Just as Mr. Clarke picked up his fork, a chunk of plaster fell off the ceiling and plopped into his food. We looked at the plate, and at each other. Since Mr. Clarke was speechless, I yelled for Betty. She came over, and I said: "Betty, look at that!"

She bent over, looked closely, and straightened up. "That wasn't on the plate when I gave it to you," she declared, and marched off.

It was at Louie's one night, as we all sat drinking and playing "Tom Swifties," that one of the nuts who roamed the area preaching and shouting, threw open the doors and stood dramatically before us, his arms upraised.

We all swung around and the bearded character, staring sternly at the dissolute barflies before him, lowered his arms, pointed at us, and declaimed: "APENT! RETONE!"

As soon as he said this, he realized his words weren't quite right. We were looking at him open-mouthed. He muttered to himself, "Apent? Retone?" shook his head, shrugged his shoulders apologetically, and beat it out of there. From then on, there was hardly a day I didn't get a call from somebody asking me if I wanted to meet him at Louie's for a little apenting and retoning.

One of the best parts about being in Nic's city room in those days was the great schmoozing we used to do.

Josie DiLorenzo and I sat next to each other and became close friends. Neither one of us was consumed with ambition and spent our spare time telling stories to each other instead of plotting our futures.

She had a loving, close-knit Italian family and I came from a loving, close-knit Jewish family, and we would entertain ourselves for hours talking about them.

My favorite Josie story was the one about her grandmother stuffing the Thanksgiving turkey with pasta and insisting that this was how Thanksgiving turkey had always been prepared in Italy. When the rest of the family pointed out that Italy didn't celebrate Thanksgiving, the grandmother ordered them to be quiet, what did they know about Italy, they weren't born there, in the old country everybody stuffed Thanksgiving turkey with pasta! So the DiLorenzos always had pasta-stuffed turkey on Thanksgiving—an old Italian tradition.

I told her about my father bringing home all kinds of pets, from a bear to a monkey, to add to the joy and confusion of a household filled with eleven kids and dogs and cats and birds, including a famous "watchdog" who let everybody and anybody walk into the house, day or night—but then attacked if they tried to leave. For a while there, we had an awfully crowded house, with the milkman, the postman, delivery boys, our friends who dropped in to pick us up for school, my father yelling he had to get to work, my mother handing out cups of coffee; all of us milling around trying to escape the dog who wouldn't let us.

Swapping favorite newspaper stories was another way we entertained each other. One of mine was about the timid witness in a federal case I was covering who spoke so softly that the jurors had to cup their ears and strain forward in their seats to hear her.

The prosecutor repeatedly asked her to speak up, but she kept looking down shyly and whispering her answers into her lap. Finally, hoping he could get her to answer his questions in the direction of the jury box, he said to her: "Please, Miss Jones, speak to the jury!"

Miss Jones lifted her eyes, blushed, and obeyed. "Hello!" she chirped out to the startled jurors.

Another courtroom classic was about the judge in a southern court who was polling the jurors after their verdict was rendered. The court: "If that is your verdict, so say you all." The jurors: "You all."

One story I loved came from Henry Lee, who told us that when he was a young reporter in Connecticut during the Depression, he went to his local bank to try to get a loan.

"Everything was going along fine," Henry said, "until this stuffed-shirt banker asked me what I did. I told him I was a reporter. That was the end—it was like I threw a skunk on his desk. The banker wanted me to know that they didn't make loans to reporters, he wanted me to know that reporters weren't the kind of people bankers dealt with.

"So, since I knew I wasn't getting the loan anyway," Henry continued, "I told this banker: 'Yep, I'm a reporter, and I cover a lot of stories about people who embezzle, and you know what? Not one embezzler I ever wrote about was a reporter. They were all bankers.'"

Everybody in the business in those less-than-respectable days had stories. Fran Lewine, who covered the White House for the AP, told me a tale of how she had left a bathing suit in her desk at the newspaper where she started. When she returned, she discovered one of the old drunken-and-talented staffers sitting at his desk, hard at work, wearing her bathing suit over his clothes.

At the newspaper where I started, the *Evansville Press*, I had left a shopping bag on my desk when I had to run out on a story. When I came back, the bag was empty. Frantically looking around the room for my purchases, I noticed several of the men casting their eyes skyward. Hanging from the ceiling pipes were two brassieres and a pair of lace-trimmed panties. I had to call the carpenter to bring his ladder and remove my unmentionables, which he handed to me with his eyes averted as everybody applauded, including the guys from the composing room who had come in to watch. Boy, we were wild in those days!

Then there was the day at the *Press* when we stashed a bottle of bourbon in the men's room to mix with our colas toward the end of the day. Someone asked me to run in and get the booze—the bathroom was unoccupied, and everybody else was busy. As soon as I got into the bathroom, the rest of the staff blockaded the door with filing cabinets. I screamed and yelled and I didn't get out until the editor, Frank Ford, came back from wherever he was and heard me beating on the door and ordered me released. He never asked me what I was doing in there.

There were wonderful stories about things that had happened years before, as well. At the *News*, I heard about famed former staffers like Paul Gallico, whose books became bestsellers, and John McNulty, whose short stories were published in the *New Yorker*. At some time before he came to New York, the legend went, McNulty, who enjoyed drinking, was working at the *Columbus Citizen*. One day, after going out to lunch, he disappeared. After about two weeks, a telegram arrived at the city desk from some burg miles away. It read, "Please send $100 and my middle initial. Am going to join local Elks. John McNulty."

When Nic was still an assistant city editor, Gallico wrote a story about him and the way he worked which was published in *Vanity Fair*. It was supposed to be fiction, so Gallico changed the spelling of Nic's name but the piece—"City Editor Nicholls"—was as true in its description of Nic in 1932 as it was when he was my city editor 20 years later. (In all the years I knew Nic, he never mentioned this piece, which had made him a legend. He would have hated it, being described as a legend, for chrissakes.)

> His skull is packed with the lore of the vast city he covers, every highway and byway, means of transportation, neighborhood and locality is spread out before his mental eyes like a map. He soaks them all up, the rumors and tips and the leads, the flashes, the whispers and the clanging alarm bells. They pass through his system where they are separated, valued, ticketed and channeled, and they emerge as news and stories in the paper. . . .
> He has the mechanics of news-gathering and story coverage and the ability to move reporters swiftly to the scene of action at the tips of his fingers, but the spark is inspiration, love of work and the most sensitive schnozzle for sniffing out news in the business . . . like a juggler he can keep five stories in the air at one time and never turn a hair, or miss a drag on his butt.
> They hand him telephones in relays and he usually wears out about two a week. He starts at top speed and increases the tempo as he approaches closing time, and I never remember him getting flustered or sore, or violent, or unpleasant with his colleagues and reporters, or behaving like the movie version of a city editor.

The city desk is the heart of the newspaper, it was the only desk Nic ever wanted to sit at, and when he left, the gusto and the joy left with him.

On Dec. 31, 1969, after 47 years with the *News*, Nic left the city desk at precisely 6 P.M. for the last time.

He was 73, but he never looked it, and in all the years he was my city editor I don't remember him taking a day off for illness. Once he arrived at his desk a few minutes later than usual; this was such a rare occurrence that we all came up to him, worried. He had just left the dentist's office where he had been through major oral surgery.

The hot shots who came in to "improve" the *News* pushed Nic out because, among other things, he wouldn't change his style. They didn't appreciate the fact that he ignored the executive meetings they began scheduling every day; he kept telling them he couldn't leave the city desk and waste time yakking with them when news could be breaking and reporters needed to talk to him.

Imitating other more formal papers, the new executives also met to discuss and schedule upcoming stories, which Nic also considered a waste of time. Why bother with meetings and conferences and schedules, when any fool knew the best stories were the unexpected ones that could break at any time? Nic wanted to be there at the desk when they broke.

After they took the *News* away from Nic—he was not ready to leave—he became a recluse. They took away a big part of Nic's life, and only a short time later his remarkable health and stamina failed. In early 1971, slightly more than a year after he left the city room for the last time, he died, of what his staffers knew was a broken heart.

We cried when Bob Shand had died in 1966, and we cried, a lot, at Nic's funeral. We didn't know it then, but we were also crying for the *News*. It was the end of an era.

10

Going Crazy
With Charlie

The main reason the Charles Manson trial was totally different from any other I ever covered was because it was the only one where everybody went a little bonkers—judge, jury, reporters, lawyers, deputies, and spectators.

Of course, the four defendants were bonkers already.

Charlie was the weird end product of our prison system, having been institutionalized since he was eight, and the three Manson Family "girls" were as nutty as street drugs and garbage food could make them. I still believe that, to this day, the girls—Susan Atkins, Patricia Krenwinkel, and Leslie Van Houten—don't have a clue why they did what they did. Or that, immediately after the murders, they had more than a vague recollection of how and when they committed the deeds that turned them into monsters.

The girls were a trio of freaked-out acidheads, and they came from a distorted '60s world where a sawed-off redneck like Manson could make fairly well-educated, middle-class girls fight for a chance to sleep with him and obey his orders to sleep with anybody else who wandered in.

But why did the rest of us go a little meshuga?

Maybe the length of this trial and its total unpredictability did us in.

Ten months in that gloomy old Hall of Justice in downtown Los

Angeles listening to testimony that went from horrifying to ludi-
crous . . .

The testimony itself, punctuated with outbreaks from the defendants, supplemented by outbursts from the audience . . .

The jurors, ranging in age from 25 to 74, locked up so long in
hotel rooms that one of them threatened to tie sheets together and
escape out of window . . .

Threats of self-immolation and other destruction outside the
Hall of Justice, where the Manson Family members still at large
held their daily vigil, the girls' shaven heads turning burnt orange
from the sun . . .

A defense attorney disappearing, his drowned body undiscov-
ered until many months later, on the very day that the defendants
received death sentences from the jury . . .

Witnesses with names like "Lotsapoppa," "Snake," and
"Ouish." Another witness who described himself as "an emissary
from God" . . .

A monomaniacal prosecutor under such strain he screamed at
another woman reporter, calling her a "cocksucker," and then was
forced to publicly apologize to her under threat of being taken off
the case . . .

Was there ever a trial in which a murder suspect arranged to
surrender to his "Family" on a street corner during a noon recess
of the trial with the entire press corps as witnesses, after which the
deputies arrested him? The TV, radio, and newspaper reporters
then formed a procession down the street and into the Hall of
Justice, led by the suspect, the deputies, and the Manson Family
followers singing one of Charlie's songs.

One woman juror wore a different wig nearly every day. When
Coroner Noguchi testified, her wig was a jet-black bouffant and
looked exactly like something out of *Madame Butterfly*.

When ever was there a murder trial where the jurors were
sequestered for seven months, and with the trial still on, unse-
questered and allowed to go home, and then once more were
ordered back into sequestration at another hotel?

Those of us who covered the Manson trial became like battle-
scarred buddies, friends forever who went through intense fire
and survived. Names that mean nothing now to anybody else, like
"Elmer" and "Herman's Kids" and "Julie Shapiro," send us into

joyous recall.

"Elmer" was the pet marijuana plant that was nurtured at Spahn's Ranch, the Family's country residence. There was a lot of testimony about "Elmer."

"Herman's Kids" was the name the jurors gave themselves in honor of their foreman, Herman Tubick, a retired mortician. After the trial, Tubick called a press conference to deny that any of his "kids" were "promiscuous" while sequestered at the Ambassador Hotel, as charged by a fellow juror, and to tell us "If anybody was having any hanky panky, I don't know about it!"

"Julie Shapiro" was the beautiful woman from Chicago who came to be a faithful spectator at the trial. She first attracted attention when she came to court in a see-through blouse with nothing under it but lots and lots of Julie.

The court did not look kindly on this distraction. In fact, it didn't look kindly on anything during this trial, being notably humorless, high-strung, and touchy as all get-out. Some hapless deputy was ordered by Judge Charles Older to give Julie the word that she was not to come to the trial bra-less anymore.

Julie obeyed the judicial edict and came properly attired after that, sorely disappointing many in the courtroom. She didn't cause any more trouble until months later, when she took issue with the prosecutor during his closing arguments, and from her seat in the spectator section angrily called him a liar.

Instead of just ordering her ejected, Judge Older told his deputies to arrest her, book her, and hold her for a contempt of court hearing when the day's session ended.

As Julie was being hustled out, obviously startled that she could be treated this way, she plaintively asked her reporter friends: "What's the matter? I'm wearing a brassiere. Why can't I stay here?"

Because the judge had ordered a contempt hearing for Julie, which we had to cover, it was necessary to get Julie's background and vital statistics. It was then she told us she was studying witchcraft here under Morlock the Warlock.

We ran to the telephones with this wonderful little story. I began dictating the details about how "a witchlet who said she is studying here under Morlock the Warlock" had disrupted the Charles Manson murder trial. Next to me I could hear Sandi Mettetal dictating at top speed to City News Service, and Linda Deutsch of the

Associated Press doing the same thing. Morlock the Warlock. How could you resist?

We all hung up about the same time, and our wry grins told the same tale. All of our editors had had essentially the same reaction: "Morlock the Warlock? You've been on this trial too long!" But of course the editors loved it. The *News* copy desk borrowed my "witchlet" description for the headline, and it was displayed nicely for our delighted East Coast readers, who by this time were convinced that what was happening at the trial of Charlie and his three helpmeets represented the 1960s, the druggies, the dropouts, the flower children, and the whole zany West Coast.

The deputies, who had started out somewhat hostile and suspicious of the press corps, over the months relaxed a great deal around us. Apparently, they realized that we were just there to do a hard job as well as we could, and that we were really quite harmless, if goofy.

The Manson Family members were on the street outside the courthouse threatening all sorts of dire consequences, and the prosecution did not discourage early rumors that they were planning to break in to the courtroom to rescue their guru and the girls. But we were in a heavily guarded courtroom, everyone went through a body search every day (despite my complaints that "no reporter ever killed a good story, why are you searching us?"), and nobody I knew ever felt they were in real danger. Although there were a lot of spectators who created brief interruptions with drug flashbacks or other problems, the trial proceeded without any trouble from them or from the Manson Family.

In fact, the only time we heard screaming and shouting in the hall, it turned out to be a spillover of a fight that had started in some other trial in an adjoining courtroom. When something happens right outside the courtroom, one reporter usually goes out to check while the rest stay behind to continue taking notes. In this case, we whispered to Earl Caldwell of the *New York Times* that he should be our pool reporter, and we'd cover for him inside. Earl agreed.

Shortly after, the judge called a recess since the noise was continuing outside. As soon as the judge left the bench, we dashed out to the corridor and saw a bunch of people hitting and hollering at each other. There was Earl, our intrepid representative, perched high atop the tables where we had our telephones, asking no questions, taking no notes, and staying well out of the way of the yelling mob below him.

"I wasn't going to mess with those people. You could get hurt down there," Earl told us righteously when we chided him for his lack of journalistic curiosity. He was right. If it *had* been the Manson gang, he certainly could have gotten hurt asking questions, and since it wasn't the Manson gang, standing on top of the telephone tables was just as good a place for him to be as anywhere else.

Another time we selected a pool reporter was when we were advised during a trial session that a sanity hearing for Charles (Tex) Watson, Manson's top lieutenant, was scheduled in a nearby courtroom. Tex, the onetime high school athlete and all-American boy, had been imprisoned in his Texas hometown and brought to Los Angeles as one of the murder suspects—the one, in fact, who had led the murder raids on the Sharon Tate house, where the actress and four friends were butchered, and the next night at the house where Leno and Rosemary LaBianca were killed.

We agreed that we would leave one of us behind at the Manson session while all the rest of us went to cover the Watson hearing. We had learned that anything could happen at this trial, like when Charlie suddenly leaped screaming at the judge brandishing a pencil in his little fist. By this time the trial had gone on so long that we thought one of the jurors would leap out of the jury box next, screaming, "Oh God, make it stop!" the way prosecution witness Linda Kasabian burst out when she described the killings at the Tate house.

Sandi Mettetal under promise of eternal sainthood was our proxy in the Manson session, and the rest of us trooped down the hall to Judge George Dell's courtroom. There we saw the 6'2" Tex, down to a shadowy 110 pounds, mouth agape, his headlights out. The judge declared him "insane," "a vegetable," and near death, and had him committed to a state mental hospital with orders that he be tried if and when he recovered. (He did recover, and was later convicted on all charges and is serving life like the others.)

When we came back to the Manson courtroom to give Sandi the news, she met us out at the phones, nearly purple with suppressed laughter. It seems that as she sat there alone, Charlie's lawyer,

Irving Kanarek, in the course of one of his interminable objections, told the jurors for the zillionth time that his client's rights were being prejudiced by the international publicity emanating from the huge press corps covering the trial.

Apparently unaware that we had left, Irving dramatically swept his arm back, telling the jurors that "there sat the world press." The entire jury, the judge, and everybody else in the courtroom turned and stared at Sandi, sitting all alone surrounded by rows of empty seats, almost comatose from Irving's harangue, "and with cobwebs coming out of my hair" as she described it to us. Some world press!

Poor Irving. He never did figure out why, from then on every time he mentioned the "world press" the jurors would stare at Sandi. She would turn bright red and we would crack up.

Besides Julie Shapiro there was another disruptive spectator, a talented artist who had been doing sketches in the courtroom for magazines (no cameras allowed in those days) and who freaked out one day toward the end of the trial, in the third day of an excruciatingly boring summation by Charlie's mouthpiece. She opened the doors and marched into the trial room, holding a Bible and chanting, "I am the Whore of Babylon! I have come to defend my brother!"

The deputies weren't as skittish as they had been at the outset of the trial, and their reaction time was further slowed from having to listen to Kanarek's less-than-dazzling oratory, and our artist got almost to the well of the courtroom before the deputies roused themselves.

"Arrest that woman!" hollered Judge Older, his cheeks flushed at this insult to courtroom decorum. He was the only judge I knew who took these things personally. Once again, he ordered the woman booked so that he could try her for contempt.

Early in the trial, disruptions like these were big news, but we had had months of weird behavior to write about and we were a little jaded. Where once we would have dashed out after the artist, now we began bickering amongst each other: "You go get her background." "No, you go." "Why me?"

As we hissed and muttered while taking down testimony, one of the deputies who had schlepped the artist out returned to his seat near us.

"Any information on that lady?" somebody whispered to him.

He shook his head, and then with a straight face he said, "We just ran a check with the Babylon PD, and they don't have a thing on her."

Whenever national interest flagged during the many months of the trial, we knew something would happen to spark interest again in Manson and his followers. But we never knew when it would happen or where it would come from, which was why the *News* kept me on the case every day, unlike the *New York Times* and some other out-of-town papers.

There was the day that President Nixon unexpectedly took a hand in the case. During a press conference in Denver, Nixon noted that at his recent vacation in San Clemente, California, he had been inundated with Manson trial coverage on the radio, TV, and in the newspapers.

"Front page every day in the papers," Nixon told the reporters at the conference. "It usually got a couple of minutes in the evening news.

"Here is a man who was guilty, directly or indirectly, of eight murders without reason," Nixon continued.

"Here is a man who, as the coverage was concerned, appeared to be rather a glamorous figure, glamorous to the young people whom he had brought into his operations, and also another thing that was noted was the fact that two lawyers in the case, two lawyers who were, as anyone who could read any of the stories could tell, who were guilty of the most outrageous, contemptuous actions in the courtroom, and who were ordered to jail overnight by the judge, seem to be more the oppressed and the judge seemed to be the villain."

After getting this off his chest, Nixon went on with his press briefing.

Thank God the *News* had Paul Healy traveling with the President. Being the intelligent reporter he was, Paul realized instantly that Nixon had made a terrible boo-boo—publicly branding as guilty a man who had not yet been convicted and who was therefore still presumed to be innocent. Paul realized that this gaffe had implications far more important than anything else Nixon was doing in Denver, and he notified the desk in New York. The editors immediately swung into action and sent an urgent message to my telex in the courthouse pressroom.

It was lunchtime, which was deadline for me because of the three-hour time difference, and I always used the noon recess to file a story for the first edition with all the details of the morning session.

Most of my colleagues went out of the building to eat, along with some of the lawyers, and so I was pretty much alone when the message came over the wire. As soon as the lawyers came back, I told the desk, I would get reaction from them. The desk would send me Nixon's complete statement so that I could show it to the lawyers.

I left the pressroom and hurried to my phone outside the eighth-floor courtroom, hoping to grab any of the prosecutors or defense team. As luck would have it, the first lawyer off the elevator was Ron Hughes, the bearded, 250-pound, prematurely bald flower child of a defense attorney.

Poor Ron, who lived in somebody's basement and had to borrow a jacket from a reporter when he went into the judge's chambers, was always in hot water with Judge Older. His wreck of a car kept breaking down, making him late for the sessions, and he wasn't given to lawyer-like demeanor in the courtroom. Judge Older had put him in jail for contempt for telling the prosecutor he was "full of shit" during an argument at the bench about whether or not the prosecutor had shown the defense a photograph before trying to introduce it as evidence. That was one of the "outrageous" actions the President was referring to.

"Ron!" I yelled. "Quick! I'm on deadline. President Nixon just made a speech and he called Charlie guilty. We need a statement from you."

"He did what?" Ron asked. I read him the Nixon quotes about Manson being "guilty, directly or indirectly, of eight murders" and told him my office had just gotten the information from our political reporter.

"Come on, Ron. I need a comment for this first edition. I can't wait for the other lawyers to get back. What's your reaction to what Nixon said?"

"Well, fuck him!" said Ron. "That's my comment. Fuck him!"

"Oh for God's sake!" I said. "I can't send that. Now come on, aren't you going to consider asking for a mistrial? Aren't you dismayed that the President of the United States, a lawyer himself, would violate a defendant's rights and call him guilty while he's still on trial? Aren't you angry that the President would jeopardize a lengthy and expensive trial with such a thoughtless remark? Isn't that what you want to say?"

"Yeah, yeah!" Ron cried, all fired up by my remarks. "And fuck him, too!"

So, with Ron listening to me and nodding agreement, I dictated to New York, not having the time to go back downstairs to the pressroom to type it and send it on the telex. The *News* had the first react story from the Manson trial to insert in Healy's story in time for our early edition.

Ron loved every word of it, especially when I told the desk "that defense attorney Ronald Hughes had been so aggrieved by this injustice on the part of the President that he had burst out with an expletive, which of course, we couldn't use."

"What did he say, Theo?" asked Sid Feingold, my editor, who I knew was beaming because we had beaten the wire services and all of the other newspapers on the Los Angeles end of this story, thanks to Healy's acumen and the fact that I didn't have the time to go out to lunch and Ron Hughes didn't have the money to go out to lunch.

I handed the telephone to a beaming Ron, who had heard Sid. He bellowed into my startled editor's ear, "I said, 'Fuck him!'"

I took the phone back in time to hear Sid utter a bemused, "Uh, thank you very much, Mr. Hughes."

"Everybody will be coming back from lunch soon," I told Sid. "We should have some more reaction before we get back into the courtroom. I'm sure Paul Fitzgerald (the chief defense attorney) will ask for a mistrial before they bring the jury back in."

I ran back to the pressroom to get the telex with Nixon's full remarks, and then returned to the eighth floor. As the reporters and lawyers began returning I filled them in, showing them the Nixon statement.

By then, of course, Nixon's remarks and his retractions of the remarks were being received by newspapers throughout the country.

In the next day's "night owl" or first edition (Aug. 4, 1970) of The NEWS, Paul Healy's Page 2 story from Denver was headlined "NIXON, IN AD LIB REMARKS, CALLS MANSON A MURDER-ER."

The fourth graf started: "In Los Angeles, where Manson, 35, and three of his girl followers are standing trial for the murders of actress Sharon Tate and six other persons, Ronald Hughes, the defense attorney for one of the accused, Leslie Van Houten, 19, looked shocked when informed by News Correspondent Theo Wilson of Nixon's remarks.

"'President Nixon is a lawyer," said Hughes, 34. "He should know better than that.' He indicated that he and the defense attorneys . . . would seek a mistrial.

"A few minutes later, Hughes added:

"'I am going to make a motion that this case be dismissed. The fact that the President of the United States thinks that it is necessary to comment on the guilt or innocence of the defendants in this murder trial shows that the case has been prejudiced by pre-trial publicity to the point where we cannot get a fair trial.'"

Below this, under a typical NEWS headline: "LINDA FLIPS HER TOUJOURS DEMURE!" was my early trial story sent at lunchtime for that edition, about 1000 words of Linda Kasabian's cross-examination, in which I stated that the star witness had "finally lost her cool" and "for the first time had raised her voice since her cross-examination started" the week before.

By the time the four-star final edition came out, the Nixon-Manson story had become a page one story throughout the country. Our Page 1 headline was: "NIXON BRANDS MANSON KILLER, THEN 'CLARIFIES'; MISTRIAL ASKED."

On Page 2 there was a picture of Hughes and Fitzgerald talking "to newsmen about remarks made by the President", and another of Nixon and Attorney General John Mitchell in Denver as he made his "comments on Manson trial under way in Los Angeles."

Also on Page 2 were three Manson stories: Paul Healy's, now datelined from Washington, "President Calls Manson a Murderer; Then Amends Remark Amid Furor"; Michael McGovern's from Los Angeles (Mike was double-staffing with me at the time) "Defense Demands Mistrial; Judge To Eye Nixon Words"; and mine from Los Angeles, "Kicked Drugs & Manson: Linda", which was more lengthy testimony from Kasabian's cross-examination, added to what had already been sent to make the day's trial story complete.

In that story, I noted that the jurors presumably were the only ones in the courtroom unaware of the flap caused by Nixon's remarks and that no reference was made to it in open court. The mistrial motions, of course, were made with the jury absent.

In Mike's story he wrote that "Manson, sitting in court, read a Daily News telegram of Nixon's remarks during the bench conference on the mistrial motion. His face remained composed. Judge Older then ordered the telegram read into the record."

Then a *L.A. Times* page 1 headline became famous and a part of the trial itself.

The headline read: "MANSON GUILTY, NIXON DECLARES." Charlie saw the newspaper on a chair at the counsel table and held it up so that the jurors could see the headline, and this created a whole mess in the courtroom. When Judge Older learned that Korean-born defense attorney Daye Shinn, known to the press as the "Korean Tiger," was the one who had left the newspaper in the trial room, he sentenced him to three nights in jail for contempt.

After his first night in jail, Shinn kvetched to the judge that he couldn't sleep because the bunk was so narrow he thought he'd fall out of bed. Older suggested he use a two-hour lunch break for a nap.

Shinn was just as unsuccessful the next day, when he told Older that he ought to be allowed to go home to sleep that night because his wife didn't read English and therefore couldn't learn from the newspapers about his incarceration and would think he was with some other woman. The judge ignored Shinn's problem. It was suggested to Shinn that he use a recess to telephone his wife and explain his sudden absence.

Then he had another argument about why he shouldn't have to return to jail after court. He couldn't do a good job for his client, Susan Atkins, he said, because he was exhausted from being "on guard duty" in the jail.

Asked to explain, Shinn told the judge that his cellmates were criminals and he had to be on watch all night, so again he had gone without sleep. Need I say that the Korean Tiger spent the third night in jail?

Later, the *L.A. Times* headline also became famous when The *L.A. Free Press* transposed it to read: "NIXON GUILTY, MANSON DECLARES" and used it that way for a page 1 headline. Of course, we cut that out and posted it in our press room.

All trials are unpredictable, but the Manson trial was filled with more surprises than any other I had covered. The disappearance of Ron Hughes was the one that stunned all of us. Even today, it's

hard to believe that it happened. A lawyer vanishing just before
final arguments were to be heard and the trial was about to conclude? Who could have imagined such a twist? As it turned out,
Ron himself had predicted a disappearance, leaving an eerie message on my typewriter.

The judge had declared a Thanksgiving recess the last ten days
of November 1970; when we returned, the defense and prosecution lawyers were scheduled to give the jurors their final arguments.

Before I took off for New York and we all scattered for the holiday recess, a bunch of us gathered in my hotel room for a little
farewell party, and Ron joined us.

He told us he was going to Sespe Hot Springs so that he could
concentrate on writing his closing statement, the first he had ever
made in his short legal career. He was all excited about it. While
Sandi Mettetal, Mary Neiswender, Linda Deutsch, Bill Farr, Earl
Caldwell, and some others sat around noshing and drinking, Ron
went over to my typewriter and pounded out a "news story"
which I read, stuck away somewhere, and promptly forgot.

Two weeks later, when we came back from the holiday recess,
we learned that Ron had never returned from Sespe. We were told
there had been a flash flood, and it was feared that he had been
caught in it and drowned. But nobody knew.

As soon as we heard about the disappearance, Linda Deutsch
said to me, "Do you remember what Ron wrote in your hotel
room?" I didn't. She said, "Get that story!" and when I found it, we
all reread it together. It gave us goose bumps:

FLASH!!!BULLETIN!!!!
November 18, 1970. A woman who claimed she was the missing Theo Wilson was arrested today . . . for impersonating the famed
columnist. . . . Miss Wilson has been missing since last week when
she failed to show up in her regular seat at the Los Angeles Manson
Trial.

In searching her hotel room Los Angeles police were unable to
find any clues as to her mysterious disappearance.

The FBI, called in because of the fact that Miss Wilson worked
for a New York paper, are dusting a large catnip plant for prints of
possible abductors. . . .

Naples. April 18, 1978. The right honorable Charles Manson
was crowned Pope today in the New Roman See . . . Manson, who
quit Helter Skelter for one year to locate the famed Theo Wilson,

remembered by many for her exciting coverage of the Manson trial
. . . renamed Watson Square Wilson Mall. . . .

With Ron missing, the prosecutor, of course, put out the usual bull that the murderous Manson Family probably had killed Ron on Charlie's orders, speculating that Ron and Charlie had disagreed about the defense. This was nonsense, because Ron was closer to the Family than any of the other lawyers, and there was no reason to harm him. But it always helps to scare the public into thinking that a defendant is so evil and powerful he is capable of ordering murder from behind bars.

The prosecutor also told two Los Angeles reporters whom he disliked that they may have caused Ron to commit suicide because they had influenced a national magazine to publish an article dumping on the defense, and that hurt Ron's feelings. These reporters didn't even work for the magazine, so how they could tell it what to print was not explained by the prosecutor.

The body of the 35-year-old lawyer was not discovered until four months later. He was identified, from dental charts, on the same day the jurors, having found the four Manson defendants guilty, returned verdicts of death for all of them.

That was the same day that Lieutenant William Calley was found guilty of murder in the My Lai massacre. The trials had been running concurrently, and I never forgot a chilling similarity: At the court-martial, when Calley was asked about the My Lai killings, he said, "It was no big deal." At the Manson trial, when Susan Atkins was asked about the Tate killings, she said, "It was no big thing.")

Ron's disappearance was one of the reasons the trial lasted so many months; Leslie Van Houten's new lawyer, Maxwell Keith, needed to familiarize himself with the thousands of pages of trial testimony before he could take over her defense.

During the search for Ron, his family in Englewood, New Jersey began to call me—they had been following the trial in the *News* and knew my byline—and I tried to give them as much information as I could, though it wasn't much.

In early April, 1971, Ron's parents, Anita and John Hughes, came to bury their son in Los Angeles, where he had been born and where his friends were, they told us.

We went to the funeral services with them, and to Westwood Memorial Park (Marilyn Monroe's crypt there had a single fresh rose from Joe DiMaggio in front of it) and tried to comfort them. We all had loved Ron, he was such a good-hearted bear, and maybe it helped them to know it and to be told stories about him, including how he had started buying movie stars' clothing after the MGM auction, showing off $5 suits that had been worn by husky guys like Walter Slezak, Raymond Burr, and Spencer Tracy.

We were always glad that Ron was still with us when Mary, Sandi, Linda, and I threw a trial party that was, like the trial itself, unlike anything else before or since. It was on October 24, 1970 in a suite at the Hilton.

It was a "Helter Skelter Party," and the printed invitations, illustrated with a sketch of Manson by artist Bill Lignante, used some of the catch phrases of the trial.

We called the venue "The Bottomless Pit" (Charlie's proposed desert hiding place when the race war he expected broke out). After the date was, "We have no calendars"; after the time was, "Night is day and day is night and I am you and you are me" (both quotes from the Manson Family philosophy.)

We decorated the suite elaborately with such things as a hotel plant that resembled "Elmer" and a toy replica of Spahn's Ranch, the Manson Family headquarters outside Los Angeles where Charlie and his group lived at the time of the murders.

The judge, defendants, and jurors were about the only ones missing. Nearly everybody except the defense lawyers and prosecutors came dressed up in trial-related outfits.

I was Linda Kasabian, who had been described by the grateful prosecutor as "a little hippie human being," despite the fact that she twice drove the killers to the houses where the murders were performed. I wore a blonde wig with long pigtails and a demure peasant dress, and carried a doll with the name "Tanya" on its tiny headband, representing Linda's daughter, whom she left temporarily at the ranch when she fled after the murders.

Sandi Mettetal, who is tall, came as Juan Flynn, the 6'5" Panamanian part-time actor who gave as his occupation "manure shoveler" at the Spahn Ranch. Linda Deutsch, wearing oversized glasses and carrying a big plastic hamburger, came as myopic Barbara Hoyt, the Family member who was fed an LSD-laced hamburger in Honolulu. Mary Neiswender came as defendant Susan Atkins, aka Sadie "The Snitch" Glutz, in dark "creepy crawlie" clothes over her slacks. (The Manson girls called their black slacks and shirts "creepy crawlies" because they could creep about without being seen in the dark.)

Since we were all dressed like hippies and had cross marks on our foreheads like the defendants and the other Family followers, the Hilton house detective became extremely nervous. As we were setting up the party, he came roaring into the suite and warned us "hippies" he was keeping an eye on us. It seems that a religious group had hired the suite across the hall, and he didn't think they would appreciate our big "Bottomless Pit" sign on the front door, welcoming one and all to free booze and free everything else. It took a couple of calls to the manager to calm down the poor house dick, who was nervously patrolling the corridor as dozens of oddly dressed guests arrived.

The night gave us some release from the truly awful events unfolding every day in the courtroom, letting us laugh in spite of the tragedy that had brought us together. There were certain moments we will never forget. For starters, Ron, who was always hungry, emptied an enormous tray of hors d'ouevres all by himself before most of the other guests arrived. Mary and Linda watched him, faces frozen in horror, their eyes moving in unison from tray to mouth, tray to mouth, as each expensive tidbit disappeared. Ron chatted away all the while, absolutely unaware of the effect his gastronomic feat had on the two hostesses.

The cute costume award went to TV reporter Chuck Boyd and his wife, who arrived at the party handcuffed together. It got cuter when they couldn't figure out how to get the cuffs off, and they were still chained together when they left.

The chief prosecutor and the defense attorneys engaged in a few acrimonious exchanges during the party, but the other prosecutors and everybody else had a great time. It helped us get rid of a lot of pressure. Like all these parties it was for fun. And like all trial parties, it was strictly off the record and not one word about it ever surfaced.

Linda Kasabian was, as I wrote, "a prosecutor's dream witness." When Susan Atkins recanted on her confession and refused to cooperate with the state, the prosecution went after Kasabian, who had fled the ranch after the two murder nights in which she had participated, and she agreed to tell all. It was the luckiest break the state could have gotten.

"In 10 days on the stand," I wrote, "she has been a dramatic, articulate, remorseful, and reformed girl who never forgets to place the blame for seven violent murders right where the state wants it—on Charles (Messiah) Manson, the little man who wasn't there when any of the killings happened."

Without Kasabian's testimony, the state would have had almost no case at all, especially against Charlie, who had not been in the houses when the killings took place and who, the girls insisted, had issued no murder orders.

In return for her testimony, Kasabian was granted immunity and seven murder charges against her were dropped. Of course, if she had decided not to talk, she would have been convicted along with the others; she had driven the gang the first night to Sharon Tate's house, and the next night, even though she knew murders had been committed, she drove them to the Leno LaBianca home where two more killings took place.

Don't ever fault a prosecutor when he has to give a criminal participant immunity. If you want to convict, you sometimes must make deals, and if it hadn't been for Kasabian—the only witness to the murders who would talk—the outconme of this trial could have been different.

Kasabian was near the end of her testimony when she was released from custody and we learned the next morning that she had celebrated her freedom by cooking a spaghetti dinner.

That morning, Saverio LoMedico, a Los Angeles-based correspondent for *La Stampa,* the Turin, Italy newspaper, came into the courtroom late and asked me for a fill-in. I read him my notes of the testimony he had missed, and he listened rather languidly. As an afterthought, I mentioned that we had been told Kasabian had made a spaghetti supper the night before.

LoMedico was galvanized. Spaghetti? She made spaghetti? What kind of pasta was it? With what kind of sauce? I told him I really hadn't thought to ask, and he raced from the trial room.

A few minutes later Bruce Russell of Reuters came in and told me that he had just heard LoMedico on the telephone, excitedly dictating to Italy the big story: In honor of her release from prison, Linda Kasabian had cooked a freedom dinner and for it she had chosen spaghetti with marinara sauce! It was the most excited LoMedico ever got.

*   *   *

After being at the trial for months, I couldn't take seriously the myths about Charlie, his scary eyes, his sexual prowess, and his hypnotic power over others. Once, during a recess when the judge was off the bench and the jury was out of the room, Charlie, sitting alone at the defense table, started muttering. He stared at me, Sandi, Mary, and Linda chatting together and called out something about our karma coming down on us. "Oh, shut up, Charlie!" I snapped at him. The next instant I gasped, "What am I doing, yelling at a defendant? We're going nuts here!"

Sitting behind us was a young reporter on his first day at the trial. He heard what Charlie had said and reported to his wire service that Manson had threatened women reporters covering the trial. We found out about it later when our editors asked why we hadn't mentioned the threats in our reports. Stunned, we all explained that it was just old Charlie yakking, that there was no story. Thank God the kid ran out before he heard me tell the evil defendant to shut up.

Charlie did have a power over the druggies and dropouts who became part of his Family. A lot of them were runaways looking for something, and Charlie gave them what he figured each one wanted. It was the way runty Charlie had survived as an unwanted, neglected kid, and as an inmate in the institutions where he had spent most of his life.

I realized the hold Charlie had on the girls when I heard Patricia Krenwinkel's testimony. Patricia was known in the Manson Family as Katie. She had a hormonal problem that left her body covered with hair. She was not an unloved or neglected child, but when you are a hairy and not-too-pretty girl, no matter how much your parents love you, you want to hear flattery from a young man. Charlie gave her that flattery.

She testified how they met at the beach, how he took her with him, how he told her to take her clothes off and stand naked in front of a mirror, how he told her she was beautiful and made love to her. And that was the end of the normal life of Patricia Krenwinkel. She followed Charlie so fast she never even picked up her last paycheck at the bank where she had a steady job, and she never came home again. I guess with Charlie, and only with Charlie, she was "beautiful." So she did whatever Charlie wanted.

Susan (Sadie Glutz) Atkins was a girl in need of a family, and Manson gave her one. She was in constant need of attention, also, which is why she hinted to a cellmate about the Manson Family's involvement with the Sharon Tate killings, giving the cops the first break in the case. If Susan could have kept her mouth shut, the Tate and LaBianca killings may very well have remained one of the most sensational and frightening mysteries of our times.

The police work on the case was so bad that evidence was being found by TV reporters and other civilians, including a precocious little kid who found one of the Family's guns near his house and turned it over to his father, who notified the authorities. Through some foul-up, nobody came to get it until long after the find was reported.

My room at the Hilton was tiny, with a walk-in closet as its only asset, but it soon became the after-hours press headquarters for both the local and out-of-town reporters, where we could meet after everybody had filed, and have drinks and plan where to go out for dinner.

The prosecutor had already irritated some of the reporters by telling them how to write their stories, and berating them for not recognizing the importance of his work in the courtroom. He also said, in all interviews with him, that he was dedicated so totally to the prosecution of the Manson Family that he had little time for his own family. So we didn't feel concerned about not inviting him to share our after-hours get togethers, although sometimes the other attorneys dropped by.

The hotel added a small bar to my room, and after a while I had so much stuff in Room 905 that it was a true home away from home. Photos and souvenirs were taped to my mirror. Extra glasses and ashtrays covered the dresser. My manual typewriter occupied the dressing table. Vases of flowers cheered up the place.

Maybe that's why I received special treatment after the earth began to shake.

Dates mean absolutely nothing to me and I never remember when anything happened, but the date of the big earthquake is unforgettable. It was February 9, 1971, my son's birthday.

The night before, I had received some strange information. Defense attorney Paul Fitzgerald, who had joined in some of our gab sessions, called me from the hotel lobby. He needed to talk about something very disturbing. Upstairs, he told me he had just come from the Sybil Brand Institute, the women's jail downtown where Krenwinkel, Van Houten, and Atkins were held during the trial.

We now were into the penalty phase of the case, when the jurors, having convicted all four of murder, were hearing testimony to determine life or death for the defendants. Paul told me that the three women, who had never testified, now had decided to take the stand and confess the murders, to "save Charlie." They were going to describe exactly what they had done to the victims, how they had stabbed Sharon as she pleaded for her unborn baby, how they had written *pigs* and other words in blood inside and outside the house.

Paul said neither he nor the two other defense lawyers who were trying to save the women from the gas chamber could dissuade them. Susan Atkins, he said, would be the first to take the stand, to implicate herself and the other two women, and to swear that Charlie had nothing to do with the killings. Fitzgerald said he had spent most of the night arguing, but it was hopeless and he was exhausted.

When he left, I realized it was too late to call anybody, and I figured I would tell my buddies this news first thing in the morning, when we gave each other early wake-up calls.

I went to bed, and the next thing I remember was seeing wild lightning-like flashes outside of my window, and thinking: "My God, the astronauts have fallen on the hotel!" (The Apollo 14 mission was under way, and just the day before I had been talking about covering the early Mercury space shots and how the space program had changed since the old days at Cape Canaveral.)

Then I heard a grinding within the walls, my big bedside lamp started to fall on me, and as I sat up and grabbed it, I saw all of my clothes in my closet suddenly sway up, up, up until the hems were almost vertical to the ground, and then, just as slowly the dresses swung back, back, back to the other side. It was 6 A.M.

The grinding inside the walls was incredible. Just as I thought the room would crack apart, it stopped. I knew it was an earthquake, I had been through another smaller one in Los Angeles the year before.

I was lucky. My room, at the very end of the old section of the hotel, was absolutely untouched. Later I found out that other people couldn't get their doors open, that floors and walls had cracked in their rooms, and that many guests had become hysterical trapped inside.

I also found out the manager's secret. I was the only guest who was not evacuated from the ninth floor and above.

I didn't even know, in fact, that I was all alone on the ninth floor until reporters from throughout the country came flying in to cover the killer quake, and several of them later that night told me they had asked for rooms near mine and were informed that nobody was being housed above the eighth floor.

The manager apparently had discovered there was no earthquake damage in my room and, without bothering me, just went ahead and evacuated everybody else on that floor and above. He must have seen the contents of my household in Room 905. It would have taken weeks just to move me to another floor.

When the first shake stopped, I was lucky enough to get a long distance telephone line. I had planned all along, because of the birthday, to call my son in New York and I got through.

"Delph," I said, "this is mom. Happy happy birthday."

"Thanks ma," he said. "How are you doing?"

"Well, listen carefully," I told him. "You have to do some things for me, okay? We've just had a big earthquake and I don't know how bad it is or anything, but I have to get word to Sid Feingold as soon as possible, and I'm not sure I'll be able to get a long distance line again."

I told my son to tell Sid that I had received information late the night before that Susan Atkins was going on the stand, and for the first time at the trial she would confess to the murders and describe how she killed Sharon Tate and the others.

There was no way I could leave the court to cover the earthquake, when we were going into one of the most dramatic sessions of the trial, and Sid should send another reporter out right away. The earthquake was not a story that was going to go away after a few hours.

We talked a little more, and the very next thing I did was telephone Sandi and Linda to tell them that Susan Atkins was taking the witness stand to confess and describe the murders. Like me, without this information they would have gone to cover the earthquake, which was becoming by now the most important story in the country. The final death tally was 65.

As Al Slagle was flying in from New York for the *News*, along with reporters from all over the country, Sid said he'd use the wire services until Al could file, but meanwhile, if I got the chance, would I write something about my own experience in the earthquake?

Susan, on the stand, not only was admitting the Tate and LaBianca killings, she also said she had killed musician Gary Hinman, a crime for which handsome Bobby (Cupid) Beausoleil, a Manson Family member, was imprisoned.

But she was going through a lot of her background, and this gave me a chance to dash off an earthquake story for the *News'* first edition, which started:

It sounded as if the plaster in the hotel walls was grinding to pieces. The rolling, shaking, pitching of the room seemed endless.

And most horrifying to me, half-sitting in the dark room and holding a huge desk lamp to keep it from crashing onto my bed, was what I thought were lightning bolts outside my ninth-floor windows in the downtown Hilton Hotel.

Lightning isn't supposed to accompany earthquakes, and this is what made me—and hundreds of others, I learned later—believe something worse had happened to the city shortly after 6 a.m.

The brilliant white lights came from power arcs—electricity flashing from transformers heaving during the quake . . .

When I was able to get up and went to my window, lights were flashing in windows all over the hotel. People were running and yelling in the halls, but as I started for my door there was another shake, and I fell onto the bed.

I reached over and put on the all-news radio station. Nothing. I tried to telephone. Nothing.

Then there were the sounds of sirens, fire engines, ambulances, police emergency cars.

By this time there were only a few after shocks and I went for a glass of water. Dark brown water poured out of the faucets. But the lights stayed on, there were no cracks in my room, the hotel was standing.

The news came on and then I was able to telephone New York and get dressed and go to the Hall of Justice for the trial. In the old court building were huge cracks, plaster on the floor, people in little knots . . .

AP reporter Linda Deutsch met me near the trial room. She told me one book had been tossed out of her shelves during the quake. It was the Bible.

And outside the Hall of Justice, Charles Mansons's girls, X-

marks on their foreheads, were proudly telling anyone who would
listen: "Charlie predicted this earthquake. He told us about this two
days ago."

Later that day Linda came over to me and told me she had been
talking to Jules Loh, the AP special feature writer who had flown
in to cover the quake.

"Jules said to tell you," Linda said, "that he read your story, and
he'll buy the brown water coming out of the faucet, and he'll buy
the stuff about Charlie predicting the earthquake—but what's this
crap about Linda Deutsch having a Bible?"

The Hilton was downtown, not too far at that time from the rundown sections of the inner city, and as a walker, I ran into all kinds
of street people.

In those days, the homeless were not as heartbreakingly visible as
they became in the 1980s and 1990s, and the street people I ran into
around the Hilton were eccentric regulars like the man who stood at
bus stops and used a megaphone to yell religious speeches at hapless
passengers who were captive audiences inside the buses.

One old guy used to walk up and down Seventh Street, shouting one sentence over and over. One day he decided to follow me,
and I'll tell you, you haven't suffered until you've scuttled up a
busy street followed by an old coot who keeps shouting "You're a
liar!" at you. That was the one sentence he loved to repeat.

Another time, as I was standing on a corner waiting for the light
to change, a sort of wild-eyed fellow on the opposite corner called
over to me: "Say hello!"

I didn't say anything, but I was the only person on the corner he
was facing, and again this character screamed across to me: "Say
hello!" and again, "Say hello!"

Just then the light changed, and as we started toward each other
I figured I'd make this looney-toon happy and do what he asked.

"Hello," I said to him, as we passed.

"Don't you talk to me!" he screeched, and then, as other people
turned to see what was happening, he screamed again, "Don't you
talk to me! Don't you ever talk to me!" and marched off as everybody glared at me.

Within walking distance of the Hilton was a small market where
I was able to buy fruit and cheese and crackers to set out for the
gatherings in Room 905.

Early on in the trial, as I walked to the market, I passed a vagrant sitting in a little open area that had one bench, one tree, and a lot of pigeons. He was a typical Skid Row denizen: tattered coat held together by a safety pin, unshaven chin, watery eyes, broken-down shoes, straggly hair.

Since somehow I attract street people, I wasn't surprised when this one nodded, got up, and walked into the grocery store the same time I did. He gallantly got a shopping cart for me, and pushed it wherever I went.

He never said a word. Neither did I. As we walked past the wines, he reached over and put into the basket a small bottle of the cheapest wine on the shelf. He looked at me for a reaction, and I just walked on, finishing the shopping.

At the checkout counter, he left the cart and waited for me as I paid. I had the wine put into a small paper bag, and after we left the store, I handed it to him. He went his way and I walked back to the hotel.

From then on, every time I went to the market, which was about once or twice a week, the guy was there and we repeated the whole silent episode—him pushing the cart for me, adding to it a bottle of cheap wine, me paying for it, handing him the bag, and separating outside the store.

One day he wasn't there. I looked up and down the street, but my poor, smelly "private bum," as the other reporters called him, was not in sight. I went into the grocery, got my goodies, and as I pushed the cart to the checkout counter, the clerk there looked up, glanced around, noticed that my usual escort was missing and asked me, "Where's your husband today?"

When you are covering a trial, your life is in another world, encompassed by the courtroom and dominated by everything within it. This unreal world is peopled by the witnesses you meet when they identify themselves in the witness chair. Some of them come and go and are barely remembered, like people you see at a big gathering and forget right away, while others become an important part of this unreal world, either because they are weird (like a lot of the witnesses at the Manson trial) or are so interesting, or unusual, or entertaining, or informative that you remember them a long time, even if you never see them again.

I don't think anybody out in the real world remembers now when Charlie testified, with the jury absent. He was on the stand for two hours, and I took down just about every word.

He rambled, he was sometimes incomprehensible, but considering that he was unlettered, uneducated, deprived of any kind of teaching or exposure to normal educational advantages, his was one of the most astounding speeches I have ever heard from a witness box.

At 5'3", Charlie was a survivor of the prison system; he had learned to survive by telling people what they wanted to hear, and it was this talent that had made him the leader of those poor dumb girls who followed him out to the desert and into madness.

Charlie would never discuss his parents or his birthplace, but the officials said he was born to a teenager, possibly a prostitute, in a small Kentucky town, and that from birth he had been a neglected and unloved runt, kicked around among relatives, foster homes, and finally penal institutions.

When Charlie was sworn in as a witness, to testify at his own request and over the objections of his attorney, the jury was not in the courtroom. Advised that Charlie wanted to talk, and that his defense attorney protested against this, the judge said he would listen to Manson's statements and then determine if this testimony should be heard by his jurors.

Charlie walked to the front of the courtroom, raised his hand as ordered, and while the three women co-defendants sat silently at the defense table, took the oath to tell the truth "so help me God."

Charlie sat down, looked over at Judge Older, said "Hello, God," and began to talk:

> There has been a lot of charges and a lot of things said about me and brought against me and brought against the co-defendants in this case, of which a lot could be cleared up and clarified to where everyone could understand exactly what the Family was supposed to have been.
>
> I have spent my life in jail, and without parents.
>
> I have looked up to the strongest father figure, and I have always looked to the people in the free world as being the good people, and the people in the inside of the jail as being the bad people.
>
> I never went to school, so I never growed up in the respect to learn to read and write too good, so I have stayed in jail and I have stayed stupid, and I have stayed a child while I have watched your world grow up, and then I look at the things that you do and I don't understand.
>
> I don't understand the courts and I don't understand a lot of

the things that are brought against me.

You write things about my mother in the newspaper that hasn't got anything to do with anything in particular. You invent stories, and everybody thinks what they would do, and then they project it from the witness stand on the defendant as if that is what he did. . . .

I don't think like you people. You people put importance into your lives. Well, my life has never been important to anyone, not even in the understanding of the way you fear the things you fear and the things that you do.

I cannot understand you, but I don't try. I don't try to judge nobody. I judge what I have done and I judge what I do and I live with myself every day.

I am content with myself.

If you put me in the penitentiary, that means nothing because you kick me out of the last one. I didn't ask to be released. I liked it in there because I like myself. I like being with myself.

But in your world, it's hard because your understanding and your values are different.

These children that come at you with knives, they are your children. You taught them, I didn't teach them. I just tried to help them stand up.

Most of the people at the ranch that you call the Family were just people that you did not want, people that were alongside the road, that their parents had kicked them out or they did not want to go to Juvenile Hall, so I did the best I could and I took them up on my garbage dump and I told them this, that in love there is no wrong. . . .

You make your children what they are. I am just a reflection of every one of you. . . .

I have killed no one and I have orderd no one to be killed. I don't place myself in the seat of judgment.

I may have implied on several occasions to several different people that I may have been Jesus Christ, but I haven't decided yet what I am or who I am.

I was given a name and a number and I was put in a cell, and I have lived in a cell with a name and a number.

I don't know who I am. I am whoever you make me, but what you want is a fiend, a sadistic fiend because that is what you are. You only reflect on me what you are, inside of yourselves. . . .

My father is the jail house. My father is your system. . . .

No matter how crowded you may think you are in a room with a lot of people, you are still by yourselves and you have to live with that self forever and ever and ever. To some people that would be hell; to some people it would be heaven. I have mine, and each of you will have to work out yours, and you cannot work out by pointing your fingers at people.

I have ate out of your garbage cans to stay out of jail.

I have wore your secondhand clothes.

I have give everything I have away, everything.

I have done my best to get along in your world and now you want to kill me, and I look at you, and look how incompetent you all are, and then I say to myself, "You want to kill me, ha, I'm already dead, have been all my life."

I've lived in your tomb that you built.

I did seven years for a $37 check. I did 12 years because I didn't have any parents, and how many others do you think you have in there? You have many sons in there, many many sons in there, most of them are black and they are angry. . . .

Sometimes I'm thinking about just jumping on you and let you shoot me. Sometimes I think it would be easier than sitting here and facing you in the contempt that you have for yourself, the hate that you have for yourself, it's only the anger you reflect on me. . . .

I don't dislike you, I cannot dislike you, I am you. You are my blood. You are my brother, That is why I can't fight you. If I could I would jerk this microphone off and beat your brains out with it because that is what you deserve. Every morning you eat that meat with your teeth. You are all killers. You kill things better than you, and what can I say to you that you don't already know? . . .

I live in my world and I am my own king in my world, whether it be a garbage dump or in the desert, I am my own human being. You may restrain my body and you may tear my guts out..do anything you wish. But I am still me and you can't take that . . . you cannot kill the soul. . . .

We have to find ourselves first, and second kind—k-i-n-d— comes next, and that is all I was doing, I was working on cleaning up my house, something Nixon should have been doing. He should have been on the side of the road picking up his children, but he wasn't. He was in the White House, sending them off to war. . . .

I survived 25 years in every torture chamber you have in this country, and I survived by bringing the good out in each human being I meet. . . .

I have done the best I knew how, and I have given all I can give and I haven't got any guilt about anything because I have never been able to see any wrong.

I never found any wrong. I looked at wrong and it is all relative. Wrong is if you haven't any money. Wrong is if your car payment is overdue. Wrong is if the TV breaks. Wrong is if President

Kennedy is killed. . . .

I don't care what you think about me and I don't care what you do with me. I have always been yours anyway. I have always been in your cell.

When you were out riding your bicycle I was sitting in your cell looking out the window and looking at pictures in magazines and wishing I could go to high school and go to the prom, wishing I could go to the things you could do, but oh so glad, oh so glad, brothers and sisters, that I am what I am.

Because when it does come down around your ears and none of you know what you are doing, you better believe I will be on top of my thought. I will know exactly what I am doing . . . In my mind I live forever, and in my mind I have always lived forever. . . .

I have not broken your rule because I learned a lesson a long time ago, this man (pointing to Judge Older) is God. If you don't believe he is God you stand up in the courtroom and he will show you. He is the most powerful thing in the face of this earth, and I accept this power because I have no power greater than his. . . .

Charlie spoke on, describing the prosecutor, Vincent Bugliosi, as a genius and a lawyer who had everything except a case and "were I allowed to defend myself, I could have proven this to you. . . .But I am inadequate in education . . . so I am forced to sit here and just ramble on. . . .

Describing prosecution witness Linda Kasabian, he said:

You set her up here to be a hero, and that is your woman. That is the thing that you worship. You have lost sight of God. You sing your songs to women. You put women in front of men.

Woman is not God. Woman is but a reflection of her man.

But a lot of times, man is a reflection of his woman. And if a man can't rise above a woman's thought, then that is his problem. It is not my problem. But you give me this problem when you set this woman against me.

You set this woman up here to testify against me. And she tells you a sad story, how she has only taken every narcotic that it is possible to take. She has only stolen, lied, cheated, and done everything that you have out there in the book.

But it is okay. She is telling the truth now. She is telling the truth now. She wouldn't have any ulterior motive like immunity for seven counts of murder. . . .

Referring to the court-martial of Lt. Calley, Manson said of the soldiers in Vietnam: "We train them to kill, and they go over and kill, and we prosecute them and put them in jail because they kill. . . . If you can understand it, then I bow to your understanding." Then Charlie got back to his own case:

I look at the jury and they won't look at me. So I wonder why they won't look at me. I look at them. Have they judged me already?

Before the case was presented they would not look at me. They are afraid of me, and do you know why they are afraid of me? Because of the newspapers.

You projected fear. You made me a monster. And I have to live with that the rest of my life because I cannot fight this case.

If I could fight this case, and I could present this case, I would take that monster back and I would take that fear back. Then you could find something else to put your fear in, because it's all your fear.

You look for something to project it on, and you pick a little old scrawny nobody that eats out of a garbage can, that nobody wants, that was kicked out of the penitentiary, that has been dragged through every hell hole you can think of, and you drag him and put him into a courtroom.

You expect to break me? Impossible. You broke me years ago, you killed me years ago. . . .

I went to jail when I was eight years old and I got out when I was 32. I have never adjusted to your free world. I am still that stupid, corn picking country boy that I always have been. . . . You can send me to the penitentiary; it's no big thing. I've been there all my life anyway.

But what about your children? . . . there is many many more coming in the same direction; they are running in the streets and they are coming right at you.

Allowed to cross-examine Manson, again over repeated objections from defense attorney Irving Kanarek, the prosecutor concluded by asking Charlie, "You testified you wanted to go back to the desert with your children, is that right?"

Kanarek: I object, your Honor.

Manson: That is a very good question. I wouldn't object to it.

Older: State your objection.

Kanarek: On the ground that it is a solicitation of a conclusion. What he testified to is in the record.

Older: Overruled. Proceed.

Kanarek: I have another point to make, your Honor.

Older: Sit down, Mr. Kanarek, and remain seated until the next question is asked.

Bugliosi: Is that right, you want to go back to the desert with your children?

Manson: I would like to be a good father and do what my children would like me to do.

Bugliosi: Who are your children?

Manson: Everyone that loves me. Anyone that will return my love.

Bugliosi: Mr. Manson, are you willing to testify in front of the jury and tell them the same things you testified to here in open court today?

Manson: Tell them the same things? . . . Do you know how impossible that would be?

Older: You may step down, sir.

The judge then asked the three women defendants if they wanted to testify and all said no. He asked Charlie if he wanted to speak in front of the jury, and Charlie asked: "Your Honor, is it possible that we could read that (the entire testimony he had given) back to the jury? . . . To repeat what I said would be like I didn't even say it. You know, to repeat it over twice.

Older: I am asking you if you want to testify before the jury.

Manson: Testify before the jury? I have already relieved all the pressure I had.

Older: You don't want to testify, is that right?

Manson: Your Honor, I would mostly like to get it over with, one way or the other.

Older: Answer the question, sir. I am trying to find out what you want to do. Do you want to testify in front of the jury?

Manson: I'd like to offer a whole defense.

Older: Well, I understand your answer to be that you do not want to testify.

Manson: This testimony doesn't count?

And that is where this session ended.

Manson never spoke to the jurors, they were unaware he had even taken the stand (they were sequestered and newspapers, TV and radio news was censored by their guards) and we often wondered if it would have made any difference had they been able to listen to Charlie under oath.

I personally think nothing would have been changed. I think that no matter what Manson told them, the jurors would have sentenced him to death with the three women, as they did after the penalty phase. (The death sentences were changed to life imprisonment during that period when death was outlawed by the U.S. Supreme Court.)

The Manson case, to this day, remains one of the most chilling in crime history. And as Charlie predicted, to the world he has remained a monster. Even people who were not yet born when the murders took place know the name Charles Manson, and shudder.

11

The Queen of the SLA

I have a wonderful souvenir from the Patty Hearst trial in San Francisco. It is a cartoon by *News* artist Joe Papin, and it shows Patty, wearing a crown, merrily waving a scepter, and smiling toothily from inside a garbage can borne by two grinning gunmen.

"Queen of the SLA," Joe entitled this cartoon, his goodbye gift to me at the end of Patty's bank robbery trial. No cameras were allowed inside the federal court where it was held, so Joe had been sent out to illustrate the stories I filed.

At the trial we were told that when Patty was kidnapped by the Symbionese Liberation Army and was being sought by the FBI, she was moved by her kidnappers from safe house to safe house hidden inside a garbage can, scared to death. That was before she opted to stay with the SLA, having become, as the prosecution explained it, enamored of the dangerous and exciting radical life she had so unwillingly been dragged into. It sure beat making casseroles for her lover Stevie Weed at Berkeley.

Her title came from one of the psychiatrists who testified for the prosecution. He said he believed the heiress had become a dedicated member of the SLA. She was exhibited as their superstar convert, in effect becoming "The Queen of the SLA."

Joe's cartoon, showing a garbage can converted into a royal carriage, told better than any words what Patricia Hearst really is. She is a survivor, the queen of survivors.

She survived the kidnapping by the self-styled "soldiers" of the

SLA, who dragged the screaming teenager from the Berkeley apartment she shared with her professor boyfriend. She survived life with the SLA, changing her name to Tania, robbing a bank, toting a gun, issuing vitriolic anti-establishment statements with the rest of them. She survived a police fire-bombing that killed nearly everybody else in the SLA; she survived nearly two years hiding out as the FBI hunted her as an indicted fugitive, and eluding newspaper reporters trying to find her so they could have the scoop of the century. And when she was finally caught, she was allowed to plead no contest and walk away from weapon charges in Los Angeles that could have sent her to prison for life, and after being tried and convicted in San Francisco of armed bank robbery, she was released early from prison, thanks to a commutation from President Jimmy Carter.

Another souvenir: I opened my mail not too long ago, and there was a newspaper photo of Patty, now a housewife and mother (she married one of her former bodyguards) taken at some gala. She is wearing gorgeous long pearls, her head is thrown back, she is laughing, she looks great. Across the top of the photo, Ronnie Claire Edwards, the actress who mailed it to me, had written: "Little Tania, happy at last!"

"Blow in My Ear, I'll Follow You Anywhere" we titled a musical we wrote about her, watching her change from tough Tania, underground soldier, to subdued Patricia, victimized heiress.

She was one interesting kid when she was out there, first as kidnap victim, then as SLA "soldier" Tania, and finally as militant prisoner, giving us a grin and a clenched-fist salute and signing herself into jail as a "self-employed urban guerilla" the day she was arrested.

Once in jail, she was Tania long enough to demand a feminist lawyer, and to confide to her best friend Trish Tobin, in a taped jailhouse conversation filled with bravado and gutter language, how "pissed off" she was at being caught, and to promise her, "When I get out, man, there are stories I can tell you!"

The jury heard this jailhouse tape at the very end of the trial, after the defense lost a bitter fight to keep it away from them, and it clinched Patty's conviction.

Trish had testified that her poor friend could barely talk to her in jail, was almost inaudible; but then the jurors heard the tape, I could tell from their faces they were offended by the two girls' excited laughter and the vulgarity of their language. Patty tried to explain this away by testifying that she laughed and talked the way she did only because SLA member Emily Harris was nearby and she was afraid of Emily. Unfortunately, the prosecution produced jail records showing that Harris was locked up in another part of the jail.

Whether Patty ever told Trish those stories we'll never know, because Patty dropped the Tania role and quit talking tough as soon as it was made plain that the Hearst millions would not be used to defend a loud-mouthed feminist revolutionary. Patty's folks, especially her very proper mother, were not going to accept the fact that Patty's mouthings as Tania—she called the Hearsts "pigs and clowns"—were voluntary. Patty dropped her request for a feminist lawyer, forgot her status as self-employed urban guerilla, and went along with the family's choice, the celebrated F. Lee Bailey. Patty even changed her hair color (from brassy dyed red to Hillsborough deb brown) to try to convince her jurors that every single rotten thing she said and did with the SLA was done only because she was in terror of the SLA, only because her life was in danger every minute of the time she was with the SLA.

Unfortunately, that did not explain for the jurors why the defense claimed Patty was brainwashed. If she had been brainwashed she would have agreed with the SLA and gone along with them. Someone who is brainwashed doesn't need to be threatened with death, as Patty claimed she was. Thus, her testimony about continual terror was contradictory.

There were other unanswered questions: Why did Patty took the Fifth when asked about a certain period of her underground life? Why did she empty two guns from a van parked outside a Los Angeles sporting goods store to rescue fellow SLA member Bill Harris from arrest as a shoplifter? Why didn't she leave San Francisco and just go home to nearby Hillsborough once the SLA (except for Bill and Emily Harris and Patty herself) had been exterminated in a fire bombing by the Los Angeles police? And why didn't she even once send a card, a note, to her parents just to tell them she was alive and well?

Patty was advised, wrongly as it turned out, that the only way she was going to escape prison was to repudiate everything she had done as Tania. And being Patty, by the time the trial was over she apparently hated the SLA and everybody in it who had gotten her into this mess, even Willie Wolfe, the young man known as Cujo who Patty grieved for in a moving farewell speech she released after the fire-bombing that killed him and the others.

She hated him, she told prosecutor James Browning, and she swore to her jurors that she had said all those beautiful things about Cujo after he died only because she was in fear of her life from Bill and Emily Harris.

How could Patty and her defense team know that Browning would tell the jurors, as part of his successful prosecution, that when Patty was arrested in San Francisco, she still carried in her purse the Olmec Mexican monkey carving that Cujo had given her when they became lovers in the SLA? Or that Browning would remind the jurors that Patty had mentioned this little souvenir in her public tribute to Cujo, saying that he had a similar one on his body in the ashes of the Los Angeles house where he died?

Later, some of us asked Bailey's co-counsel, Al Johnson, why, if Patty hated Willie so much, she was carrying around his gift a year after he died. Poor jolly Al—he tried. Patty had kept Willie's gift with her, long after Willie was killed, Al told us with a straight face, because she was an "art lover."

It was on February 4, 1974, a few weeks before her twentieth birthday, that the publishing heiress was kidnapped by a band of underground revolutionaries made up of white, middle-class, anti-establishment young men and women, with one black man, ex-convict Donald DeFreeze (known as Cinque) as their proclaimed leader.

Two years to the day later, the U.S. Attorney prosecuting Patty made his opening statement in a huge, packed courtroom and said he would prove that Patty had been a willing bank robber named Tania when she was photographed, gun in hand, at the scene of the crime.

Because of what had transpired during those two years, this was a case unlike any ever tried before. And there never will be one like it again.

The press coverage was massive. Even Adela Rogers St. John, that legendary Hearstling, came to cover a portion of the trial, making big news by her very appearance. As had been her wont at all the big trials in recent decades, she told us, "This is *not* the trial of the century. That was the kidnapping of the Lindbergh baby!"

I understood Adela's fixation, because Charles Lindbergh was an American hero whose solo trans-Atlantic flight had captured the imagination of the world. There had never been anybody quite like the lanky, shy, boyish Lindbergh before; his historic feat had brought joy and great pride to his fellow Americans, and he was as famous as any of today's movie megastars. His marriage to an ambassador's daughter was big news, as was the birth of their first son. The disappearance of that beautiful little boy and the eventual discovery of his body was a worldwide tragedy, culminating in a trial of the alleged kidnapper, which Adela and every other writing star of that time had covered. To Adela it remained the one big trial of all time.

But the Patty Hearst story was more than an internationally sensational kidnapping. The Hearst case was remarkable because it exposed every facet of our society as it was in the 1960s and 1970s. In criminal history, it was unique.

This was a case that could have happened only in the United States of that time. It involved the very rich, the very poor, the middle class, the famous, the unknown, the establishment, Vietnam protesters, the militant underground, blacks, whites, prisoners, sports figures, church leaders, liberals, reactionaries, revolutionaries.

If it had just been the kidnapping of a wealthy girl from a famous family by criminals demanding the customary ransom, it would have been a great but predictable story, and of interest mainly to those people rich enough to have to fear such criminal threats.

But how many poor people, how many middle class, how many radicals, how many blacks would have followed it with the fascination that the Hearst case evoked, with its poverty food program, its SLA membership of black ex-convicts, feminists, and disenchanted white middle-class college graduates, its scathing communiques from Patty, spewing that mixture of idealism and anger so typical of those times?

This was a story that never quit. Every time we thought it had died down, some dramatic and unexpected event broke and Patty was once again front-page news.

First, the kidnapping: College student Patty of the famous Hearst family torn out of the apartment she shared at Berkeley with Weed, who fled, unable to save her. Then the first comminque declaring that Patty was a prisoner of war of the SLA. After that, the mind-boggling ransom demand ordering Randolph Hearst, Patty's father, to use the Hearst millions to set up a food giveaway for the poor. Next, the announcement that Patty had been offered her freedom, and had refused, and Patty's own declaration that she was rejecting her family, had taken the name Tania, and had become an SLA soldier. Then the bank robbery, featuring Tania photographed in full battle gear inside a branch of the bank owned by the family of her longtime friend, Trish Tobin. The revelation that Patty had used guns to protect her SLA companions at a Los Angeles store, and then a fiery police raid on live TV made more horrendous by the fear that Patty was among those dying in that raid. Next a very moving taped eulogy from Patty mourning her dead comrades, particularly her lover Cujo, and finally the disappearance of the heiress who had turned into a law-breaking, gun-toting revolutionary.

From that federal courtroom in San Francisco I wrote thousands and thousands of words about the Patty Hearst case, and still people say to me, "Tell us about the Hearst trial."

I know what they want.

They want me to describe things I saw but never wrote about when I was covering the trial, unimportant but interesting things I didn't put into the newspaper because at that time I needed the space to write what Patty Hearst said, how she looked when she was testifying, what the jury was doing as she spoke, how the prosecutor cross-examined her, and how the defense attorney tried to protect her.

I tell them: the Hearsts never touched each other.

Catherine, the newspaper publisher's wife who loathed the press, and Randolph, the courteous gentleman who seemed more a hapless victim than Patty, sat near their daughter's defense table, in the first row of courtroom spectators. Sometimes another of their daughters sat with them.

There never was, during those long long weeks, a spontaneous gesture of affection, a hug, a kiss, a hand reached for and held tightly. They were living through the same nightmare, but they could not share its terrors. The ritual of the Tic-Tac was their only communication.

Each day Mrs. Hearst would reach into her purse and then hand around the small plastic case of Tic-Tacs. They would take some of the spicy little refreshers, pop them into their mouths, and return to their space capsules.

Maybe Mrs. Hearst had decided she would not allow the reporters the satisfaction of writing anything juicy about her. Maybe she was trying to play the role of a Jackie Kennedy: the noble, tragic, disciplined great lady who did not weep or scream or moan like some vulgar peasant.

But Catherine Hearst was no Jackie Kennedy. Jackie, with her remarkable sense of style, was one of the few women in this world who could carry off that aristocratic role and evoke universal admiration. And Jackie, as all of us saw and remembered, touched her children during the funeral; she made it plain she always knew they were there.

So in her efforts not to be common, Catherine Hearst became a stone in that courtroom, tight-mouthed, bitter, hostile to reporters who once had nothing but compassion for her. She was a lady, damn it, and no "ghouls"—her own word for the reporters, including those who worked on her husband's newspaper—were going to see her make a display of herself.

One time she fled the courtroom in tears, a few minutes before the doors were locked so that Judge Oliver Carter could read the charge to the jurors at the end of the trial. Later she said, "I'm afraid I chickened out. I didn't do too well," as if weeping from tension and worry over her child was some kind of flaw.

When the verdict was returned, Patty's sister Anne was sitting with her parents, and when she heard the clerk say "Guilty" she began to cry and then, as if she suddenly realized what was happening to her sister, to her, to her family, she crumpled forward, her face in her hands, weeping so piteously that I felt a sick clutch in my stomach.

Mrs. Hearst, sitting next to her, stared straight ahead. She did not look at Anne, turn to her, or make one motion of quiet comfort, not even to pat her knee. But I saw her lips move; she was whispering something to her daughter.

Later, a reporter who had been sitting behind her, told me what she had said. "Stop it, Anne. They are looking at us."

She didn't start out that way. When Patty was first kidnapped, I didn't go to the Hearst estate in Hillsborough. I stayed first in Berkeley, the scene of the kidnapping, and then at the Federal Courthouse in San Francisco waiting for the SLA tapes, but the reporters on the chilly, round-the-clock stakeout at Hillsborough often spoke of the kindness and cooperation of the grieving Mrs. Hearst.

The Hearsts put up graciously with the crush of newspeople on their grounds, and had used them to make public appeals to the kidnappers. During the stakeout the reporters had telephones installed on the estate, and one of the few jokes during those first anxious days was for one reporter to yell to another, "Hey Jack! Your tree is ringing."

Cookies and coffee and hot soup were brought out by the Hearsts' cook during those early days when we were writing only about the brutal kidnapping, the pleas from the parents, the demands of the SLA, and Patty's first plaintive tapes.

But after the bank robbery; the release of Patty's pictures with the SLA; her announcement that she had become a revolutionary and did not want to return to her former life; her caustic tapes denouncing her mother, her father, her fiance Steve Weed, and "the pigs and clowns" of the establishment, Mrs. Hearst began to hate the messengers. It was as if she blamed the media for writing all of the terrible things that were happening.

I never spoke with Catherine Hearst, nor ever saw any need to after she indicated she wanted nothing to do with us once Patty's status changed from kidnap victim to indicted bank robber and fugitive. Walking down the courtroom aisle one day during the trial, I reached the gate that separates the well of the court from the public section and began to walk through to get to the jury box where some of us were assigned seats. (The jurors sat in the main jury box way across the room from us in the huge courtroom.)

Mrs. Hearst started through at the same time and as I stepped aside for her, this woman I had never met or talked to shot a look at me out of blue eyes blazing with such hatred that I froze. We never looked each other in the face again, and I never forgot that icy stare.

Randolph Hearst was a man in torment, but he had manners. He never failed to greet by name his own reporters from the *San Francisco Examiner*, he would join us for a smoke sometimes during short breaks outside the trial room, he posed in the corridor for the *News* artist, and he would nod if he caught your eye when we first entered the courtroom.

He was such a decent man, in fact, that when a guest house at Hearst Castle was bombed during the trial, Rosalie Ritz, the multi-talented artist-sculptor who was drawing the trial for TV, felt bad for him and wanted to say something nice.

As she passed him getting to her seat, she told him: "I'm really sorry about the bombing, Mr. Hearst. I hope your castle is okay." She told us later that as soon as the words popped out, she realized that this was just about the weirdest condolence she had ever offered anybody.

We all agreed that having a castle bombed was not your every-day problem, and that Rosalie had done the best she could under the circumstances. There were certainly no sympathy cards in the stores saying "Sorry about the bombing" or "In sympathy for your castle."

It was this bombing, and others before and during the trial, that convinced me that San Francisco was a violent city under that facade of beauty and elegance—much more so than Los Angeles, which was more dingbat than murderous. In Los Angeles nobody paid much attention to the infrequent bomb threats we would get while working at the various courthouses, but in San Francisco, when the deputies came up to the press room one noon and ordered us out of the building because of a bomb scare, everybody scrammed. Everybody, that is, except Linda Deutsch in the AP office and me at the *News* desk.

When the rest of the corps returned (there was no bomb) they were horrified that Linda and I had stayed behind.

"Are you crazy?" Rosalie yelled. "Don't you know that they're not kidding around up here?"

When we told Rosalie that nobody paid attention to that stuff in L.A., she reminded us that we were in San Francisco now, and the radicals in the Bay area weren't playing when they sent bomb threats.

Sure enough, the underground blew up a few places while we were there, and the next time we were ordered out of the court-house on a bomb threat, we out-of-towners dropped everything and ran out just as fast as everybody else.

*   *   *

They say: tell us about the Hearst trial.

I tell them there was this secret jailhouse tape of a conversation with Patty and her parents on the day she was arrested in San Francisco. Although she wet her pants in fright when the FBI grabbed her, she recovered enough on the ride to jail to give the smile and clenched-fist salute that hit the front pages of newspapers everywhere.

This tape was never used at the trial. Some of us heard it after the trial was over, but nobody wrote about it. The conversation on that tape revealed a mother and a daughter who were totally out of touch with each other, and a father/husband who was trying to keep the peace.

This was the parents' first meeting in 19 months with the kidnapped child, but it was no warm, emotion-choked reunion. It was understandably not the most joyous of meetings; even so, it was so brittle.

Randolph Hearst was evidently walking on eggs, trying not to upset his irritable and nervous daughter. (Later, when Patty's two younger sisters visited her in jail, they said they felt as if they were "on thin ice . . . we kept changing the subject if things were getting tense . . . we didn't want to make her defensive.")

At this first reunion with her daughter, Catherine Hearst acted as if brassy-haired Tania was still Hillsborough deb Patty, and she talked about history books and clothes, quickly driving Tania/Patty right up the jailhouse wall.

At one point, when Randolph left the room to get some information, Catherine said that she would bring Patty a book she had just been reading which she thought her daughter would also enjoy. I think it was a book on the history of art, I have forgotten the title. In any case it held no appeal for revolutionary-feminist Tania, and she told her mother she didn't want it. Catherine persisted, and again Patty said, impatiently, she didn't want the book. Catherine still thought it would be a good idea, and through gritted teeth Patty said, "Mother! I don't want it!" at which point Randolph returned and moved the conversation into smoother waters. The book Patty did ask for, and got from a friend, was *Ruby Fruit Jungle* by Rita Mae Brown, which is about as far from an art history book as you can get.

Months later, when Mrs. Hearst testified in her daughter's

defense, she told the jurors that she and Patty "shared a mutual enthusiasm for art, so we always had a great deal in common."

We had learned that even before the kidnapping Patty thought her ultra-conservative, Old South mother was hopelessly out of tune with the world, and friends said that her imitations of Mrs. Hearst were hilarious.

As a young girl living in the South, Mrs. Hearst had been one of the pretty but naive belles who had tried out for the part of Scarlett O'Hara during the big "talent search" below the Mason-Dixon line that was part of the publicity hype for *Gone With The Wind*.

She was a practicing Catholic as well as a Southern lady, and so we wondered how she had handled Patty's affair with Steve Weed, with whom Patty moved in when she was 17.

Even though it was no fault of his, Steve's inability to save Patty from the kidnappers must have rankled. The Hearsts would have been more than human if they did not, even subconsciously, blame him for escaping while Patty was being torn out of their lives.

Steve stayed with the Hearsts at Hillsborough for a short time after the kidnapping to help the FBI agents who had moved in while waiting for the first ransom demands, and we were told that Mrs. Hearst couldn't stand him.

Somebody told us, that at one point, Mrs. Hearst lashed out at the generation of young men embodied by Steve Weed: "Why are there no more Rhett Butlers in this world?" she said. That sort of indicated where her head was at while Patty was sending "Greetings to the people. This is Tania. . . . I would never choose to live the rest of my life surrounded by pigs like the Hearsts. . . . Patria muerte . . . Venceremos! Death to the Fascist Insect that Preys Upon the Life of the People."

They say: tell us about the Patty Hearst trial, and I tell them how we had watched Patty shrink from a mouthy urban guerilla to a withdrawn Hillsborough deb, giving names to the FBI of people who had tried to help her when she was a fugitive, and telling what she tried to do to Steve Soliah, the young house painter she had been living with in San Francisco when the FBI caught her.

Soliah was on a job when he heard that Emily and Bill Harris, who lived several miles away, had been arrested, and instead of taking off to save his own skin, he raced back to the house he was sharing with Patty to warn her.

He was too late. By the time Soliah arrived, the FBI had arrested Patty and their other housemate, Wendy Yoshimura, the house was crawling with agents, and he was taken into custody, since he had been harboring a fugitive.

Then Soliah was charged with committing a bank robbery in Sacramento in 1975, during which a woman customer had been shot to death.

The "missing year" in Patty's underground life was 1975. She refused during her trial to answer any questions about that time, invoking the Fifth Amendment 42 times, even refusing the trial judge's orders to answer under threat of contempt.

There was a good reason for her silence. Patty, the Harrises, and other SLA members were living in Sacramento at the time of the bank robbery and fatal shooting, and as was brought out at the Soliah trial, the SLA was involved in that bank robbery and murder.

At his own trial in Sacramento, which took place after Patty's conviction, Soliah insisted he was not an SLA member and had not been involved in the robbery. He admitted that he had befriended Patty when she was a fugitive, they had become lovers, he was helping to support her while she remained underground in San Francisco during the months before her arrest. The jury believed him and acquitted him.

We learned that Patty, through her defense attorneys, had offered to become a government witness and would testify that Soliah had been stationed outside the bank during the robbery as a lookout.

The U.S. prosecutors in Sacramento turned down Patty's offer, which would have contradicted government witnesses who placed Soliah inside the bank at the time of the robbery. Unofficially, they told us they didn't want Patty to testify for the prosection because she was not a credible witness. Officially, they said they rejected the offer because "there is a rational reason for disbelieving a woman who wants to look out for her boyfriend . . . who gave up his own life and what he was doing to look after her best interests."

Since Soliah swore he was not even in Sacramento during the fatal bank robbery—testimony that the Soliah jurors ended up believing—Patty's offer to tell his jurors that he was one of the lookouts outside of the bank didn't seem all that friendly to the defense. As Soliah's attorney, Sheldon Otis, noted, "With friends like that Mr. Soliah doesn't need enemies."

If the U.S. attorney in Sacramento had accepted Patty's offer and called her as a prosecution witness, he would have put himsel in a very odd position.

He would have had to try to convince the Soliah jurors that they should believe everything Patty told them, while only a month earlier his colleague, the U.S. attorney in San Francisco, had succeeded in convincing her own jurors that she was a liar. Patty's lawyers were trying to make points with the government, but, like her defense strategy at the trial, it just didn't work.

When I first learned about the kidnapping and was preparing to leave Los Angeles for Berkeley, I called Mary Neiswender, then the top investigative reporter for the *Long Beach Independent Press-Telegram*, to see if she was going north on the story.

She wasn't, but she told me to ask the cops in Berkeley about a radical militant group that I had never heard of before, something I spelled "Cymbionese Liberation Army" in the first story I dictated to the *News* before grabbing a plane.

In Berkeley, the cops became intensely interested when I asked them if the "Cymbionese Liberation Army" was involved, telling me nothing while demanding to know what I knew, which was nothing. But their reaction tipped me off that Mary was on to something, and pretty soon I got the name straight and had learned more about the Symbionese Liberation Army than I ever wanted to know.

I remember with what excitement we received the first word from the SLA after the kidnapping, how we studied the tape, pored over it, and how the newspapers, including the *News*, obeyed the SLA command: "All communications from this court MUST be published in full in all newspapers, and all other forms of the media. Failure to do so will endanger the safety of the prisoner."

Every word of the first SLA communiques was news, and every word was used. The SLA had a worldwide forum.

We didn't have to be urged to use the first SLA communiques in full: the kidnapping—followed by the revelation that Patty was being held by a radical group as a "prisoner of war," followed by the SLA demand that the Hearsts provide $70 worth of food for every needy person in California—had become a sensational news story throughout the United States and abroad.

(California's governor, Ronald Reagan, demonstrated the compassion he was to later show his fellow Americans who were hungry or needy. When the Hearsts tried to comply and organized a $2 million food giveaway in San Francisco, Reagan said of the crowds that came that he hoped they would all come down with botulism.)

The *News*, thank God, sent Alton Slagle out from New York to double-staff with me. The SLA tapes came at all hours, and since our last deadline in New York was midnight in California, Al and I were stuck every night in the press room on the top floor of the Federal Courthouse.

We stayed there because the FBI agents were on duty all night in the same building, and we could check quickly for new information. It was the FBI that released copies of the SLA communiques to all of us, and those communiques could come at any time.

The reporters assigned to the Federal Courthouse beat by the the wire services and the local newspapers could knock off and go home at the end of each day, since there were staffs on night-shift duty at their main offices to watch the Hearst story, but Al and I had to wait through the night, just in case anything broke before the *News* went to bed.

The press room in the San Francisco Federal Courthouse is one of the most handsome in the country, with a gorgeous view from a wall of windows overlooking downtown San Francisco. It has a refrigerator and sink and stove, and many cabinets painted in earth tones.

The beat regulars at that time—Tom Hall of the *Examiner*, Bernie Hurwitz of AP, Don Thackery of UPI, Bill Bancroft of the *Oakland Tribune*, Bill Cooney of the *Chronicle*, and Phil Hager of the *L.A. Times*—adopted me into their press room, allowing me to install our own *News* desk and telephones.

One night, fatigued from our 15-hour days and more than a little stir-crazy, Al and I amused ourselves by making up our own SLA tape. This was when Patty still was making frightened pleas to her parents, urging them to get her home as quickly as possible. The tape was more prophetic than we guessed.

Al took the part of nonstop talker Cinque, the SLA leader, who had announced in an early communique, "I hold the rank of general field marshal in the United Federated Forces of the Symbionese Liberation Army."

I took Patty's role, but I made her a revolutionary, a member of the SLA, kvetching to Cinque that I was sick and tired of sitting in the kitchen stuffing bullets with cyanide—I wanted to get out there and shoot like everybody else. Al, as Cinque, made pronouncements, issued orders, and kept telling Patty to "shut up, woman, and stuff those bullets."

The next day we played it for the reporters in the press room. They thought our tipsy tape was hilarious, if far out. But it all came true when a communique from Patty announced to the world that she had become Tania, soldier of the SLA.

Whatever made me think of Patty as a revolutionary? Maybe because it was the most impossible twist I could imagine, like something from *Saturday Night Live*.

After a while, as more tapes were received, we became less enamored with them, and listening to the windy rhetoric of the SLA communques became a tedious part of the job.

More and more newspapers, including the *News*, decided not to obey the terrorists' demands and did not use the messages in full, mostly eliminating the repetitive, rambling propaganda which always ended with the SLA signoff: "Death to the fascist insect that preys upon the life of the people." However, that became one of the favorite phrases in the press room. If one reporter was arguing with another, the ultimate put down was, "Ah shaddup, you fascist insect that preys upon the life of the people!" And when we had a birthday party in the press room, the cake we ordered had inscribed on it, "Happy Birthday and Death to the Fascist Insect. . . ."

Two years later, with Cinque and most of the SLA dead, Patty on trial, and her two comrades, Emily and Bill Harris, in prison, we were back in that same press room where we had spent so many hours waiting for word from the SLA. Now we were waiting for another kind of communique—the jury's verdict.

The jurors had begun deliberating the day before, Friday, March 19, 1976. Since it was Saturday and all the courtrooms were locked and dark, there was a surreal quiet in the big building. It was empty except for us jittery newspaper, radio, and TV staffers on the twentieth floor, the jurors working in their locked and guarded deliberation room, the judge, his court officials, and the prosecutors in their offices.

Lee Bailey had just been in the courthouse and had made some brief remarks in the seventh-floor press room, indicating that it was a little too soon for the jurors to reach a decision. Maybe there would be one on Sunday, Lee said, and left. He and the rest of the defense team were waiting in their hotel.

It was about 2:30 P.M.

The seven women and five men jurors had come from their hotel to the courthouse at 8:45 that morning, and about three hours later, at their request, lunch had been brought to them from a near-by McDonald's.

As usual when awaiting a verdict, I was glued to my desk and telephone, not even going downstairs to hear Lee's impromptu press conference.

Margaret, the Western Union operator who sent all of my copy to the *News* telegraph desk in New York, was at her machine.

The others in the crowded newsroom represented most of the massive press corps that had been on the case since the first day of jury selection, January 26. The trial had received enormous daily coverage, and the largest courtroom in the federal building had been turned over to this event.

As Bailey had said downstairs, it really did seem a bit early for a jury verdict, considering how much testimony had been heard from too many psychiatrists and the defendant herself, but the morning newspaper staffers—including myself and the reporters from the *L.A. Times* and the *New York Times* and the Hearst-owned *San Francisco Examiner*—had been striking terror into the hearts of the afternoon paper staffers by hoping aloud for a Saturday verdict.

For a morning newspaper, of course, nothing could be better than a Saturday verdict that will be published in the big Sunday editions. A Sunday paper goes out to the most readers, and it usually has lots of space for a story of the magnitude of a Hearst trial.

Afternoon papers do not publish on Sunday, so the morning newspapers have the exclusive story. So for a jury to bring in a verdict on Saturday is the nightmare of trial reporters on afternoon papers, for their papers can't publish the story until Monday, when it is old news.

And it happened.

In mid-afteroon, reporter Tom Hall of the *San Francisco Examiner,* the dean of the courthouse beat, opened the door of his office and called out, "Judge Carter's clerk just telephoned. There is a verdict!"

Instant pandemonium.

I was on the telephone to my office. I had sent them two advance leads—one for guilty, one for acquittal—to be used if we were on deadline and had to ram in the story.

They knew the Western Union operator would be standing by: if I had to stay downstairs in the courtroom to get quotes and other reaction, she was to send just one word, *Guilty* or *Innocent* to the *News,* as soon as the other reporters returning to the press room told her what it was. The editors could begin the layout of our front page, and use the lead I had sent until I could do a new one.

The wire services already had their helpers downstairs near the trial room, holding open the telephones to their bureaus. I had no helpers, but since my information went straight into the *News* telegraph desk I usually was ahead of the wire service bulletin. On deadline, those extra minutes are like gold to editors trying to work with a big Page 1 headline and main stories, which was why the *News* always leased a direct Western Union wire when I was on a national trial out of New York.

Bob Rose of the *Chicago Sun Times,* an afternoon paper, looked sick. He caught my eye, I shook my head in sympathy while talking into the telephone, and he shrugged philosophically.

Later he told me that knowing he had to listen to a verdict being brought in on a day when his paper wasn't publishing was only part of the frustration. The other grinding part was that while he could hear the rest of us excitedly talking to our editors, there was nobody in his Chicago office that he could even talk to about the big news. And if he did reach an editor, what was there to do but commiserate?

"If you need anything, I'll help you," Bob said at last, which were the most wonderful words I could hear at that time. Being from out of town, Bob had to work alone too, and he knew how tough it was. You're not just filing a verdict story; you also have to try to get reaction and quotes from the defendant and jurors and family and attorneys. That's why the wire services and local papers, with access to whole staffs, send a phalanx of helpers to handle the color and the sidebars.

Rob Navias, the radio reporter, also had assured me that if I were tied up filing the verdict story when the jurors were talking, he'd play back the tape for me.

My desk was a bedlam. The radio reporters who kept their telephones on it were screaming into them.

As I was getting my gear together, some of the reporters were yelling to me: "What do you think? What is it? Isn't this kind of fast?"

It was kind of fast. The old rule of thumb is that a jury usually deliberates one hour for every day of testimony. There had been 39 trial days in the Hearst case.

You learn, during a jury deliberation, to keep a careful score of the hours and minutes that a jury is actually working. By law, the jurors can discuss the case only while inside their locked deliberation room. So we always arranged for a court offical to keep us advised of exactly when the jurors enter the room, when they go out to lunch, when they return, when they go back to their hotel at night. Their exact hours of deliberation are posted and kept updated in the press room.

The Hearst jury, our figures showed, had deliberated slightly more than 12 hours.

When a verdict comes in that fast, your first thought is acquittal, only because it seems easier than having to convict.

"I don't know," I said, starting to run out of the press room, "this was fast. Maybe they've acquitted. Maybe they believe Patty."

On the Sunday before the trial had started I had written my curtain raiser for the readers:

> The case is officially entitled "United States of America vs. Patricia Campbell Hearst," but when it goes to trial this week, its true name will become obvious: "Tania, Underground Terrorist vs. Patty, American Princess."
>
> Sitting in the Ceremonial Courtroom, on trial as the most famous bank robber since Willie Sutton, will be Patty—the heiress, the kidnap victim, the hapless young girl taken prisoner of war by a revolutionary mob so ruthless that it forced her to become a common criminal and a fugitive running for her life.
>
> But also in that federal courtroom will be Tania—her voice, her

pictures, her philosophy—brought before the jury by prosecutors determined to prove that the defendant, a foul-mouthed, gun-toting enemy of the establishment, willingly helped steal $10,600 from a neighborhood bank and meant it when she told the world on tape: "My gun was loaded . . . I am a soldier in the people's army."

Of all the witnesses the government intends to present at this trial, it is Tania who is the most important to the prosecutors, the most threatening to the defense. There were many eyewitnesses to the bank robbery, and they will testify, but in its possession the government also has hundreds of photos of Tania in the bank, and hundreds of Tania's words on tape.

The defense lawyers trying to save Patty from conviction and a possible 35 years in prison have already said that Patty was coerced, brainwashed and threatened with death by her Symbionese Liberation Army captors. When she declared war on "the ruling class," referred to her father as "Pig Hearst," and spoke about her love for her "comrades," she was, according to chief defense lawyer F. Lee Bailey, "reading from a piece of paper" drawn up by the SLA.

Out of Tania's own mouth, however, the jurors will hear: "As for my being brainwashed, the idea is ridiculous to the point of being beyond belief."

They will hear Tania explain that during the robbery: "I was positioned so that I could hold customers and bank personnel on the floor . . . at no time did any of my comrades intentionally point their guns at me."

And now, two months and many thousands of words of testimony later, this is what it had boiled down to, this is what the jury had to decide: Was Patty the heiress telling the truth when she swore to her jurors that she had never joined the SLA but had remained an unwilling, terrified captive, forced into bank robbery and life in the underground under threat of death? Or, as the government contended, had Patty after her kidnapping become Tania, the convert who wanted to live like a revolutionary, learned to fire a gun, to plan and carry out a bank robbery—and had savored the intrigue and the danger?

Patty's own testimony had been the highlight of the trial, as it always is when a defendant chooses to take the stand.

This is when you write down every word, every question from the lawyer, every answer from the defendant, so that you can intersperse your newspaper story with Q and A dialogue. But while you are scribbling away, you also have to keep looking up at the jurors, at the opposing counsel, at the relatives and friends in the trial room, to get their reactions when the defendant says something particularly shocking or revealing.

You have to be taking it all down, and you can't stop, no matter how shocking or graphic the testimony is. So many times after an extraordinary statement by a witness, I have glanced up and seen some of the reporters immobilized, mouths open staring at the witness, pens unmoving in frozen fingers. "Write! Write!" I whisper to them, or jab them with an elbow if they're within range.

When Patty testified that she had been raped, I was able to write into my story that her father pressed his head into his hands so tightly that he left red fingerprints on his face.

(The alleged rape was questioned by the prosecutor, who pointed out to the jurors that the SLA women were feminists who never would have allowed it. He also noted that the alleged rapist, Willie Wolfe, was Patty's beloved in the SLA, as she proclaimed after his death, and everyone including Patty, when she still was Tania, described Willie as a gentle soul.)

Patty was a wispy, sour and not very convincing witness in her own defense, and I often wondered how much better she would have come off with her jury if she had told them what I really believe to be the truth: When she was kidnapped she was an apolitical kid barely 20 years old, totally naive about the hard world outside her sheltered home and college life. But she was aware and intelligent enough to question and rebel a bit against the rules and mores of her stuffy upbringing as a rich Catholic deb, as suggested by her decision to move in with a lover—though a pedantic one—at age 17.

And further, that she became radicalized, not brainwashed, by the dedicated young men and women who had banded together to right what they considered the country's wrongs. She found with them a purpose and an edge to her life that had been lacking in her pleasant but insipid role as Weed's live-in girlfriend. She was so young she could not dispute or dismiss the terrible facts of life that she learned from her companions, facts about injustice and corruption and poverty and inequity. She became Tania willingly, she truly mourned Cujo, and she remained underground because she wanted to, not because she "had nowhere to go" and still feared the Harrises, as she testified.

This was the 1970s, remember, during the anti-Vietnam War protests. I wonder what would have happened if Lee Bailey had told the jurors that this was a very young and impressionable girl, living in a time of youthful anger and disillusionment; and that her kidnappers, although totally misguided, included some bright, convincing, and charming people, which we discovered when the Harrises came to trial.

If Patty had told her jurors that she now realized she had been duped, that she had been seduced by the excitement and intensity of a world totally alien to her, and now deeply regretted everything she had done as Tania, and if she had pointed out that none of this would have happened had she not been kidnapped, would the jury have acquitted her?

I don't know. But I do know this: she certainly would have been a more believable, a more sympathetic defendant, and she would have made it absolutely impossible for the prosecutor to punch so many holes in her story, to make her out to be a liar under oath, which he did so successfully.

When the Harrises, college sweethearts and typical midwestern middle class Americans who became radicalized after Bill fought in the Vietnam War, came to trial in Los Angeles, they were so steadfast and so likable that the prosecutor took the unusual precaution of warning the jurors, before they began their deliberations, not to be taken in by their charm and personalities. Even so, the jurors reduced several of the charges. The Harrises received sentences of 11 years to life in connection with the sporting goods store incident. Their charges were less serious than those that Patty faced, but in Los Angeles the heiress was allowed to plead no contest and was placed on probation for five years. The probation was ended two years early.

When we raced to the trial room for the jury's verdict, I took my seat and saw Lee Bailey looking over at me from the defense table. Apparently he thought the quick verdict meant an acquittal, and he gave me a victory sign, a thumb's up. I nodded, sat down, and in longhand began writing out an innocent verdict.

Then the jury came in, and none of them looked toward Patty. I knew they had convicted her.

The lead I wrote that wild Saturday afternoon for the *News'*

Sunday editions was simple. "Patricia Hearst, daughter and granddaughter of millionaires, was convicted as a bank robber today. Her jurors took less than two days to reject the heiress' sworn testimony and to agree with the government that she was a voluntary robber and a willing 'soldier' in the Symbionese Liberation Army."

Once again a jury had listened, had paid attention, had made the court system work. Those jurors later heard a lot of garbage from people who didn't know one fact about the case, from the kind of people who got up petitions for Patty's release, contending that the poor thing was a hapless victim of thugs and goons who kept a gun at her head for 19 months, the very defense that had been used at her trial and that had been rejected by the 12 persons who knew more about her case than anybody else—her jurors.

12

Jean and the Diet Doc

February 24, 1981, White Plains, New York. The telephone rang on my desk in the chilly courthouse lobby, and instantly there was silence in the improvised press room, messy with coffee and food cartons, jammed with computers and cameras, reporters and writers, photographers and technicians.

We had been waiting eight days. During that time, so long as the jurors were in deliberation upstairs, I had never gone more than a foot away from my desk in the drafty lobby of the Westchester County Courthouse. Judge Russell Leggett had agreed to telephone either me or Tara Connell of the Gannett Westchester Newspapers as soon as he learned the jurors had reached a decision. Every time the phone had rung on her desk or mine, the laughing and yelling and typing and noshing and gossiping had stopped as if turned off by a faucet.

Each time, Tara or I had shaken our heads "no" as we talked, letting the others know it wasn't the judge, and each time within seconds the din had returned to the lobby.

But not this time . . .

"Theo, this is Judge Leggett. There is a verdict. Will you tell everybody to come upstairs as quickly and quietly as possible?"

"Yes. Yes. Thank you, Judge," I said, and began to call out to the others, "There is a verdict. The judge wants us to come upstairs as quietly as . . ." and was drowned out in the uproar of running and shouting as the press corps prepared to learn— and then spread to the world—the fate of Jean Harris, accused

217

of murdering her lover, Dr. Herman Tarnower of "Scarsdale Diet" fame.

Like every other reporter there, the first thing I did was call my newspaper and tell the editors the jurors were coming in with a verdict. I reminded them I would be out of communication because we would be locked into the tenth-floor courtroom while the verdict was being read. I would file the story as soon as I could get back downstairs to my desk in the lobby.

As I grabbed my notebook, gave last-minute instructions to the other *News* staffers who had been sent out to help, and raced for the elevators, I wondered if I would make it this time without throwing up.

All those years covering big trials, as soon as a jury began deliberating, my stomach got queasy and stayed that way as long as the jury was in the deliberation room. The moment we were told a verdict had been reached, the queasiness would churn into real nausea, which would last until I got into the courtroom.

I guess it always stopped then because the drama was unfolding so inexorably that I forgot everything except the urgency of putting together—as seamlessly, colorfully, accurately, and quickly as possible—the page 1 verdict story that, for the *News* at least, was guaranteed to sell out every edition.

Now a verdict had been reached, the courtroom was being unlocked, and we were about to witness the climax to a case that had become an international sensation even before it went to trial more than four months before.

The victim: Herman "Hy" Tarnower, a well-to-do cardiologist made famous by his best-selling book, *The Complete Scarsdale Medical Diet.* The book gave the 69-year-old, bald, hard-eyed bachelor celebrity status with the ladies he met at home and abroad. Writers described him as "vulturine."

The accused killer: Jean Harris, the 56-year-old headmistress of Madeira, a posh school for young women in McLean, Virginia. She was a white bread WASP often described as "starchy" and "genteel." In one of my stories, I described her as a lady "who doesn't look as if she could pick up the wrong fork, much less a loaded gun." She was the last person you'd expect to be charged with a murder, committed, according to the state, in rage and jealousy over Lynne Tryforos, a younger mistress.

While the jurors had deliberated in their guarded room we had

not been allowed in the trial room upstairs, and those of us waiting for a verdict had occupied ourselves at our desks in the
makeshift press room, often greeting old friend columnists and
reporters and commentators who had not covered the trial, but
had come in for the big story, the verdict.

During the wait, I filed a story every day with whatever information we were getting from upstairs: the written requests the
jurors had sent to the judge and what these requests indicated,
what testimony they had asked to have re-read to them in open
court, what time the jurors arrived amd what time they left, did
they eat in or go out, how much time each day had been spent in
actual deliberation.

Jurors are not allowed to discuss the case with each other or
deliberate on it anywhere except inside their guarded deliberation
room. So when they went out to lunch, or came back into court to
re-hear testimony, or retired at night to their guarded hotel rooms,
these times were carefully noted on a chart we hung up in the
lobby so that we would have an exact total of the days and hours
they had spent reaching a decision.

My colleague Bella English, who had worked with me through
the trial, was turning in color stories: an interview with the judge;
a description of how the press corps was getting through the long
days; a story about some Westchester County housewives who
had become Jean Harris groupies; the way jurors' families were
coping while the trial dragged on.

The other writers were similarly occupied. At the *New York
Times*, for instance, Jim Feron's daily stories were supplemented by
features by Dudley Clendinen, such as an interview with the eight
artists who had been sketching the trial for TV and newspapers,
including the *News'* remarkable Joe Papin. (No cameras were
allowed at this trial.)

Gannett's drama critic, Jacques le Sourd, who arrived to write
about this "final act," was lucky enough to be there on one of the
days when the jurors asked for a readback. Everybody, including
the defendant, had to be present for that.

"Our Man on the Aisle at the Harris Trial" was the headline of
le Sourd's piece, and he described the ways reporters mark time,
such as casting roles for a movie:

> Who will play Jean Harris in "The Scarsdale Story? Deborah
> Kerr is 60, three years older than Jean. But wouldn't she be perfect?

Lauren Bacall? Too tough. Joan Fontaine? Lee Remick is too young.
Julie Harris perhaps, dyed blond. As for Tarnower? Maybe Werner
Klemperer, provided he sheds a few pounds on the Scarsdale Diet.
And in the role of Lynne Tryforos: Mary Crosby, who shot J.R. on
TV. Make her a blond, too.

As it turned out, a television movie *was* made about the trial.
Ellen Burstyn portrayed Jean Harris, Martin Balsam played
defense attorney Joel Aurnou, Peter Coyote was cast as prosecutor
George Bolen, and Richard Dysart was Judge Leggett. Since the
film stuck strictly to the courtroom action and the trial testimony,
there were no Tarnower or Tryforos roles.

In his description of some of the reporters, the drama critic
described me as "bright, instantly lovable." Tara Connell was "the
leader of the pack." Of course, this immediately became ammunition for our irrepressible colleagues. "Good morning, Pack
Leader!" they would bray when Tara walked in, or "Will the Pack
Leader please call her desk?" "Hey, Instantly Lovable," they
would shout, "will you answer your goddamn phone? It could be
the judge, you know."

We trial reporters had been casting our own version of *The
Scarsdale Follies* while testimony was still being heard. Joyce
Wadler wrote for the *Washington Post*: "The press corps, which
casts the movie in quiet moments, sees Lee Remick as the young
Harris; Elke Sommer as Lynne Tryforos, Bruce Dern for the role of
George Bolen, the preppy prosecutor; in the role of Dr. Herman
Tarnower, a vulpine and foreboding man, the German actor Klaus
Kinski, as seen in *Nosferatu*."

When Joyce wrote that, we were still hoping that Lynne
Tryforos, who was Tarnower's nurse-receptionist as well as his
lover, would be called to testify as a witness for the prosecution.
Joyce had noted in her article that Lynne's appearance would
"bring this trial back to Standing Room Only . . . and courtroom
regulars speculate on what she might best wear for her day in
court."

Some vote for a white nurse's uniform with a red cross above
the bosom; some see her in widow's black. Theo Wilson, veteran
trial reporter of the Daily News, thinks her cause could best be
served if she makes her entrance in a wedding gown, angel wings
affixed, and hooked onto a pulley system that would permit her to

hover or float.

And Murray Kempton, the columnist, feels the costume is moot. "The only way Tryforos could lose this case for the prosecution," he says, "is if she chews gum and calls the judge "Toots.""

We weren't being hard-hearted or insensitive; this was our way of relieving the daily pressures of covering a trial many of us saw as "a sad and ugly story" (in Jean Harris's words) of wasted lives, with no heroes, no heroines, and no happy ending for anybody.

While waiting for the verdict, I filed the background of the trial (dates, highlights, a summary), which was held at the *News* for use when the verdict came in, either as part of the main verdict story I would write or as a sidebar to run elsewhere in the paper. Because the trial was in the *News'* metropolitan area, there were fellow staffers available to prepare for the coverage which is routine on a verdict day, and which I had to handle by myself when I was elsewhere in the country.

First and most important were quotes from the jurors. We hoped that the jurors would have a press conference in the courthouse after the verdict; if they refused, some reporters would have to follow them. We needed reaction from the defense team, from Jean, from her relatives and friends, from people at the Madeira School, and from Lynne Tryforos. (Good luck!) We needed to get comments from the two prosecutors and from their boss, the district attorney. Somebody had to call Tarnower's sister, who had attended every day of the trial, for her reaction.

But right now we had to hear the verdict, and we were on deadline.

There was a mob scene at the elevators. For some reason, the deputies were not letting the reporters get on, causing confusion and complaints until word came down to let the press go up to the trial room. I was just taking deep breaths and hoping I didn't throw up on my colleagues.

Once in the courtroom, we scrambled for our regular seats, reserved for those of us who had shown up for every day of the trial. Jean Harris was at the defense table, looking terrible; she was haggard and bleached out from the strain of the agonizing days of jury deliberation. Tall, white-haired Judge Leggett was standing in the well of the trial room, apparently waiting for everybody to be seated before making an announcement. In minutes, every seat was taken.

Although nothing was "happening," I was taking notes: the time Leggett called (5:45 P.M.); the total hours of jury deliberation (47 hours, 57 minutes); how Harris looked (no expression, dazed); what she was wearing (brown skirt, brown suede jacket, hair pulled back with a tortoise-shell headband); who was in the courtroom (no Harris or Tarnower relatives); the judge's remarks (a thank you to the press for helping him conduct a dignified trial and a warning to the spectators against outbursts); the time Leggett took the bench, the doors were locked, and the jurors began to file into the box (5:59 P.M.)

While I scribbled these last notes I stared at the jurors. They were solemn, grim, as they took their seats. A couple of them darted their eyes toward the prosecutors, Bolen and his assistant, Tom Lalla. Not one of them looked at the defendant or her counsel, and I whispered to the person next to me:

"They've convicted her."

On page 1 of the *News* the next morning, the headline consisted of one word: GUILTY! It was in two-inch letters, superimposed over a photo of Jean, her hands clasped, sitting in a police car next to a uniformed officer.

> Jean Harris was found guilty of second-degree murder yesterday by a jury that agreed—after nearly eight days of deliberation—that she had intentionally shot to death her lover, Dr. Herman Tarnower, in a jealous rage over his younger mistress, Lynne Tryforos.
>
> While some of her defense attorneys wept, the 57-year-old former private school headmistress sat absolutely without expression, almost dazed, as she heard the jury foreman, at 6 P.M., answer "guilty," "guilty," "guilty," when asked by the court clerk the verdict on the three counts of the indictment.
>
> The murder conviction, which carries a prison sentence ranging from 15 years to life, indicated that the eight women and four men jurors did not believe the sworn testimony of the frail, blond defendant when she told them that Tarnower's shooting on March 10, 1980, was an accident and that her lover died trying to prevent her suicide.
>
> And it indicated also that they believed Prosecutor George Bolen when he described Harris as a jealous woman whose "rage and frustration" exploded in gunfire in the doctor's bedroom at his Purchase estate.

Harris was declared guilty of three crimes—second degree murder and two charges of criminal possession of a weapon. In my
article, I tried to tell our readers everything that happened inside
the courtroom during the verdict, informed them that Jean—who
had been free on bail—had been taken into custody as required by
the law, and made it plain she probably would not get the maximum life term but the minimum 15 years. The tip-off for this last
came from the Westchester County District Attorney, Carl Vergari,
who was quoted as saying he was not going to press for the maximum. If the judge thought 15 years "is fair and proper," Vergari
said, "then we definitely would not object." So it was no surprise
to faithful *News* readers when, on March 20, Leggett sentenced
Harris to the minimum 15 years.

Nor were faithful *News* readers surprised when stories began to
come out about Jean having been sedated. In my verdict story,
defense attorney Joel Aurnou was revealed for the first time that
his client had been "heavily medicated during the trial, and for the
verdict."

The *News* printed an extra 100,000 copies on February 25, 1981,
the day of the verdict story. The entire run, plus the extra 100,000
copies, sold out.

Ever since the conviction of Jean Harris, I have been asked the
same questions, over and over, by people who are fascinated with
the story but are unable to figure out why certain things happened.
The questions go something like this:

Was the jury right in convicting her of second degree murder?
Yes.
Was justice served with that verdict?
No.
Should she have been sentenced to 15-to-life?
Yes.
Was justice served with that sentence?
No.
Did she kill Dr. Tarnower?
Yes.
Did she plan it, premeditate it, do it "in cold blood"?
No.
Was it a shooting committed in "the heat of passion"?

Yes.

Then, shouldn't she have gotten off with a lesser conviction, a shorter sentence?

Yes.

Then why didn't she?

Neither the conviction nor the sentence Harris received were the ones she deserved, but the jurors who convicted her and the judge who sentenced her acted properly; because of legal restrictions imposed on them by the defense, they had no options.

Justice would have been better served if the jurors had been allowed to consider a verdict of first degree manslaughter in this case. But because of defense tactics, the jurors were foreclosed from even considering that verdict during their deliberations.

A few days after the verdict, for the March 2 editions of the *News*, I quoted medical and legal experts who agreed that the Harris case "had all the elements of a classic 'crime of passion,' and the jurors who convicted her of cold-blooded murder should have been given a chance to consider this. . . ."

I wrote that Harris should have let her jurors consider first degree manslaughter, but "proud, refined, and adamant about the truth of her story, [she] apparently will insist forever that the shooting was an 'accident' and that the famous diet doctor died trying to save her from suicide."

Sure enough, in her own book, written in prison and published in 1986, Harris told the same story that put her in prison for so many years. To her, this was the truth, she had to cling to it, and she always will. Despite the evidence.

To this day, Jean Harris cannot admit that she had killed a cold and unjust lover in an unplanned, uncontrollable explosion of blinding, consuming outrage. The genteel headmistress could not let the public see what she had become, a powerless and obsessed woman, filled with anger and self-pity, pleading, crawling, begging for crumbs at the table of Hy Tarnower.

Instead, she wanted to believe, and she asked her jury to believe, that she and her longtime lover enjoyed a civilized, cerebral relationship—and that he died trying to save her life, accidentally receiving every single one of the bullets she had intended for her own suicide. Hy Tarnower dying nobly, a dedicated doctor trying to preserve a life, was the only palatable story for Jean Harris in her role as a lady too well-bred to stoop to so crass an emotion as violent jealousy over an unworthy rival.

Palatable as it was for Jean, it was impossible for her jurors to swallow.

The worst disservice to Harris's case was her own insistence that she had done nothing to cause her lover's death. But there were just too many bullets, all of them in Tarnower's body, for a jury to believe that. As somebody asked, "Hey, what kind of a gun is this that every time you point it at yourself it shoots somebody else four times?"

European reporters at the trial asked me after the verdict why there is no such thing as a crime of passion in this country; according to them, Harris would not have been so harshly dealt with abroad. The fact is that we do have provisions for crimes of passion, and Harris could have offered what is known as an "affirmative defense" of first degree manslaughter—a defense completely bolstered by testimony the jury heard from Jean's mouth and from that 15-page "shriek of pain" known as the "Scarsdale Letter."

First-degree manslaughter is a killing committed in what used to be called "heat of passion" or "sudden passion." For her jurors to consider Hy Tarnower's killing to be a crime of passion, however, Jean Harris would have had to admit to them, and to the world, her suffering and her degradation; she would have had to make admissions intolerable to her. She would have had to reveal her hated role as a rejected, jealous, tormented, aging mistress; she would have had to admit "intent."

After all the testimony was in and before the jurors began their deliberations, the lawyers for both sides met with Judge Leggett to argue over the judge's charge to the jury—the legal instructions the jury was to follow in its deliberations. At one of these meetings, assistant prosecutor Lalla had asked Leggett to include first degree manslaughter as one of the possible lesser verdicts for the jurors to consider.

If it had been included, the jurors would have been instructed that New York law provided that a defendant could be found guilty of first degree manslaughter when, "with intent to cause serious physical injury to another, he causes the death of such person," or "with intent to cause the death of another person, he causes the death of such person . . . under circumstances which do not constitute murder because he acts under the influence of extreme emotional disturbance."

The important words are intent and *extreme emotional disturbance*. First degree manslaughter is the only lesser charge that includes the word *intent*, and since the jurors eventually agreed there was intent, it is very possible they could have convicted Jean Harris on this charge. Such a conviction carries a 2-to-6-year minimum, 25-year maximum sentence. Jean Harris was no threat to society, and the judge probably would have given her the minimum. She could have been a free woman in a short time.

But defense attorney Aurnou opposed including the charge, and the judge accepted the defense request. The only lesser charges given the jurors to consider were second degree manslaughter and criminally negligent homicide. Neither of these include intent, and they were never considered during deliberations.

In a go-for-broke defense, Jean Harris had asked the jurors to either acquit her or find her guilty of the maximum offense charged against her—second degree murder. Given the testimony they had heard, especially Jean's "Scarsdale Letter," there was no way the jurors could find Jean Harris innocent. Once the jurors brought in the only possible verdict, the judge had no choice either, and pronounced a sentence required by the law.

If Jean Harris had given them the facts to work with, they could have considered evidence showing that although she had shot the doctor, and had in fact the intent to shoot him at that uncontrollable and passionate moment of outrage, it was because she was suffering "extreme emotional disturbance" and so had committed not murder, but first degree manslaughter.

Because I believe that jurors really seek the truth and work hard to bring in fair and just verdicts, I think the jurors would have understood the tragedy of Jean Harris; that at the time of the shooting, she was a basket case, worn out and sick, in misery at the Madeira School, and in constant emotional turmoil for years from the callous treatment she felt she was receiving from Tarnower.

There was something so pathetic and at the same time so infuriating watching headmistress Jean sink herself on the witness stand, trying to convince her jury about what a compatible, intellectual couple she and Hy were. They were worldly wise and sophisticated; they had elegant friends. Jean indicated she even thought that Tarnower's best-selling diet book was somehow beneath a cardiologist who read Herodotus "for fun." This was such a tolerant, high-class couple that the only time they had quarreled, she said, was about "the use of the subjunctive."

She threw out this pretentious little statement while describing the fatal events in the doctor's bedroom, and her timing was terrible. It came in the midst of a description of physical violence, breaking glass, gun explosions, and blood in the last minutes of Tarnower's life. She testified that as Tarnower lay dying, she told him she thought the bedroom telephone was broken. Then, she continued: "Hy said, 'You're probably right.' That was the only civil thing he said all night and it was the last thing I heard him say. I guess we both were thinking how sad this was to happen to two people who didn't argue about anything—except the use of the subjunctive."

Maybe that was what she thought as she looked at her bleeding lover. But Tarnower was dying, he had struck her and called her crazy (she said) before the gunfire, and I really doubt that his last thoughts were of this allegedly wonderful and non-argumentative relationship.

Jean also told her jurors that she did not consider Lynne Tryforos to be a rival. She and Hy, she wanted them to believe, had a relationship above that sort of pettiness, just as Jean, socially and intellectually, was above Lynne. Hy had lots of women and Lynne was just another bit of fluff on the Tarnower hit parade, not worth thinking about. Jean even had her lawyer read to the jurors a Christmas poem she had written for the doctor in which she poked good-natured fun at the doctor's penchant for the ladies.

But the "Scarsdale Letter," mailed shortly before she made her disastrous last trip to her lover's home, contradicted everything Harris said. In it, she described Lynne in the terms of degradation a woman uses about another woman only if she despises her: she called Lynne "a vicious adulterous psychotic," "whore," "a self-serving ignorant slut," "slave," "thieving slut," "sick playmate," "dishonest, ignorant, and tasteless."

When this immensely important letter was read into the trial record after months of suspense and legal debate, the *News* ran it in full. The *New York Times*, which had been doing remarkably good trial coverage for the *Times*, printed only excerpts of the letter.

At one point in the letter Harris warned her lover that she intended to be a guest at a testimonial in his honor even if he was inviting Lynne Tryforos.

Poor desperate Jean claimed that their friends agreed that she, not Lynne, was the one who deserved to be at the dinner, and she said she had assured them she would be at the banquet "even if the slut comes—indeed, I don't care if she pops naked out of the cake with her tits frosted with chocolate."

The Times, in a fit of prudery, replaced *tits* with "----." The day the stories came out, I got calls from friends who had seen only the *Times* and couldn't get the *News* because it was sold out. They wanted to know what filthy four-letter word had been blanked out. When I asked them what they thought it might be, most of them guessed *cunt;* nobody could believe it was something as innocuous as *tits.*

The letter made it clear that Harris was being driven into suicidal depression by the thought that the doctor was going to humiliate her before all of their friends by bringing Lynne to an important banquet in his honor scheduled for April 19, thus showing the world that Jean Harris was a castoff and that her 14 years with him meant nothing.

The letter contrasted directly with what Jean said on the stand under direct examination by her lawyer:

> Did your feelings about Lynne Tryforos and Dr. Tarnower have anything to do with your being in Purchase, N.Y. on March 10, 1980?
> No, they didn't. I think it depressed me to see Hy was less than I thought he was. That could have been part of my depression, but it had nothing to do with Hy. I had a feeling about myself, my own integrity.
> . . . Actually, I thought it [the affair with Tryforos] denigrated Hy, but then I thought the book did, too. . . .
> [Tarnower was] the only person I could turn to . . . I drew a great deal of strength from him. A lot of people did. He was the person who made me feel safe.

But in that long letter, Jean was obviously in anguish over the doctor's affair with the younger woman. She fearfully tried to flatter him while pouring out her fury and hurt and hatred. She misspelled Lynne's name as Lynn throughout, and referred to the doctor as Hi, not Hy.

> Hi. I will send this by registered mail only because so many of my letters seem not to reach you. Or at least they are never acknowledged so I presume they didn't arrive.
>
> I am distraught as I write this—your phone call to tell me you preferred the company of a vicious, adulterous psychotic was topped by a call from the Dean of Students ten minutes later and has kept me awake for almost 36 hours. I had to expel four seniors just two months from graduation and suspend others.
>
> What I say will ramble but it will be the truth—and I have to do something besides shriek with pain.
>
> . . . I haven't played the slave for you, I would never have committed adultery for you—but I have added a dimension to your life and given you pleasure and dignity, as you have me. As [a friend] says: "Hi was always such a marvelous snob. What happened?"

Jean wrote that she received a copy of Tarnower's will just four weeks earlier with "my name vigorously scratched out, and Lynn's name in your handwriting written in three places, leaving her a quarter of a million dollars and her children $25,000 apiece—and the boys and me nothing. It is the sort of thing I have grown almost accustomed to from Lynn—that you didn't respond to my note when I returned it leaves me wondering if you sent it together. It isn't your style—but then Lynn has changed your style. . . ."

> It didn't matter all that much really—all I ever asked was to be with you—and when I left you to know when we would see each other again so there was something in life to look forward to. Now you are taking that away from me too and I am unable to cope—I can hear you saying, "Look, Jean—it's your problem. I don't want to hear about it."
>
> I have watched you grow rich in the years we have been together, and I have watched me go through moments when I was almost destitute. I have twice borrowed fifty cents from Henri [Tarnower's houseman] to make two of the payments on the Garden State Parkway during those five years you casually left me on my hands and knees in Philadelphia. And now—almost ten years later—now that a thieving slut has the run of your home you accuse

me of stealing money and books . . . The many things your whore
does openly and obviously (to your friends and your servants! Sadly
not to you) you now have the cruelty to accuse me of. . . .

Twice I have taken money from your wallet—each time to pay
for sick damage done to my property by your psychotic whore. I
don't have the money to afford a sick playmate—you do.

Jean had testified that Tarnower had given her an engagement
ring early in their relationship, but they had never married,
although at one time she had planned on it. She said she returned
the ring to him, but from the Scarsdale Letter the jurors learned
more painful details than she revealed on the stand.

As for stealing from you, the day I put my ring on your dresser my income before taxes was $12,000 per year . . . I desperately
needed money all these years. I couldn't have sold that ring. It was
tangible proof of your love and it meant more to me than life itself.
That you sold it the summer your adulterous slut finally got her
divorce and needed money is a kind of sick, cynical act that left me
old and bitter and sick. Your only comment when you told me you
had sold it (and less than two months before you had assured me
you would get it from the safe so I could wear it again) was "Look,
if you're going to make a fuss about it you can't come here anymore.
I don't need to have anyone spoil my weekend." Too bad Somerset
Maugham didn't get hold of us before he died. He could have come
up with something to top *The Magnificent Obsession.* [Jean meant *Of
Human Bondage.* In court she said that she knew the difference but
was so upset she'd misnamed it.]

. . . Going through the hell of the past few years has been bear-
able only because you were still there and I could be with you
whenever I could get away from work, which seemed to be less and
less. To be jeered at, and be called "old and pathetic" made me seriously consider borrowing $5,000 just before I left New York and
telling a doctor to make me young again—to do anything but make
me not feel like discarded trash—I lost my nerve because there was
always the chance I'd end up uglier than before.

You keep me in control by threatening me with banishment—
an easy threat which you know I couldn't live with and so I stay
home alone while you make love to someone who has almost totally destroyed me. I have been publicly humiliated again and again
but not on the 19th of April. It is the apex of your career and I
believe I have the right to watch it—if only from a dark corner near
the kitchen.

. . . I wish 14 years of making love to one another and sharing so much happiness had left enough of a mark that you couldn't have casually scratched my name out of a will and written in Lynn's instead. But for God's sake don't translate that into begging for money. I would far rather be saved the trial of living without you than have the option of living with your money. Give her all the money she wants, Hi—but give me time with you and the privilege of sharing with you April 19th . . . Please, darling—don't tell me now that it was all for nothing. She has you every single moment in March—for Christ's sake give me April—T. S. Eliot said it's the cruelest month. Don't let it be, Hi. I want to spend every minute of it with you on weekends. In all these years you've never spent my birthday with me—There aren't a lot left—it goes so quickly. I give you my word if you just aren't cruel I won't make you wretched, I never did before until you were cruel—and then I just wasn't ready for it.

She said she had tried to reach Tarnower on the telephone several times on Saturday, March 8, but was unsuccessful. This was after she had learned from him that he intended to bring Lynne to the April gala. She said she wanted to talk to him because she felt as if she were falling apart, and she insisted it was because of the problems at the school. But as the letter showed, she obviously was much more consumed with her anxiety over not attending the banquet and her deteriorating relationship with the doctor than with any school crisis. In that entire lengthy letter, she mentioned the school problems just once. The letter is about her hatred of Lynne (who Jean even accuses of spreading human feces on one of Jean's dresses) and about the doctor's lack of sympathy for Jean.

She also told the jurors that as soon as she mailed the letter from the campus post office on Monday, March 9, she regretted it and called Tarnower to tell him so.

"I had wanted to be good company and not a whiner," she said. "I told him when it comes, throw it away and don't read it."

From the letter we learned that Hy was running their affair, punishing Jean by "exiling" her when she complained or got out of line, favoring her younger and prettier successor in his bed, ignoring her pleas for more of his time, and there wasn't one goddamn thing Jean could do about it. What was worse, she had once been in charge. At the beginning of their relationship, she told us when she testified, Hy had been doing the pursuing and the sweettalking, and now here she was completely at the mercy of a man who didn't need her anymore. He had become a celebrity, the famous "diet doctor," with a young and pretty mistress to accompany him on trips and be shown off to his friends.

If Dr. Tarnower had lived to get the Scarsdale Letter, I think he would have become furious, and would have crumpled it up and thrown it away without reading it all the way through.

I am sure that when Jean left the Madeira School and drove through the rain to Westchester, she intended to tell the doctor of her undying love and then kill herself near the daffodils on his pond.

Tarnower no longer was in love with Jean Harris, if he ever had been more than just attracted to her WASP blond looks and style, and so her complaints, her pleas, her calls for help, her reminders of happier days were only annoyances that made him feel guilt and irritation. Jean had become a royal pain in the ass. How could this proud lady admit this publicly?

God knows what actually happened after Jean burst into the doctor's bedroom, waking him up to tell him that she was going to kill herself. We know that she found Lynne's curlers and night clothes; Jean was not expected that night, so Lynne's belongings had not yet been put away by Tarnower's discreet housekeeper. This must have been the last push for a woman already eaten up by the anger that filled the letter she had just written.

She testified that when she told him she was so miserable she wanted to kill herself, instead of giving her sympathy Hy told her she was crazy. I think that Jean then must have begun ranting about Lynne, repeating everything she had just put into the letter, calling the younger woman a slut and whore. I think that she hurled Lynne's things around, breaking a window in the process; she told us that Tarnower struck her, but I think he also told her to quit bad-mouthing her rival, told Jean he wanted her off his back, told her he didn't want her at his testimonial dinner, and maybe, not even meaning it but just wanting to get rid of Jean, even told her he was considering marrying Lynne.

And that, I think was when Jean, who really had intended to commit suicide on the Tarnower grounds (what a sweet revenge on the old goat, to have her body found there and let him explain that to the police!) went over the edge.

If ever there was a heat of passion shooting, it was this one.

I have been asked why her lawyer went along with her and didn't insist on offering the jurors a first degree manslaughter option.

Jean was adamant about certain things about her defense. For instance, before the trial started, she ordered her attorney never to say anything bad about Tarnower. If Aurnou had not gone along with this, she would have fired him. There are plenty of other competent defense attorneys eagerly waiting in the wings for a high-profile case like this one to catapult them into newspapers all over the world. Jean could have replaced Arnou in a moment.

There were other reasons. As veteran lawyers pointed out to me at the time, if Aurnou's go-for-broke defense had worked and the jurors had acquitted Jean because they could not convict her of a cold-blooded murder (she certainly was no hit man), then Aurnou would have been hailed as a brilliant legal tactician. Plus, Jean would have been able to collect the $220,000 Tarnower had left her in his will.

But a lawyer and a defendant have to give the jurors who are friendly to them something to fight with when they get into the deliberation room. Jean and Joel gave the jurors nothing except her insistence that the bullets which finished off Hy Tarnower were all meant for her.

During the Harris trial, the *News* was in chaos, what with the disastrous attempt to publish a new edition called *Tonight* and the fact that there were new people on the desk who neither knew nor cared about how to handle a story as complicated as a trial for a stylish tabloid like the *News*. One veteran editor, who disliked stories about people and had never figured out why *News* readers were captivated by trials, often was in charge of the Harris case. This editor gave it short shrift, even though it was the one sort of story left on which a newspaper could beat television. At that time, TV never gave the story enough time to bring out the color and details and testimony that make a trial come alive.

But instead of giving New York readers the best daily coverage in town, as we always had, these alleged editors chopped, and cut, and deleted, and buried, and ruined the stories.

I don't think they understood one thing I tried to explain. For instance, they couldn't comprehend that the "curtain raiser" I wrote was supposed to get readers so hooked that they couldn't wait for the next day's edition. We had learned through the years to set the stage, give the readers an idea of what was awaiting them in this courtroom, and let them know that a mystery was slowly going to be unraveled for them in the pages of the Daily News.

This curtain raiser was particularly interesting because not only did I take our readers into the courthouse with me, but for the first time, I gave them a look inside the house where Tarnower was murdered. Jim Van Sickle of NBC News had smuggled me in with him to see the Tarnower house, which had been bought by a lady who was not allowing any newspaper reporters in. Jim passed me off as a member of his TV team, and I was able to see for myself the layout of the house and grounds—a big help when testimony came later in the trial about where Tarnower was found lying in his bedroom, where the housekeeper was standing when she heard a shot on the intercom, and where Jean entered the house after her drive through the rain from Virginia.

In the curtain raiser, I explained the circumstances leading to the upcoming trial, described the courthouse and the courtroom itself, wrote how Jean looked, what the judge was like, the issues that were going to be presented to the jurors, and then wrote about Tarnower's house.

> Few outsiders have been in the house where the diet doctor lived, where he entertained his ladies, where he gave his dinner parties and where he was shot to death.
>
> The house is handsome and uncluttered. Its new owners, who are in commodities, have renamed it "Limit Downs," a financial expression.
>
> It is approached on a private drive, landscaped to ensure privacy, with a lovely pond on the right. . . .
>
> The master bedroom, where Jean Harris and "Hy" Tarnower had a confrontation that ended with a fatal shooting is on the second floor. . . . Tarnower's bedroom had twin beds facing a picture window, a patio, and a lovely view of the pond and surrounding countryside. He was in pajamas, lying between the beds, when the cops came upstairs with Harris and the doctor's housekeeper and butler, Suzanne and Henri Van Der Vrecken.
>
> The bedroom ceiling is beamed. Behind it, in a dressing room area filled with built-in wardrobes and dressers of Honduran mahogany, are two bathrooms, one with a shower, the other with a tub.
>
> There are bookshelves over the beds and at the sides of the room. There is a fireplace in the corner. There is nothing else on this floor.

I described the "extremely narrow winding staircase" leading from the living room to the bedroom, and explained that "it was down these steep wooden triangular steps, which encircle a black iron pole, that the mortally wounded doctor was carried by police who came to the scene, thinking at first that a burglary was in progress."

Tarnower was a big-game hunter and downstairs he had a trophy room. I remember wondering, as I looked at the trophies, why a not-so-handsome man would want to display in his home the heads of such magnificent, beautiful beasts.

I described for our readers the other rooms, tying it in with some of the pretrial information we had received about the night of the shooting:

> Downstairs, at a table in the foyer near the dining room . . . Harris was questioned by police and reportedly told them she had shot the doctor. The kitchen is on the right off the foyer. It was there that an officer said he could not get a dial tone on a telephone, after Harris said she wanted to talk to a lawyer. [Jean had explained that she ran from the Tarnower house after the shooting because the telephone didn't work and she was trying to find a telephone to call for an ambulance.]
>
> She was then taken through the dining/trophy room area, down a narrow hall with a red tile floor, to the Van Der Vrecken bedroom. . . . It was in [this] bedroom that Harris reportedly told an attorney friend on the telephone: "My God, I think I've killed Hy," and then, "Henri is looking at me as if he wants to kill me."
>
> Walking down the narrow hall, back to the foyer, Harris reportedly saw herself in the large mirrored wall over the double sinks, and according to both a cop and Mrs. Van Der Vrecken, she touched her bruised face and said: "He hit me. He hit me a lot."

The curtain raiser should have been displayed so that the *News* readers would know that a sensational trial was about to unfold. This always guaranteed an increase in readership—people who seldom read the paper bought it when we were covering a big trial. But it was so badly edited and so poorly displayed there wasn't a chance to entice readers to start looking for the trial story.

It turned out that my newspaper was on the self-destructive course that finally resulted in the loss of its long-held position as Number 1 in the country in circulation, and the handling of the Harris trial was worse than I could have imagined. There were days when the story was cut so carelessly that the last paragraphs made no sense. There were days when the *Times*, which often did such a terrible job covering trials, gave more space to the day's events than the *News* did.

If there was color in the story, it was removed. If there was high drama, it was flattened. If the story could be buried in the back of the newspaper, it was buried.

In addition to the editorial bungling, the feuding, politicking, and back-biting made the once happy *News* the most depressing office I've ever seen.

I survived this period because I didn't have to go into that dreary newsroom, but could stay up in White Plains most of the time. And there were days—such as when Jean testified—when the copy I was sending was so irresistible that even the disinterested editors had to let it ride.

Another reason was that there was a good press corps. Spending every day with professionals like Jim Feron, Bella English, Jim Van Sickle, and Lally Weymouth helped. There was Joe Nicholson of the *Post*, who was conscientious and hard-working and sometimes had terrible things done to his stories by his editors, who had turned that once-respectable, liberal paper into a British-type penny dreadful.

One day we all wrote about testimony from a detective who was one of the first to arrive at Tarnower's house after the shooting. Under Joe's byline, the Post story had the detective announce to "a hushed courtroom" that "Mrs. Harris murdered her unfaithful lover, Dr. Herman Tarnower, to get revenge and then tried to disguise her crime as a botched suicide attempt."

Such prejudicial words, of course, never could be spoken by any cop on the witness stand, not if he had all his marbles and didn't want to be held in contempt. Cops don't tell jurors that a defendant "murdered" somebody and then lied about it. It was hard for us to conceive how even a *Post* editor could be so dumb.

Poor Joe. He told us that he had tried to explain to an editor the prosecution theory of the Tarnower killing. Somehow, the editor decided that this theory should become part of the detective's actual testimony, and, without Joe's knowledge, just wrote it into the third paragraph.

As usual, the true testimony was better than anything an editor could invent. The detective quoted Harris as saying that Tarnower "slept with every woman he could, and I'd had it." That single line became this *Post* headline banner: "The Amazing Sexual Appetite of Diet Doc, 69."

Lally Weymouth, writing for *New York* magazine, kept getting interesting tips which she shared with me. The two of us running them down together were a sight to behold. Lally is tall and I am not, and even we thought we looked funny trying to sneak out of the courthouse together to some clandestine meeting with principals in the case; we'd become convulsed with laughter. The cameramen spotted us immediately and would come loping over to ask where we were going.

Lots of words were written about Jean Harris and her trial, in books and magazines and newspapers. But my very favorite coverage of the trial was a "special report" printed in the January 26, 1981 issue of *The Monday News* under the head: "Chief Attends Harris Trial."

This mimeographed paper, to which I was a paid subscriber, was edited by Lally's daughter, Pamela, the 12-year-old "chief," and it contained photos, movie reviews, and news from New York and Washington staffers.

The "personal coverage" by Pamela included a photo of Jean Harris and this account, which certainly captured the flavor of a typical day in the life of any trial:

> Last Friday January 23 Mrs. Harris sat on trial for the murder of Dr. Herman Tarnower. The Jury sat on one side of the room chewing bubble gum. Jean Harris sat next to her defense attorney Joel Aurnou, and further down the table sat prosecutor George Bolen.
>
> The issue under discussion was whether or not Tarnower had been holding up his hand when he was shot in the chest. The first witness Albert Ackerman after a few hours came to the conclusion that the 3 fragments of tissue in the chest did not come from the hand but that one of them had to have been cartilage. When questioned by Bolen, Ackerman said that he was not an expert in cartilage but that the difference between hand tissue and cartilage was not hard to see. "It's like the difference between a Volkswagen and a Rolls Royce!!!"
>
> Ackerman was one of the many Pathologists (doctor for skin and tissues) that rose to the witness stand. By the time the 3rd Pathologist appeared (the 6th since the beginning of the trial) I was surprised to find the jury still awake!
>
> When the last witness Dr. Michael Janis came to the stand and

was asked his profession he said he was a pathologist, and he thought that we knew what a pathologist does! Later Bolen asked, "Do you belong to any normal medical societies?" Then Janis answered, "I don't know what you mean by 'normal,' I don't belong to any abnormal society!" At this point the whole court was up in laughter, even Judge Leggett who was holding his hand over his mouth to try and stop himself. After he made a few more jokes, Bolen said, "Have you ever worked as a stand up comic?" By this time even Jean Harris was on the floor with laughter.

The thing that struck me as quite bizarre was that here is this woman on trial for murder—and sitting in a court room with the jurors who are trying to decide if she spends the rest of her life in jail, or gets off free!

And, they can't even keep a straight face!

It is hard to tell what will happen next . . .

From the looks of how things are going it is hard to tell just what the jury thinks . . . accident or homicide.

At the end of the Harris trial, the reporters who had sat through the trial together threw a farewell party for each other and for the principals in the case. I had told my colleagues about similar get-togethers at the other trials I'd covered, and they enthusiastically planned it with me at the Coachman Hotel, where some of us had stayed throughout the case. The judge, prosecutors, investigators, and defense attorneys were promised, as always, that this would be strictly off the record, and it was. But unlike all the other times, I received an excited message from the *News* after the party. The editors had heard about "the press party I threw in the jail" and I was to write a story about it!

It took some doing, because they couldn't quite understand, but I finally was able to explain that not only was there no party in the jail, there was no party to write about—it was all off the record.

I used to rush back to the *News* city room to schmooze with editors and colleagues after I was away on a trial or a story, but as soon as I could after Jean Harris was sentenced I left New York and returned to Los Angeles. I could not face that now joyless newsroom. After the first Claus von Bulow trial, the next year, I quit. I never walked into the gorgeous *Daily News* building again.

FINAL ★★★★

DAILY  NEWS

NEW YORK'S PICTURE NEWSPAPER ®

 15¢

Vol. 57. No. 201   New York, N.Y. 10017, Saturday, February 14, 1976★   Sunny, 33-43. Details p. 39

Sobs on Stand

PATTY'S STORY OF KIDNAPING:

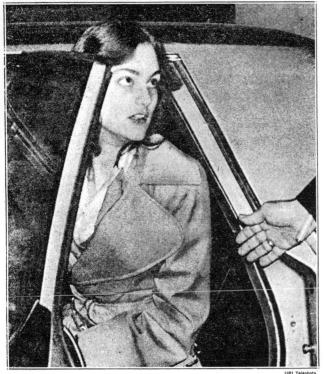

Patty Hearst gets helping hand from U.S. marshal as she arrives at court.

UPI Telephoto

● The doorbell rang, looked over, and I saw person standing there .

● She grabbed me ar put a pistol in my face .

● I was screaming ar then I was struck . . .

● He just said, 'Bitc better be quiet or we blow your head off . .

● He pinched . . . on n breasts . . . and down .

Stories on page 3